Homer's People

This book examines the role and character of Homer's people, *laoi*, in Homeric story-telling, arguing that Homeric poetry is crucially concerned with the people as a basis for communal life. Both the *Iliad* and the *Odyssey* are read as sustained meditations on the processes involved in protecting and destroying the people. The investigation draws on a wide range of approaches from formulaic analysis to the study of early performance contexts. From a close reading of the Homeric epics, Homer's people emerge as a community without effective social structures. When this is viewed from the perspective of Homeric performances in the *polis*, a contrast between Homer's *laoi* and the founding people of ritual emerges. While the former typically perish, the survival of the latter is secured by the establishment of successful institutions.

JOHANNES HAUBOLD is a Research Fellow at Girton College, Cambridge.

CAMBRIDGE CLASSICAL STUDIES

General Editors
P. E. EASTERLING, M. K. HOPKINS,
M. D. REEVE, A. M. SNODGRASS, G. STRIKER

HOMER'S PEOPLE
Epic Poetry and Social Formation

JOHANNES HAUBOLD
University of Cambridge

CAMBRIDGE
UNIVERSITY PRESS

PUBLISHED BY THE PRESS SYNDICATE OF THE UNIVERSITY OF CAMBRIDGE
The Pitt Building, Trumpington Street, Cambridge, United Kingdom

CAMBRIDGE UNIVERSITY PRESS
The Edinburgh Building, Cambridge CB2 2RU, UK   www.cup.cam.ac.uk
40 West 20th Street, New York, NY 10011–4211, USA   www.cup.org
10 Stamford Road, Oakleigh, Melbourne 3166, Australia
Ruiz de Alarcón 13, 28014 Madrid, Spain

© Faculty of Classics, University of Cambridge 2000

This book is in copyright. Subject to statutory exception and to the provisions of relevant collective licensing agreements, no reproduction of any part may take place without the written permission of Cambridge University Press.

First published 2000

Printed in the United Kingdom at the University Press, Cambridge

Typeset in Times 11/13 pt [AO]

A catalogue record for this book is available from the British Library

Library of Congress Cataloguing in Publication data
Haubold, Johannes.
Homer's people: epic poetry and social formation / Johannes Haubold.
p.   cm. – (Cambridge classical studies)
Enlargement of author's thesis (Ph.D.) – Cambridge University.
Includes bibliographical references and indexes.
ISBN 0 521 77009 2 (hardback)
1. Homer – Political and social views. 2. Epic poetry, Greek – History and criticism. 3. Politics and literature – Greece – History. 4. Literature and society – Greece – History. 5. Social structure in literature. 6. Community life in literature. 7. Oral – formulaic analysis. I. Title. II. Series.
PA4037.H38   2000
883'.01 – dc21   99-37676 CIP

ISBN 0 521 77009 2 hardback

CONTENTS

Preface   *page* ix
Abbreviations   xiii

Introduction   1
   Between the omnipresent hero and the absent *polis*

1 *Laoi* in early Greek hexameter poetry   14
   'Shepherd of the people'   17
   Privilege and obligation   20
   An epic ideal   24
   The failed ideal   28
   Social structures   32
   An incurable imbalance   35
   Negative reciprocity   37
   Society and the stone   40
   'The people of the Achaeans'   43
   Conclusion   45

2 Homer's people   47
   Laoi in the *Iliad*   47
      The theme   48
      Agamemnon   52
      Achilles   68
      Hector   83
      The people at the end   95
      Conclusion   98
   Laoi in the *Odyssey*   100
      The theme   102
      Laoi and companions   104
      Laoi and suitors   110
      The people at the end   125

The group dies for its leader	126
The leader kills his group	137
Conclusion	143

3 *Laos* epic in performance 145
   Some preliminary considerations 147
   Homer's people outside Homer 152
   Similarities 153
   Differences 160
   The founding people 163
   Leos ritual 173
   Ritual formulae 174
   A festival of institutional progress 183
   Laos epic in performance 188
   Conclusion 195

Appendix A. Epic formulae 197

Appendix B. Ritual formulae 202

Bibliography 203

General index 218

Index of passages cited 225

PREFACE

This book is a revised version of my Cambridge dissertation on the Homeric *laos*. I have called it 'Homer's people', because from the start I wish to draw attention to some of its wider implications. The *laos* in Homer is not a group among others: I shall argue that any attempt to understand their role and character affects our understanding of early Greek hexameter poetry as a whole, of the Homeric poems as a prominent part of the genre, and of the performance of Homer in archaic and classical Greece. My task is complicated by a long tradition of Judaeo-Christian thought, which resulted in 'Homer's people', *laos Akhaion*, becoming the 'people of god', *laos theou*.[1] Under such circumstances, the older picture could only be reclaimed in an act of detailed analysis. This is what I am hoping to provide.

Since this book is not written for Homerists alone, a few general words about its background and aspirations may be in place. In classics, as in many other social sciences, there has recently been a trend towards combining the study of (literary) texts with that of social and political (power-)structures. Prominent players within the field of postmodern hermeneutics have often approached the world as text, while at the same time emphasising the intimate link between textual communication and social formation.[2]

The present study is in many ways indebted to this development and may be viewed as a contribution to it. As I shall argue, Homer's people are both the subject and the addressee

---

[1] Handed down via the *Septuagint*, the *New Testament* and the Church Fathers; for a first overview see *EWNT s.v.*, *PGL s.v.*

[2] For an overview from outside classics see Greenblatt and Gunn (1992); for classics see e.g. Foley (1981), Benjamin (1988), Winkler and Zeitlin (1990), Dougherty and Kurke (1993), Easterling (1997).

of what may well have been the most influential reflection on society in archaic and classical Greece. At Athens, this reflection took the form of rhapsodic performances at the city's most important state festival. Homer's people, together with their local counterpart, the founding people of Attica, helped to mark out the social space within which Athenian democracy envisaged its own coming into being. No specialised knowledge is needed to see that this has potentially far-reaching consequences for our understanding of political life in classical Athens and beyond.

Yet, I must emphasise that this book is not primarily a study of the classical Greek city. Some may regret its focus on Homer at the expense of Athens, on 'text' rather than 'society'; but, as any student of antiquity knows, this would not have troubled the Greeks themselves. For them, any reflection on their lives in the *polis* quite naturally started with Homeric poetry. Homeric poetry *was* classical Greece; not least, as I shall argue here, in the specific sense that it enabled societies – the city of Athens among them – to reflect on their founding acts. What this could add to our understanding of ancient Greek ritual and politics will have to be discussed in more detail elsewhere. In the meantime, I hope that those interested in the Homeric side of the issue may find this book of some use.

After an introductory section, chapter 1 looks at the place of the *laos* in the wider system of early epic language and thought. Throughout early Greek hexameter epic *laos* denotes a social world in need of support. Support is expected to come from single agents whose function is epitomised in the formulaic metaphor 'shepherd of the people' (*ποιμὴν λαῶν[3]). Since the shepherd does not usually act as he should, the people come to be associated with communal catastrophe in phrases such as 'he destroyed the people' (ὤλεσε λαόν).

Chapter 2 forms the core of the argument, offering an extensive reading of the *Iliad* and the *Odyssey*. Discussion of the

---

[3] Phrases that are not attested in this form in early Greek epic are marked with an asterisk.

PREFACE

Iliad focuses on the plight of Homer's people throughout the poem, on the failure of three exemplary leaders, Agamemnon, Achilles and Hector, to save them, and finally on the way in which different social frames of reference are set against and accommodated within the larger context of life among the people. The *Odyssey* poses slightly different problems. Here it will be asked how the three major groups 'people', 'companions' and 'suitors' interrelate, why we concentrate on the latter two at the expense of the former, and why they are redefined as Homer's people at points of narrative crisis.

Chapter 3 is designed to complement chapter 1. Taking its cue from Simonides, it investigates how Homer's people would have fitted into archaic and classical performance contexts. I first argue that the *laoi* outside epic are seen as the 'founding people' of political and sacred institutions. In the second half of the chapter the results of chapters 1–3 are combined in an attempt to understand better what Homer's people could have meant to the audience gathered at the festival of the Great Panathenaea and so to Athenian society as a whole.

This study is cast as a search for a Homeric audience. It proceeds from historically and generically unspecific observations to a historically specific performance context. Along this path, chapter 1 draws on and discusses all epic traditions and performances accessible to us today; chapter 2 many possible occasions, but only one tradition among others (Homeric song); chapter 3, finally, one occasion for the one Homeric text. The Great Panathenaea does not answer the question of who first heard Homer. It does, however, offer an important context for the reading proposed here. Hence its function in the present work.

All Greek, apart from the appendices, is translated or transliterated. Translations are based on Lattimore (1951) and (1965) for Homer, West (1988) and (1993) for Hesiod and lyric poetry, Nisetich (1980) for Pindar, Sandys (1919) and Race (1997) for the Pindaric fragments, Jebb (1905) and Fagles (1961) for Bacchylides, Grene and Lattimore (1953–72) for tragedy, Sommerstein (1980) and (1985) for Aristophanes,

PREFACE

de Sélincourt (1972) for Herodotus and Tredennick (1970) for Xenophon. I have sometimes adapted translations for the purpose of the argument but have generally sought to adhere to versions that are currently available. The two appendices have been added for those interested in the details of formulaic language.

Many people have helped in the making of this book. I am grateful for the support and criticism of my fellow graduate students Felix Budelmann, Rachel Foxley, Barbara Graziosi, Emily Greenwood, Liz Irwin and Pantelis Michelakis. James Diggle, Robin Osborne and Michael Reeve read through the manuscript and made many helpful suggestions. My two examiners Pat Easterling and Oliver Taplin offered much-needed encouragement, criticism and advice. Above all, I am grateful to my supervisor Simon Goldhill, who has challenged and supported me throughout the years. Pat Easterling suggested that the thesis might be included in the Cambridge Classical Studies and saw the project through its final stages. Pauline Hire proposed the title and improved the book in many other ways. Susan Moore saved me from countless mistakes and infelicities. I wish to thank them all for their help. The book is dedicated to Barbara for her love and understanding.

ABBREVIATIONS

Classical authors are abbreviated as in LSJ, journals as in *L'Année Philologique*. For the scholia I have used the following editions: Erbse for the *Iliad*, Dindorf for the *Odyssey*, Drachmann for Pindar, Holwerda and Rutherford for Aristophanes, and Greene for Plato. Standard works of classical scholarship are abbreviated as follows:

Allen	*Homeri Opera V*, ed. T. Allen, Oxford 1912
CEG II	*Carmina Epigraphica Graeca II*, ed. P. Hansen, Berlin 1989
Davies	*Epicorum Graecorum fragmenta*, ed. M. Davies, Göttingen 1988
Diggle	*Euripides: Phaethon*, ed. J. Diggle, Cambridge 1970
Dindorf	*Scholia Graeca in Homeri Odysseam*, ed. W. Dindorf, Oxford 1855
Drachmann	*Scholia vetera in Pindari carmina*, ed. A. Drachmann, Leipzig 1903–27
Erbse	*Scholia Graeca in Homeri Iliadem*, ed. H. Erbse, Berlin 1969–88
EWNT	*Exegetisches Wörterbuch zum neuen Testament*, eds. H. Balz and G. Schneider, Stuttgart 1978–
FGrHist	*Die Fragmente griechischer Historiker*, ed. F. Jacoby, Berlin and Leiden 1923–58
Grammatici Graeci	*Grammatici Graeci*, eds. R. Schneider, G. Uhlig, A. Hilgard, Leipzig 1867–1910
Greene	*Scholia Platonica contulerunt atque in-*

ABBREVIATIONS

	vestigaverunt F. Allen, J. Burnet, C. Parker, ed. W. Greene, Haverford 1938
Holwerda	*Scholia in Aristophanem pars I, fasc. III.I continens scholia vetera in Nubes*, ed. D. Holwerda, Groningen 1977
IG	*Inscriptiones Graecae*
Kannicht/Snell	see *TrGF* vols. 1–2
Kassel/Austin	see *PCG*
Koster	*Scholia in Aristophanem, pars I, fasc. IA continens prolegomena de comoedia*, ed. W. Koster, Groningen 1975
LfgrE	*Lexikon des frühgriechischen Epos*, eds. B. Snell and H. Erbse, Göttingen 1955–
LSJ	*A Greek–English lexicon*, eds. H. Liddell, R. Scott, H. Jones *et al.*, 9th edn, Oxford 1996
M–W	*Fragmenta selecta*, in *Theogonia, Opera et dies, Scutum Hesiodi*, ed. F. Solmsen; *Fragmenta selecta* eds. R. Merkelbach and M. West, Oxford 1983
Nauck	*Tragicorum Graecorum fragmenta*, ed. A. Nauck, Leipzig 1889
Page	*Epigrammata Graeca*, ed. D. Page, Oxford 1975
PCG	*Poetae comici Graeci*, eds. R. Kassel and C. Austin, Berlin 1983–
PGL	*A patristic Greek lexicon*, ed. G. Lampe, Oxford 1961–8
PLF	*Poetarum Lesbiorum fragmenta*, eds. E. Lobel and D. Page, Oxford 1955
PMG	*Poetae melici Graeci*, ed. D. Page, Oxford 1962
P–W	*The Delphic oracle*, eds. H. Parke and D. Wormell, Oxford 1956
Radt	see *TrGF* vols. 3–4
RE	*Paulys Realencyclopädie der classischen Altertumswissenschaft*, eds. G. Wissowa *et al.*, 2nd edn, Stuttgart 1894–1963

ABBREVIATIONS

Rose	*Aristotelis qui ferebantur librorum fragmenta*, ed. V. Rose, Leipzig 1886
Rutherford	*Scholia Aristophanica*, ed. W. Rutherford, London 1896
Stallbaum	*Eustathii commentarii ad Homeri Odysseam*, ed. G. Stallbaum, Leipzig 1825–6
TrGF	*Tragicorum Graecorum fragmenta*, eds. S. Radt, B. Snell, R. Kannicht, Göttingen 1977–
van der Valk	*Eustathii archiepiscopi Thessalonicensis commentarii ad Homeri Iliadem pertinentes*, ed. M. van der Valk, Leiden 1971–87
West	*Iambi et elegi Graeci ante Alexandrum cantati*, ed. M. West, Oxford 1971–2

INTRODUCTION

The history of scholarship on Homeric *laos* is quickly written. In 1977 Latacz pointed out that the word was little understood and that a thorough investigation was overdue.[1] Since then some progress has been made. Welskopf collected and discussed the material as part of her study of ancient social typology.[2] Others have added further observations;[3] but useful as they may be, none of these publications have decisively changed the situation.

When Latacz declared our lack of understanding of the Homeric *laos*, he rejected the view that had been current before him. This view goes back to Jeanmaire, who argued influentially that Homeric *laoi* designate a social grouping of male adult warriors.[4] Jeanmaire's idea was taken up and elaborated among others by Heubeck,[5] who suggests a class opposition between epic *laos* and *demos*, which he traces back to Mycenean times.[6] It was this elaborated version of Jeanmaire's theory which was attacked in the late seventies

---

[1] Latacz (1977) 121.
[2] Welskopf (1981a).
[3] Contributions include Descat (1979), Nagy (1979) 69–72 and 82–4, Harmatta (1981) 156–62, Andreev (1988) 18f., Donlan (1989) 15f., Ulf (1990) 99–105, *LfgrE* s.v., Casewitz (1992), Wyatt (1994–5). Taplin (1992), Pazdernik (1995) and Martin (1997) do not study *laos* as such but in passing make a number of valuable suggestions. The variation between singular *laos* and plural *laoi* has exercised readers ever since schol. *Il.* 1.10b. It is discussed from a formalist perspective in Witte (1907) 43–5; for a recent survey see Welskopf (1981a) 163–7, Wyatt (1994–5). I have not been able to solve the problem.
[4] Jeanmaire (1939) 57, to whom Björck (1950) 318–26, Kirk (1968) 112f. and Benveniste (1973) 371–6 have little to add. Maddoli (1970) clarifies some of their misconceptions; for earlier literature see Schmidt (1886) 573–5, Witte (1907) *passim*, esp. 43–5, Güntert (1932) 39f., followed by Specht (1944) 200; Curtius (1894), esp. 466 and Kretschmer (1930) 77f. study the Attic form; Dieterich (1891) 12f. and Kern (1933) look at later developments.
[5] Heubeck (1984b), first published in 1969.
[6] Heubeck (1984b) 457; cf. Heubeck (1984a) 613, Lejeune (1965).

by Latacz and others. Latacz himself approaches the problem from the point of view of the social historian and comes to the conclusion that epic *laos* does not designate a social or military elite which can be seen in contrast with the *demos*.[7] Around the same time van Effenterre re-examined the issue from the viewpoint of the linguist. He writes at the end of his careful and detailed study:

> The *laoi* can equally well be the soldiers of an army as the members of any crowd. The only constant meaning one can ascribe to the term is that of an undifferentiated, and we might add, subordinate mass of people, viewed as being in an inferior or precarious situation.[8]

As we shall see, both the lack of differentiation and the precarious circumstances diagnosed by van Effenterre are important characteristics of the term *laos*.[9] But above all he was right to point out that the *laoi* are too flexible, too socially inclusive to form any class in the usual sense.[10] The old paradigm was refuted, and the way opened for a new beginning.

The first scholar to respond to the challenge was Nagy, who argues that our term is thematic in the *Iliad* with its focus on Achilles, the man who brings 'grief' (ἄχος) to the 'people' (λαός).[11] This thematic emphasis is further enhanced by the close formulaic link between the term *laos* and the name Achaeans.[12] It is explored in the negative interaction between Achilles, Patroclus and the Achaean people.[13]

Nagy's observations are important for what they teach us about the Homeric *laos*; but above all they mark a decisive methodological turn towards the poetic-cultural 'theme' as a focus of scholarly interest. For the first time in Homeric studies the dichotomy between 'epic poetry' and 'social background', so detrimental to our understanding of both, was

---

[7] Latacz (1977) 122.
[8] Van Effenterre (1977) 51f.
[9] Cf. ch. 1, 'The failed ideal' and 'Society and the stone'.
[10] Van Effenterre's conclusions are to some extent anticipated by Maddoli (1970) 42–4 and 47. They are further developed by Descat (1979), Geddes (1984) 21; cf. also Rihll (1986) without reference to the *laoi*.
[11] Nagy (1979) 69–72, using the etymology of the name Achilles suggested by Palmer (1963) 79.
[12] Nagy (1979) 82–4.
[13] Nagy (1979) chs. 5, 6.

overcome. Nagy's approach does not only account for both, but suggests that what is 'poetry' in Homer cannot be grasped without a thorough study of its broader socio-cultural implications and *vice versa*.

The present investigation adopts this approach. In doing so it narrows down the focus of Nagy's work in some respects but widens it in others. Nagy studied a variety of interconnected concepts such as 'the people' (λαός), 'grief' (ἄχος), 'power' (κράτος), 'the hero' (ἥρως) mainly in the Iliadic tradition.[14] The present argument, while for the most part restricting itself to the *laos*, looks at a wider range of texts and performative contexts: not only Achilles in the *Iliad*, but also Agamemnon and Hector; not only the *Iliad*, but the whole of Homeric epic, indeed, of early Greek hexameter poetry; and not only the texts as we have them, but the *Gesamtkunstwerk* of a song about Homer's people performed for an early Greek audience.

Between the omnipresent hero and the absent *polis*

Despite what has been said so far, the *laoi* of epic have continued to attract little attention. In the following section I would like to discuss briefly why this situation arose and how it can be redressed. I start by looking at two of the concepts that have so far dominated the field, the Homeric hero and the Homeric *polis*. As will appear already from a cursory overview, these two concepts are strictly complementary. For over half a century the hero and the city together have marked out the conceptual framework for discussions about Homeric poetry and Homeric society.

Under the influence of existentialist notions, 'heroes' have dominated post-war Homeric scholarship in the English-speaking world.[15] American critics in particular have used the

---

[14] Nagy (1979), cf. *id.* (1990a).
[15] E.g. Whitman (1958) and especially (1982); for earlier literature on the Homeric hero see n. 29; see also Chadwick (1912), Bowra (1930) and (1972) ch. 5. Bowra (1952) applies notions of 'the heroic' to non-Greek cultures. The custom was to become widespread.

concept for close and often illuminating study,[16] and thanks to their work 'the hero' has today become the single most important category in the reading of Homer. This situation has its drawbacks as well as its advantages. For example, there is a certain tendency in recent scholarship to heap ever new glosses on the back of the Homeric noun ἥρως ('hero').[17] The pioneering work of Whitman is symptomatic of this. Whitman presents the second half of Sarpedon's speech in *Iliad* 12[18] as a paradigm of the 'heroic paradox': 'The whole paradox is here: Honor is in action and self-risk.'[19] And further: 'The individual may, if he is tenacious enough, satisfy his heroic quest by the choice and assertion of his own death. Society, in contrast to the heroic individual, seeks continuity.'[20] Without wishing to enter into a detailed discussion of Whitman's claims, I would like to ask: who, precisely, is this 'heroic individual'? Sarpedon is not introduced as a 'hero' (ἥρως) in *Iliad* 12 nor is Glaucus (in fact, neither Sarpedon nor Glaucus is ever explicitly called a hero in the *Iliad*), nor indeed does Sarpedon mention any 'heroes' (ἥρωες) in his speech. The anonymous Lycian speaker in the lines not quoted by Whitman is interested in 'kings' (βασιλῆες), Sarpedon in his own voice makes reference to a 'mortal' (βροτός), but where and how the 'heroic individual' comes into the picture remains unclear.

I do not suggest that Sarpedon and Glaucus *could* not be called 'heroes' (ἥρωες). Nor do I wish to promote a heuristic doctrine according to which the meaning of a text consists in the sum total of its words. Concepts such as that of the 'hero' (ἥρως) or the 'people' (λαός or λαοί) inevitably transcend the

---

[16] E.g. Redfield (1975), Nagy (1979), Schein (1984); cf. also Griffin (1980), Hainsworth (1991), Goldhill (1991), Wofford (1992), Seaford (1994).
[17] The items on offer range from the popular 'heroic code' as found e.g. in Schein (1984) *passim*, Wofford (1992) 50 and *passim*, Raaflaub (1997a) 633, Schofield (1999) ch. 1, to Hainsworth's less known 'heroic brows'; see Hainsworth (1991) 30.
[18] *Il.* 12.322–8.
[19] Whitman (1982) 28.
[20] Whitman (1982) 28.

sum of their usages,[21] and, in the end, labels such as 'heroic', 'political' etc. will do more justice to the interplay between word and world than a single term dragged out of its context. There is no question about the long-term goal, then. But the basic lexical work needs to be done first. This order of things is important. Whitman's enthusiastic paraphrase is not objectionable because it is too general. Rather, it is objectionable because it is too general too soon.

Once the precedent was set, scholars proceeded to gloss 'heroisms' into their texts wherever it seemed convenient.[22] Much of this is open to dispute, but it is one gloss in particular which needs to be clarified here. Are the Homeric heroes, or are they not, leaders of the people?[23] Do they, as 'heroes' (ἥρωες), take upon themselves the privileges and the tasks which leadership entails? Whitman left the question open, but others wanted more.

The decisive step was taken by Redfield, who, in the wake of structuralism, sought to reform the existentialist figure he inherited from the previous generation of scholars by putting his hero into a more clearly defined social context.[24] As a result he added one important assumption. On Redfield's view, Sarpedon's 'kings' (βασιλῆες) *are* in effect heroes. He writes:

Heroism is for Homer a definite social task, and the heroes are a definite social stratum. [...] This is the Homeric governing class, the propertied

---

[21] In the case of Homeric ἥρως ('hero'), it is clear that passages such as *Il.* 1.4 or *Cypria* fr. 1 (Davies) reach beyond their immediate textual surroundings.

[22] E.g. Redfield (1975), Schein (1984), Silk (1987) 69–73, Goldhill (1991) chs. 1–2, Wofford (1992) ch. 1; for a historicising view see van Wees (1988) and (1992).

[23] The long-standing debate between adherents of 'competitive' and 'co-operative' values in Homer belongs here; see e.g. Adkins (1960a), (1960b), (1970), (1972), (1982), (1987), Long (1970), Scott (1980) and (1981), Rowe (1983), Gagarin (1987), Lloyd-Jones (1987), Zanker (1990), Cairns (1993), Yamagata (1994), Schofield (1999). The present discussion can help to refocus the issue.

[24] A note on chronology: although Redfield reacts against Whitman's views of the hero (Redfield 1975 pp. 10f.), Whitman's fullest statement of the 'heroic paradox' in Homer was only published after his death and 7 years after the publication of Redfield (1975). It is implied e.g. in Whitman (1958) *passim*, esp. 199, 213; cf. also (1982) 44–65, first published in 1970.

class, and also the class on which the burden falls of maintaining the community.[25]

After this precautionary measure Redfield goes on to declare: 'The most lucid statement of the hero's role and task is Sarpedon's speech to Glaukos...'[26] It is characteristic of Redfield's scholarship that he alone attempts to justify a gloss that was to become widely accepted.[27] His solution, however, fails to satisfy. If 'heroes' (ἥρωες) and 'kings' (βασιλῆες) are coextensive in Homer – in itself hardly an attractive thought – and one of the two concepts is ideologically privileged, would we not expect Sarpedon to employ it? The fact that he does not mention 'heroes' (ἥρωες) may be excused in any other context, but it can hardly be excused in 'the most lucid statement of the hero's [NB: *not* the king's] role and task'.[28] Redfield never substantiates his claim. With his attempt to understand better the heroic world of Homer he inadvertently highlights one of its most fundamental shortcomings: epic heroes are no leaders.

What Whitman, Redfield and many other readers of Homer failed to realise, they could have learnt from scholarship which developed parallel to their own. Thanks to the work mainly of archaeologists and students of Greek religion, it is clear today that, whether in cult or in myth, the Greek 'hero' (ἥρως) is a creature of the past, always already cast as remote and therefore beyond the synchronic framework of group and leader.[29] This is why tragedy, for instance, avoids the word altogether. There cannot be meaningful interaction among 'heroes' in a genre which is fundamentally synchro-

---

[25] Redfield (1975) 99; for Redfield's attempt to gloss 'king' with 'warrior' see also Donlan (1979) and Collins (1988) ch. 3.
[26] Redfield (1975) 99.
[27] E.g. Loraux (1982) *passim*, Morris (1986) 115–29, Thalmann (1988) 5f., van Wees (1988) and (1992) *passim*, Goldhill (1991) 79, Wofford (1992) 44f., Alvis (1995) 5, Bennett (1997) ch. 5, esp. 90f.
[28] Redfield (1975) 99.
[29] Thus already Rohde (1966) 118 (2nd ed. 1897), who, however, like other scholars of his generation, was compelled to postulate a gap between Homer's heroes and the 'later' usage; cf. Farnell (1921) 16. More recent scholarship has moved away from this doctrine; see e.g. Brelich (1958) 386f., Nagy (1979) *passim*, esp. 114–17; see also Snodgrass (1971) and (1982), Hadzisteliou-Price (1973) and (1979).

nising in character.[30] Pindar and Bacchylides, too, are good examples of how the word 'hero' (ἥρως) opens a temporal/paradigmatic dimension. Epinicion would not function as it does without this other-worldly quality.[31]

If we return to early hexameter epic, we can see that Hesiod betrays a similar bias. In his account of world history in the *Works and days* he introduces as a fourth generation after that of gold, silver and bronze the 'heroic men' (ἄνδρες ἥρωες), who are described as 'more just' (γένος δικαιότερον 158) and 'better' (γένος ἄρειον 158) and who represent the 'earlier generation' (προτέρη γενεή 160) which provides a point of contrast to our own. Hesiod is not interested in social differentiation within his heroic world. As a 'race' (γένος) between gods and men his heroes all enjoy equal status. They may, as has been argued recently, fall into different groups with a different afterlife.[32] But this does not mean that any of them act as leaders.

Hesiod may be idiosyncratic in his depiction of world history, but in this particular point he only expresses what is assumed throughout Greek literature: the 'hero' (ἥρως) among heroes participates in a fundamentally amorphous social world. He gains semantic depth through (diachronic) analogy, not (synchronic) social structure. The Greek 'hero' (ἥρως) above all points to 'us', the non-heroes, *outside* his world. With slight variations Hesiod's picture conforms to what we gather from other texts, including Homer.[33]

Recent semantic analysis suggests that Homeric 'heroes' (ἥρωες) do not in this respect differ from Hesiodic ones.[34] To be sure, there are neighbouring concepts such as that of the

---

[30] The 'exceptions' A. *A.* 516, fr. 55 (Radt) and E. fr. 446 (Nauck) occur in contexts of cult.
[31] As is shown by the passages in Slater (1969) *s.v.*; for an example of how the 'king' may be distinguished from the 'hero' see Pi. fr. 133; cf. also Rohde (1966) 117 with n. 24, who cites Pi. *P.* 5.94f.
[32] Most (1997) 117–19.
[33] Against von Fritz (1966) 377f., who sees a diachronic development from Homer to Hesiod; and Brelich (1958) 348, who dismisses the passages which describe heroes as a group as 'cases of most marginal exceptionality'.
[34] Cf. *LfgrE s.v.* B: 'the retrospective character [of the term ἥρως] seems to be fundamental'; cf. Brelich (1958) 386f. and above n. 29.

INTRODUCTION

'king' (βασιλεύς) or 'general' (ἡγεμών) which do comprise leadership. Both the *Iliad* and the *Odyssey* show single agents who interact with groups of people around them. These agents can also at times be referred to as 'heroes' (ἥρωες), and one may argue that the boundaries between the 'hero' and the 'king' in particular are often blurred. However, it remains the case that no Homeric hero is ever, *qua* ἥρως, seen as a leader of other people. Had this point always been sufficiently clear, some scholarly confusion could have been avoided.

The epic 'hero' (ἥρως), then, cannot support the wealth of associations with which he has been burdened in the past. He can, of course, in Hesiod and generations of sub-Homeric authors and readers, be cast as peculiar in many ways. The heroes are more just than we are (Hesiod),[35] keep to a healthier diet (Plato),[36] need no war-trumpets, and therefore have none (Aristarchus).[37] The overwhelming majority of ancient commentators capitalise on the fact that the Greek term ἥρως ('hero') creates a point of reference for 'us', the audience. They do not, on the whole, suggest that it yields the synchronic social structure of groups and leaders.

There are two exceptions to what has just been said. Like Redfield in his attempt to reform existentialist notions of heroism, the ancient Homeric scholar Istros suggested that only the 'kings' (βασιλεῖς) in Homer are 'heroes' (ἥρωες):

ὅτι σαφῶς πάντας τοὺς Ἕλληνας ἥρωας καλεῖ, πρὸς Ἴστρον λέγοντα μόνους τοὺς βασιλεῖς ἥρωας λέγεσθαι ὑφ' Ὁμήρου.[38]

He clearly calls all the Greeks heroes; this is against Istros who says that only the kings are called heroes by Homer.

The scholiast warns us that mainstream Alexandrian scholarship resisted Istros' view. Yet he was not the first who proposed it. Already Aristotle had used the notion of the 'hero'

---

[35] Hes. *Op.* 158f.
[36] Pl. *R.* 404b10–c2.
[37] Erbse *ad* schol. *Il.* 18.219a collects the relevant passages.
[38] Schol. *Il.* 13.629 a.¹; cf. schol. *Il.* 2.110a and the parallels quoted by Erbse *ad loc.*; see also Rohde (1966) 118 n. 26.

(ἥρως) to account for the phenomenon of early kingship,[39] and in a passage from the *Problems* we read:

οἱ δὲ ἡγεμόνες τῶν ἀρχαίων μόνοι ἦσαν ἥρωες, οἱ δὲ λαοὶ ἄνθρωποι, ὧν ἐστὶν ὁ χορός.[40]

Of the ancients only the leaders were heroes [ἥρωες], the people [λαοί] where human beings; the chorus is made up of them.

As Redfield himself acknowledges, this is the ultimate source of his equivocation.[41] According to Aristotle, of the ancients only the 'leaders' (ἡγεμόνες) were heroes, the 'people' (λαοί) 'human beings' (ἄνθρωποι). I cannot here discuss in detail why this reading was attractive to Aristotle.[42] Suffice it to note that, like Redfield, he maps an analogic-diachronic model of human relationships (ἥρωες–ἄνθρωποι) onto an assumed functional-synchronic one (ἡγεμόνες–λαοί); and that the terms he uses to do this point a way out of our dilemma.

Aristotle's pair 'leaders–people' (ἡγεμόνες–λαοί) provides the epic world of groups and leaders which students of Homer as 'heroic poetry' have so long sought to find. While the 'hero' (ἥρως) gains semantic depth primarily in contrast with agents essentially unlike him, Aristotle's 'leader' (ἡγεμών) and 'people' (λαοί) differ in function, but not in analogic-diachronic essence. Had Aristotle phrased his equation in any other terms, it would be of little value here. As it stands, it points us to the Homeric word *laos*. This is my starting-point.

Much like the Greek word for hero, the metaphorical expression 'shepherd of the people' is used to denote single agents. The hero and the shepherd of the people do not appear to differ in distribution, but they differ greatly in implication. The 'hero' (ἥρως) among other heroes participates

---

[39] Arist. *Pol.* 1285b3ff., 1332b12–23.
[40] Arist. *Pr.* 922b, already criticised by Rohde (1966) 118 with n. 26; the *Problems* may not have been written by Aristotle himself. I assume that they were, but the question need not be solved here.
[41] Redfield (1975) 241 n. 3.
[42] One may start from the fact that Aristotle develops his equation in the context of a discussion of tragedy. Tragedy in turn seems to be influenced by Hesiod. See e.g. Hes. fr. 1.16 (M–W) with the interesting concept of a 'race of kings' (γένος βασιλήων).

in a fundamentally amorphous social world and thus comes to represent a 'race' (γένος) in Hesiodic or sub-Homeric accounts; while the 'shepherd' (ποιμήν) among 'people' (λαοί) is defined by a situation of social interaction between two diverse agents. There is not and could not be a 'race of shepherds' in early Greek language and thought. As a 'shepherd' the single agent is always already a social composite, combining as he does the one (ποιμήν in the singular) with the many (λαοί in the plural) in a close functional relationship.

Life among *laoi*, as epitomized by the formula 'shepherd of the people' (*ποιμὴν λαῶν) is built, above all, on social interaction. It divides the world into groups and leaders who are correlated through an unambiguously stable grammatical hierarchy. There are 'shepherds of the people' (*ποιμένες λαῶν) in the formulaic language of early Greek epic, but no 'people of the shepherds' (*λαοὶ ποιμένων). At this level, at least, the shepherd is always a function of his group. As a result, our understanding of the Homeric individual becomes closely implicated with that of the people around him.

A number of well-known passages may serve to illustrate this point. For example, Agamemnon's fame in the *Iliad* depends entirely on the well-being of the people he leads.[43] Similarly, Chryses' honour in *Iliad* book 1 and Achilles' in *Iliad* book 16 are closely linked with the welfare of the *laoi*.[44] Finally, in a passage that marks one of the pathetic highpoints of the *Iliad*, Hector decides to face death because someone might say about him that 'he lost/destroyed the people' (ὤλεσε λαόν).[45] All these passages may testify to 'heroic' values and behaviour, but if they do, it is the repeated references to the people that put into perspective such key terms as 'fame', 'honour' and 'might' (κλέος, τιμή, and βίη). In the context of the *laoi* our search for the single agent in early

---

[43] E.g. *Il.* 2.114f., 9.21f.; for discussion see ch. 2, '*Laoi* in the *Iliad*', pp. 52–68 below.
[44] *Il.* 1.454, 16.237; already quoted and discussed in Nagy (1979) 82; see here ch. 2, '*Laoi* in the *Iliad*', pp. 68–83.
[45] *Il.* 22.104–10; cf. Raaflaub (1997b) 17 without reference to the *laoi*; for detailed discussion see here ch. 2, '*Laoi* in the *Iliad*', pp. 83–95.

Greek hexameter thus becomes a search for the groups of people around him. This brings my project into close contact with a second concept which has dominated Homeric scholarship in the last fifty years: the *polis*.

Ever since the seminal work of Finley, Homeric society has been described in terms of the – however present or absent – emerging *polis*.[46] Discussion has been diverse and often illuminating, and I cannot trace it in all its ramifications here.[47] Rather than attempting such a survey, I concentrate on some points on which general agreement has been reached.

During the length of time in which the Homeric poems emerged, drastic changes occurred in the structure of Greek societies, changes which eventually transformed a world of dominant aristocratic households into the classical city-state. The Homeric poems reflect this tension between *polis* and *oikos*, combining the two strands in an often complicated balancing-act. The ensuing mixture accounts for the difficulties we have today in describing Homer's social world.

This is the *communis opinio*. There have been countless attempts to go further and assess the precise nature of Homeric society, sometimes privileging the *polis*, sometimes stressing the importance of the *oikos*. Finley himself, who recommended that we date Homer's world back to the ninth or tenth century, argued that the *polis* is absent from it.[48] More recent contributors acknowledge the existence in Homer of early 'political' elements but cannot agree on how to interpret them.[49] On the one hand, Morris influentially argues that the Homeric poems represent a pro-aristocratic manifesto at a time of sinking aristocratic repute.[50] Against him Scully and others have stressed the sympathetic attention the *polis* receives.[51] In

---

[46] Finley (1977); for earlier literature see e.g. Fanta (1882), Calhoun (1934) and (1962), Strasburger (1953) and (1954).
[47] For an historical overview see Gschnitzer (1991).
[48] Finley (1977) 34 (no city-state) and 48 (the world described in Homer reflects the tenth or ninth century).
[49] For summary and bibliography see Gschnitzer (1991), Raaflaub (1991) and (1997a).
[50] Morris (1986).
[51] Scully (1990) *passim*, esp. ch. 7; cf. Thomas (1966), Gschnitzer (1971), (1976), (1981), (1983), (1991), Raaflaub (1989), (1991), (1997a), (1997b).

the words of Raaflaub: 'Of course it [the Homeric *polis*] is not a community of citizens (koinonia politōn) in the classical ... sense, but it is developing in that direction.'[52] Raaflaub, in his somewhat forced attempt to discover political structure, goes so far as to turn the Achaean camp into a *polis*.[53] Others are more cautious.[54] Others still resort to an anthropological framework which was already implicit in Finley's work. Quiller, for instance, seeks to avoid the dichotomy of *polis* and *oikos* by introducing the concept of a 'tribal society'. While this helps him to lose some unwelcome conceptual ballast, his suggestions are on the whole too unspecific to settle the issue.[55]

The list of contributors could be extended, but enough has been said to outline the general dilemma: Homer locates his world somewhere on the way to the classical *polis*, but there seems to be no generally acceptable way of establishing just where. I do not propose to answer the question here. What I would like to offer instead is a way in which the Greeks themselves, poets, historians, and philosophers of the archaic and classical eras, would have referred to the phenomenon of an early society: *laos*, the founding people. For example, Plato's Athenian stranger in the *Laws* asks who will be the 'founding people' of the model city.[56] On this reading the *laos* (or, in its Attic form: the *leos*) represent the pre-political social world *par excellence*; they are the group that aetiologically predates social structure. This view was widely held in classical Greece. For example, Aristotle reports that Athenian political myth conceptualised the (re-)founding of its *polis* under Theseus by referring to the *leos* that was gathered on the occasion.[57] Once again we see the same basic process:

---

[52] Raaflaub (1997a) 632.
[53] Raaflaub (1997a) 629; for the Achaean camp as a mock-city see ch. 3, n. 73.
[54] E.g. Seaford (1994) ch. 1, §1.
[55] Quiller (1981), followed by Ulf (1990); Greenhalgh (1972) introduces the notion of 'patriotism', which does not help much either.
[56] Pl. *L.* 707e1f.
[57] Plutarch *Thes.* 25.1 = Aristotle fr. 384 (Rose); Plutarch is quoting from the *Athenaion Politeia*, which may not be by Aristotle himself. For convenience, I adopt the traditional view.

renewed political life starts from the gathering of the people.[58] Plato and Aristotle are relatively late exponents of an idea which is also implied in many earlier Greek texts.[59] From very early on, and with remarkable consistency through the genres of epic, lyric, iambus, elegy, tragedy, comedy, Herodotean *historie* and Platonic *philosophia*, the term *laos* is the solution the Greeks themselves had to the modern puzzle of a society before the *polis*. This does not answer the question of what 'Greece in the making' might actually have looked like.[60] But it does indicate how it entered the discourse of the Greeks themselves.

[58] For further discussion see ch. 3, pp. 170f.
[59] For references and discussion see ch. 3, 'The founding people'.
[60] Osborne (1996).

I

LAOI IN EARLY GREEK HEXAMETER POETRY[1]

The 'discourse of the Greeks' is a hypothetical construct with limited heuristic value. However, there are good reasons why it should be invoked here. As I have argued above, an uncontrolled proliferation of glosses has made the work of postwar Homeric critics increasingly difficult. Under such circumstances it seemed advisable to reintroduce some semantic clarity.[2] Another reason why this study adopts a decidedly lexical approach is more specific to its task. Who early epic *laoi* are, what they do and suffer, hope and fear, has been lost to us even at the most basic level of understanding. We know so little about these people that every argumentative step needs to be developed carefully and in close contact with the texts. Finally, and most importantly, the word *laos*, in Homer and around Homer, constantly appears as a performed word. It is a deeply un-prosaic notion, endowed with a poetic–ritual force which we find stored in well-defined grammatical, metrical, semantic and social contexts. Here, if anywhere, attention to linguistic detail will be richly rewarded. This is not to suggest that something like the essence of *laos* may be found in a close description of the term alone. Homer's people are more than a sum total of lexical usages. They are dynamic, not static, in contact with neighbouring forms of human interaction as well as with the (unlimited) possibilities of their own existence over time and genre. There is no 'definite'

---

[1] The phrase 'early Greek hexameter poetry' is used as in Thalmann (1984) xi–xxi. It implies that the texts of early Greek epic share a number of metrical and linguistic features which reflect a shared overall outlook. Unlike Thalmann I have included the earliest elegiac poets.
[2] As rightly suggested by Taplin (1992) *passim*, esp. 49f. As examples of negligent glossing I quote Ulf (1990) ch. 3 and Raaflaub (1997b), who consistently confuse the two terms δῆμος and λαός. The custom is widespread.

meaning of the word *laos* behind the textual moment. But there are tendencies, traditions, hints of semantic preference which need to be understood and set out in a basic form before we can begin to engage with the texts. This is what the first chapter hopes to achieve.

Let me begin by describing the term *laos* as it was traditionally used and understood in early Greek hexameter poetry. For this I draw on material from the *Iliad*, the *Odyssey*, the early epic fragments, the *Homeric hymns*, Hesiod and the earliest elegiac poets. Special attention is devoted to recurrent themes and motifs and, inevitably, to the use of formulaic language.

The concept of the formula, introduced to Homeric studies by Parry,[3] and further developed by his successors,[4] provides an important tool for the understanding of the Homeric poems, a tool, however, which has often proved difficult to handle. Neither the function nor the form of the formula has been clarified beyond doubt, and this has sometimes prevented it from becoming as fruitful for our understanding of the texts as it might be.

The view of the formula adopted in this study is based on two major assumptions, one positive, one largely negative. With Russo it will be held that Homer's diction forms 'an amalgam of elements covering a spectrum from highly formulaic to non-formulaic'.[5] Frequency of recurrence as well as metrical, semantic, grammatical and phonetic stability are among the criteria with which the traditional character of a phrase will be assessed, but no clear line will be drawn between what is formulaic and what is not. On the positive side, I follow Watkins in supposing that the Indo-European formula is a 'vehicle of themes' and that 'in the totality of those we find the doctrine, ideology and culture of the Indo-

---

[3] Parry (1971).
[4] Russo (1997) gives an overview.
[5] Russo (1997) 259; for the formal flexibility of the Homeric formula see also Hainsworth (1968). For its semantic flexibility see Russo (1963) and (1966). Nagler (1967) and (1974) combines the two; more recent discussion in Martin (1989) 162–6.

Europeans'.[6] Of course, not *every* formula is always equally telling. But traditional phrases such as 'shepherd of the people'[7] may, under certain circumstances, carry in themselves the seed of potential texts: 'formulas may also function to encapsulate entire myths and other narratives...'[8] and further: 'There can be no doubt that the formula is the vehicle of the central theme of a proto-text.'[9] What Watkins assumes for the Indo-European formula in general has been argued for the Homeric formula in particular by Nagy.[10] In accordance with his concept of the 'traditional theme' it will be expected that traditional epic narratives are reflected in frequent traditional phrases.[11] Such narratives may in themselves take a highly formulaic shape (e.g. 'he destroyed/lost the people), allowing us to see the surviving epics as realisations of and meditations on the themes inherent in the formulaic language of hexameter poetry.

It follows that the role played by formulae in this study will be both important and uncertain. Important, in that prominent combinations such as 'shepherd of the people' or 'he destroyed the people' are given special attention. Uncertain, because no consistent attempt is made to separate formulae 'proper' from material that can be defined as more loosely traditional. The result is a methodological balancing-act. Particularly clear examples of formulaic expression may give rise to other, more general considerations. Conversely, attention may be drawn to examples of formulaic language as part of an ongoing larger argument. It is hoped that the different aspects may complement and illuminate each other.

---

[6] Watkins (1995) 68; cf. Tannen (1982), Bakker (1993) 8f.; Kahane (1997) 111f. stresses the importance of 'sameness' for preserving cultural continuity.
[7] Watkins (1995) 45.
[8] Watkins (1995) 10.
[9] Watkins (1995) 10.
[10] E.g. in the introduction to Nagy (1979); see also Nagy (1990a) 18–35, (1996a) 22ff.; cf. the concept of 'traditional referentiality' as developed in Foley (1991) 7; see also Foley (1999), Kahane (1994) and (1997), esp. 136f.
[11] Cf. Nagy (1979) 78: 'we expect to see in Homeric poetry the automatic distribution of set phraseology appropriate to set themes.'

'Shepherd of the people'

The epic word *laos* is most often found in the formulaic phrase 'shepherd of the people' (ποιμένα/ποιμένι λαῶν), which occurs 62 times at the end of the hexameter line, 56 of them in Homer. Together with 'shepherd of the people', but less frequently, we find a number of related phrases which cover other cases and metrical positions.[12] Some of these phrases are obscure, but there is little doubt that the all-pervading image of the shepherd helps us to understand less perspicuous formations.

'Shepherd of the people' was regarded a standard example of metaphorical language in classical antiquity.[13] As a metaphor the phrase entails an element of thought-experiment. Leader and group relate to one another *as if* they were shepherd and flock; though, of course, they are not. Among other things, this means that we are offered a model of social interaction which is marked as such. What precisely this model entails will be investigated presently. For the moment we need to add one more qualification: we have a shepherd but no sheep.[14] Our metaphor is made explicit only for the single agent. Accordingly, it is the shepherd with whom I start.

The concept of a 'shepherd of the people' was widespread in the ancient cultures of Mesopotamia and western Asia, and it has been suggested that it was in fact imported into Greece from there.[15] For our purposes we can leave aside this question and concentrate on what the Greeks themselves came to make of it. I shall here concentrate on the testimony of epic

---

[12] See Appendix A.1.
[13] Schol. D.T. in *Grammatici Graeci* I.3 p. 458.26–34; cf. X. *Mem.* 3.2.1, Arist. *EN* 1161a12–15, schol. *Il.* 2.85b, Apollon. *s.v.* ποιμήν, Serv. *A.* 11.811; *pace* Benveniste (1973) 373 the title never became a 'cliché'. See also Fränkel (1921) 75f. and 113.
[14] Against Philo *Legatio ad Gaium* 76 and especially Iamb. *VP* 35.260, whose view is developed in Collins (1996) ch. 2.
[15] Pritchard (1969) collects the relevant material; see also Murray (1990) 1–7, Collins (1996) 21–3, West (1997) 226f.

alone. The *Odyssey*, the *Homeric hymns* and Hesiod, together with the pastoral simile of the *Iliad*, tell us a great deal about the role of shepherds in early Greek hexameter poetry.[16]

The first thing to note is the importance of cattle farming in the world of epic. Odysseus wipes out a generation of Ithacans because they eat up his livestock. Achilles thinks an attempt on his flocks a good reason for joining the Trojan war.[17] In Hesiod, finally, the Theban war is presented as being sparked by a quarrel over the sheep of Oedipus, and this – together with the Trojan war – leads on to the extinction of a whole race of heroes.[18] The metaphor of the shepherd is nothing less than central to a genre in which the possession of flocks largely determines a person's wealth and social standing.[19]

My second point is that the shepherd of early Greek epic is not the owner of the animals he farms.[20] Young warriors are often seen herding flocks, but they do so only until they grow up and become cattle-owners themselves.[21] The shepherds of epic typically work for payment.[22] In order to earn a living they survive on the margins of the inhabited world, in the mountains or on river-banks,[23] without a proper house,[24] without human company[25] and without the benefits of human civilisation.[26] While the master of flocks lives in his house, which occupies a central position in the city, the shepherd is

---

[16] For the relationship between the 'pastoral analogy' and the world of rural life as described in epic see Collins (1996) ch. 2, esp. 25.
[17] *Il.* 1.153f.
[18] Hes. *Op.* 184–6.
[19] Benveniste (1973) 38, Lonsdale (1990) 118–22, van Wees (1992) 49–53, esp. 51; the different role of cattle farming in Homer and Hesiod is discussed in Athanassakis (1992).
[20] Collins (1996) 22; cf. *Il.* 20.219–22, *Od.* 4.87f., where ἄναξ ('master') and ποιμήν ('shepherd') are clearly distinguished; cf. also *Od.* 14.102, 15.503–5, 16.25–8, 21.83, 188f.; the only exception to the rule is the notoriously uncivilised shepherd–master Polyphemus: *Od.* 9.182–92, 336f.
[21] *Il.* 5.311–13, 14.444f., 15.546–51.
[22] The word for 'payment' is μισθός: *Il.* 21.448f., *Od.* 10.84f.
[23] *Il.* 4.275, 13.571f., 18.575–7, 20.221, 21.448f., *Od.* 9.182–92, *h. Merc.* 286f., 491f., *h. Ven.* 54f.
[24] *Il.* 4.279, *Od.* 9.182–92, 336f., *h. Ven.* 69.
[25] This is implicit in many of the Iliadic similes; for full documentation see Fränkel (1921); see also *Od.* 9.112–15 (of the Cyclopes).
[26] Again this is made explicit in the exaggerated image of the Odyssean Cyclops.

called 'loutish' (ἀγροιώτης) or 'dwelling in the fields' (ἄγραυλος) because of his place at the margins of society.[27]

The shepherd of early Greek epic guarantees stability to his social world and so is of central importance to it. At the same time he is also marginal, sometimes a stranger, in any case remote and therefore difficult to control. Many of the anxieties that surround him stem from this paradox. The one who owns the herd and the one who looks after it do not share the same cultural values and economic interests. Hence the many stories about shepherds failing to do their duty, which culminate in an almost proverbial expression from the *Odyssey*:

> ... αὐτὰρ μῆλα κακοὶ φθείρουσι νομῆες.[28]
>
> ... but bad herdsmen ruin the flocks.

The *Odyssey* in particular focuses on the problem that those whose task it is to preserve the social fabric of a cattle-farming society fail to do what they are paid for. The *Iliad* is less damning; but although shepherds are not seen as uncooperative there, the result is equally negative. For example:

> ὡς δὲ λύκοι ἄρνεσσιν ἐπέχραον ἠ ἐρίφοισι
> σίνται, ὑπὲκ μήλων αἱρεύμενοι, αἵ τ' ἐν ὄρεσσι
> ποιμένος ἀφραδίῃσι διέτμαγεν· οἱ δὲ ἰδόντες
> αἶψα διαρπάζουσιν ἀνάλκιδα θυμὸν ἐχούσας·   355
> ὣς Δαναοὶ Τρώεσσιν ἐπέχραον...[29]
>
> As wolves make havoc among young goats in their fury,
> catching them out of the flock, when the sheep separate in the mountains
> through the thoughtlessness of the shepherd, and the wolves seeing them
> suddenly snatch them away, and they have no heart for fighting;
> so the Danaans ravaged the Trojans...

The shepherd (ποιμήν) loses his flock, because he is not mentally equipped for his task. In other contexts he is seen as too weak:

> δὴ τότε μιν τρὶς τόσσον ἕλεν μένος, ὥς τε λέοντα,
> ὅν ῥά τε ποιμὴν ἀγρῷ ἐπ' εἰροπόκοις ὀΐεσσι

---

[27] *Od.* 11.293, 16.27, Hes. *Th.* 26, *Sc.* 39, *h. Merc.* 286.
[28] *Od.* 17.246; I cannot discover any relevant difference between the two most frequent words Homeric Greek has for 'shepherd' (ποιμήν and νομεύς); cf. Hes. *Th.* 26.
[29] *Il.* 16.352–6; cf. *Il.* 15.630–8, 18.525–9.

χραύσῃ μέν τ' αὐλῆς ὑπεράλμενον οὐδὲ δαμάσσῃ·
τοῦ μέν τε σθένος ὦρσεν, ἔπειτα δέ τ' οὐ προσαμύνει,
ἀλλὰ κατὰ σταθμοὺς δύεται, τὰ δ' ἔρημα φοβεῖται.[30] 140

> now the strong rage tripled took hold of him, as of a lion
> whom the shepherd among his fleecy flocks in the wild lands
> grazed as he leapt the fence of the fold, but has not killed him,
> but only stirred up the lion's strength, and can no more fight him
> off, but hides in the steading, and the frightened sheep are forsaken.

Failure of the shepherd is the rule, not the exception. If some passages remind us that without herdsmen things would be even worse,[31] this can only strengthen our impression that the shepherd of early Greek epic stands at the centre of a paradox: he is indispensable and yet ineffective. There must be someone who looks after the flocks, but because of the peculiar nature of his task he cannot be successful.[32]

Privilege and obligation

So far I have argued that the shepherd constitutes the dominant model of social interaction in the world of epic *laoi*, and I have outlined some of the less comfortable implications this model may have. The negative aspects I have been describing deserve particular attention, because they may not be obvious to modern readers, especially those steeped in a Judaeo-Christian tradition. The shepherd of biblical narrative is a far more positive figure than the one we find in Homer, and it is he, rather than his hapless counterpart, who came to dominate the imagination of Europe and its cultural descendants.

Let me then turn to the Homeric 'shepherd of the people'. I begin by arguing that the leader of people in early Greek

---

[30] *Il.* 5.136–40; cf. *Il.* 15.586–8, 17.61–9, 18.161–4, 573–86; cf. also the passages where the shepherd is confronted with the forces of nature, which he cannot control: *Il.* 4.275–9, 452–6.

[31] In *Il.* 10.485f. and 15.323–5 the aggressor is successful because the leader (σημάντωρ) is absent. In other passages we see successful defence: *Il.* 11.548–55, 17.109–12; in *Il.* 12.299–306 the outcome is left open.

[32] This is also understood in later literature – for the 'bad shepherd' see A. fr. 132c8 (Radt) and *A.* 657; an example of the willing but unsuccessful shepherd may be found in B. 18.8–10.

hexameter poetry is obliged to look after his group in a manner similar to that of the shepherd of flocks. Let us start from the testimony of ancient readers. I have already mentioned that some of them focus on the shepherd's responsibility. Xenophon's Socrates gives perhaps the most memorable account of this. In his view the shepherd is there exclusively to satisfy his group:

ἐντυχὼν δέ ποτε στρατηγεῖν ᾑρημένῳ τῳ, "Τοῦ ἕνεκεν", ἔφη, "Ὅμηρον οἴει τὸν Ἀγαμέμνονα προσαγορεῦσαι ποιμένα λαῶν; ἆρά γε ὅτι, ὥσπερ τὸν ποιμένα δεῖ ἐπιμελεῖσθαι, ὅπως σῷαί τε ἔσονται αἱ οἶες καὶ τὰ ἐπιτήδεια ἕξουσι..., οὕτω καὶ τὸν στρατηγὸν ἐπιμελεῖσθαι δεῖ, ὅπως σῷοί τε οἱ στρατιῶται ἔσονται καὶ τὰ ἐπιτήδεια ἕξουσι καί, οὗ ἕνεκα στρατεύονται, τοῦτο ἔσται; στρατεύονται δέ, ἵνα κρατοῦντες τῶν πολεμίων εὐδαιμονέστεροι ὦσιν."[33]

One day Socrates met a man who had just been appointed general. 'Why do you think Homer called Agamemnon "shepherd of the people"? Was it because it is the shepherd's duty to see to it that his sheep are safe and have their food, and that the purpose for which they are kept is achieved, and in the same way it is the general's duty to see that his soldiers are safe and have their food and that the purpose for which they are serving is achieved – this purpose being to improve their fortune by defeating the enemy?'

From the metaphor of the 'shepherd of the people' Socrates derives an obligation (δεῖ) for a military leader to look after his group and ensure its survival. The point of comparison is the shepherd, whose task it is (once again δεῖ) to look after his flock. We need not worry here about the fact that Homer is singled out as poet and Agamemnon as leader. More important is the language Socrates employs. Agamemnon as a 'shepherd of the people' teaches a lesson. The second thing to note is the nature of that lesson itself. Socrates' narrative is teleologically stringent. He insists that the single agent has a task which informs his actions (ὅπως). The shepherd of *laoi* must ensure that his people be safe. In support of this idea Socrates abolishes any form of individual purpose. The leader has no aims of his own.

Xenophon's Socrates makes a strong case for the needs of the community. His single agent, who is called 'shepherd of

[33] X. *Mem.* 3.2.1.

the people', is there to save his group. A slightly less extreme version of the same idea is offered by Aristotle. He too sees a task rather than a privilege implied in the metaphor of the shepherd when he defines the good monarch as someone who ensures the well-being of his subjects.[34] Unlike Xenophon's Socrates Aristotle is interested in the more permanent figure of the king. Immediate salvation (σῶον εἶναι) is not the issue here. But his leader, too, is there to ensure someone else's well-being (ἐπιμελεῖται αὐτῶν, ἵν' εὖ πράττωσιν). Individual action is once again directed teleologically (ἵνα) to the advantage of the group. And like Xenophon/Socrates Aristotle sets a norm (εἴπερ ἀγαθὸς ὤν ...).

Prominent ancient readers see a number of obligations inherent in the metaphor of shepherd and *laoi*, obligations which culminate in the single agent's task of looking after and saving his group.[35] Let us now consider an alternative reading: the group serving its master. This view has often been advocated by modern readers.[36] It has some currency in the ancient debate, too, but there it takes a characteristically different form from what we have seen so far. Never, before Iamblichus, does anyone claim that Homeric shepherds act in their own interest.[37] And where the metaphor of the 'shepherd' is rejected – or embraced – as tyrannical, it is never linked with the term *laos*. A characteristic example of democratic unease may be found in Aeschylus:

Βα.   τίς δὲ ποιμάνωρ ἔπεστι κἀπιδεσπόζει στρατῷ;
Χο.   οὔτινος δοῦλοι κέκληνται φωτὸς οὐδ' ὑπήκοοι.[38]

---

[34] Arist. *EN* 1161a12–15.
[35] These readings are not without a context. Early passages which portray the Homeric 'shepherd of the people' as a caring leader tend to come from the tradition of anti-democratic thought associated with Socrates. Democratic readings are on the whole less favourable. For possible reasons see Murray (1990) 6; for appropriations of the word *laos* by and for tyrants see e.g. Simon. ep. 36.4 (Page), Pi. *P.* 3.85 and *passim*. Possible democratic tendencies to suppress the term may be seen as a reaction to such texts; cf. ch. 3, n. 182; see also the epigram found in Olbia and re-published by Lebedev (1996) 264, which turns the language of tyranny against the tyrant himself.
[36] E.g. Jeanmaire (1939) 58, van Effenterre (1977) 49, Collins (1996) ch. 2; *contra* Ulf (1990) 99–105, Taplin (1992) 49f.
[37] Iamb. *VP* 35.260.
[38] A. *Pers.* 241f.

Queen: Who is the shepherd and master over the army?
Chorus: They are called neither the slaves nor subjects of any single man.

The queen in Aeschylus' *Persians* glosses 'being the shepherd' (ποιμάνορα εἶναι) with 'being the master' (δεσπόζειν), and this is taken up by the chorus when they identify the followers of the shepherd as 'slaves' (δοῦλοι). In the patriotically charged context of the *Persae*, the shepherd becomes a tyrant-figure who owns his group as a master owns his slaves.

Some of the implications of this reading are elaborated in a different context and from a different point of view by Thrasymachus in Plato's *Republic*.[39] Thrasymachus, too, redefines the metaphor of shepherd and group. In his account the Homeric shepherd becomes an 'anybody' (τις), while the group turns into a veritable 'flock' (πρόβατα). Having thus overturned the epic metaphor, he can go on to see the shepherd (ποιμήν) as a master (the Homeric ἄναξ) who uses his belongings to whatever end suits him. The outcome is plainly anti-Homeric[40] and marked by Plato as 'wrong'; and although it gives us another important glimpse of a debate which goes back at least as far as the fifth century BC, Thrasymachus' reading contributes little to our understanding of Homer's people as depicted in Homer's texts.[41]

A more pertinent – and less violent – attempt to subsume the *laoi* under the needs of their shepherd may be found in a scholion on *Iliad* 10.79a;[42] there the fact that Nestor leads a *laos* is taken as a way of praising him (ἐγκώμιον), the more so the more people he leads:

⟨λαὸν ἄγων:⟩ μεῖζον τὸ ἐγκώμιον τοῦ Νέστορος γένοιτο, εἰ λαόν τις ἀκούοι ⟨τὸν⟩ σύμπαντα, μὴ τὸν τῶν Πυλίων μόνον.[43]

Leading the people: the praise of Nestor would be greater if one takes this to refer to the whole people, not only those of the Pylians.

---

[39] Pl. *R.* 343b–c; cf. also *Tht.* 174d, *Plt.* 271dff., X. *Cyr.* 1.1 and 8.1.14.
[40] Or Homeric only in so far as it is modelled on the monstrous shepherd–owner Polyphemus; see above nn. 25f.
[41] For a late reflex of Thrasymachus' reading see above n. 37; note that Iamblichus, too, shifts the weight of the epic metaphor.
[42] See also schol. *Il.* 2.579–80a, b; schol. *Il.* 2.579; schol. D.T. in *Grammatici Graeci* 1.3, p. 458.26–34.
[43] The optative is doubtful – Maass inserts ⟨ἄν⟩.

This is still remarkably different from what Xenophon and Aristotle had suggested. The leader is not obliged to help, but profits from the size of the group he leads. I have argued that in Greek epic the size of a flock primarily reflects the social status of its owner, not that of its shepherd. Like Plato's Thrasymachus the scholiast has effectively turned the shepherd into a master. And yet, he does not go nearly as far as Thrasymachus. The scholiast's group does not become a mere commodity. 'Status' (κῦδος) is a highly developed social criterion for the leader's actions. For Nestor to enjoy his fame, the people need to be well.

An epic ideal

In the all-pervasive formula 'shepherd of the people' the model of the epic shepherd becomes crucial for our understanding of the *laos*. This is by and large borne out by the testimony of ancient readers. Self-professedly Homeric readings focus on the single agent's responsibilities. Readers who take a different view avoid the term *laos* (Aeschylus, Plato/Thrasymachus) or imply successful social interaction (the scholiast). I next argue that early Greek hexameter poetry knows of both these approaches, but treats them differently. As we would expect in a genre which has such clear ideas about the tasks of a shepherd but is relatively uninterested in his privileges, the leader's obligation is viewed as being primary.

I start from the scholiast's reading which suggested that Homer's people can sometimes be seen as a token of social recognition. It should be noted from the outset that such cases are relatively rare and tend to attract apologetic glosses.[44] What is more, the leader's privilege is hardly ever made explicit. One of the few examples is Agamemnon's entry in the Iliadic *Catalogue of ships*:

---

[44] *Il.* 3.186 with schol. *Il.* 3.186; see also *Il.* 4.47, 165, 6.449, *Od.* 9.263, schol. *Il.* 18.301; at *Il.* 13.489–95 this is elaborated in the image of Aeneas watching his men.

> τῶν ἑκατὸν νηῶν ἦρχε κρείων Ἀγαμέμνων
> Ἀτρεΐδης· ἅμα τῷ γε πολὺ πλεῖστοι καὶ ἄριστοι
> λαοὶ ἕποντ'· ἐν δ' αὐτὸς ἐδύσετο νώροπα χαλκὸν
> κυδιόων, πᾶσιν δὲ μετέπρεπεν ἡρώεσσιν,
> οὕνεκ' ἄριστος ἔην, πολὺ δὲ πλείστους ἆγε λαούς.[45]   580
>
> of their hundred ships the leader was powerful Agamemnon,
> Atreus' son, with whom followed by far the most and best
> people; and among them he himself stood armoured in shining
> bronze, glorying, conspicuous among the heroes,
> since he was greatest and led by far the most people.

Agamemnon's status as a hero among other heroes is here guaranteed by his being 'best' and leading 'by far the most people'.[46] This may seem a clear case of the single agent taking centre stage at the expense of collective interest. *Laoi* enhance Agamemnon's status as they guarantee Nestor's in book 10. However, we shall see later that these lines from the *Catalogue of ships* are part of an ongoing struggle in which Agamemnon tries, but in the end fails, to assert himself against the more fundamental needs of his people.[47] The leader of epic can boost his status by the number of people he leads; but by the same token he cannot lose or kill them without serious consequences.

Even in the more co-operative version of the scholiast on *Il.* 10.79a, then, the leader of *laoi* is rarely allowed take over. More aggressive accounts in the vein of Plato's Thrasymachus are openly rejected. Sarpedon in the *Iliad* is criticised in a characteristic fashion for damaging the people:

> σοὶ δὲ κακὸς μὲν θυμός, ἀποφθινύθουσι δὲ λαοί.[48]
>
> but yours is the heart of a coward and the people are perishing.

For our present purposes it does not matter whether Tlepolemus is 'right' in what he says. More importantly, his speech resonates with much of what the *Iliad* tells us. Agamemnon

---

[45] *Il.* 2.576–80.
[46] *Il.* 2.579f. with Ulf (1990) 95 and n. 24; cf. *Il.* 2.675, *Od.* 13.61f.; also *Od.* 8.382, 401, 9.2, 11.355, 378, 13.38 (further developed in *Od.* 7.69–72); we may also compare Hes. *Sc.* 27.
[47] See ch. 2, '*Laoi* in the *Iliad*', pp. 55ff.
[48] *Il.* 5.643.

and Achilles weep bitter tears after having destroyed the *laoi*.[49] Hector chooses to die.[50] Earlier in the text the same Hector sharply criticises Paris for letting the people perish.[51] The actions of the already discredited prince can hardly encourage a Thrasymachean reading of the matter. While Paris may prefer the group to die for its leader's caprices,[52] it is made quite clear that such behaviour attracts blame. In this respect, at least, we can trust Hector: his brother misbehaves.

The people of epic are never allowed to be aggressively instrumentalised. One simply cannot 'own' them as a master would own his flock of sheep. *Laoi* can be viewed, under certain circumstances, in terms of their leader's social status, but this is rare and tends to create new responsibilities. There is, of course, some fluctuation across the texts. The *Odyssey*, for example, displays a marked bias in favour of the leader in charge; but even the *Odyssey* shows awareness of a stronger current of individual obligation.[53] It is to this current that I turn next.

Xenophon/Socrates and Aristotle agreed that the Homeric metaphor of the 'shepherd of the people' implies certain responsibilities. On their account the group is not there for its shepherd, but the shepherd for his group. If we turn to early hexameter poetry, we find a large array of passages which – more or less explicitly – support this view. For example, the task postulated by Xenophon/Socrates can be developed out of the following lines from the *Iliad*:

οὐ χρὴ παννύχιον εὕδειν βουληφόρον ἄνδρα,
ᾧ λαοί τ' ἐπιτετράφαται καὶ τόσσα μέμηλε.[54]

He should not sleep all night long who is a man burdened with counsels and responsibility for the people and cares so numerous.

---

[49] For discussion see ch. 2, '*Laoi* in the *Iliad*', pp. 68–83 and especially pp. 72f.
[50] For discussion see pp. 92ff.
[51] *Il.* 6.325–9.
[52] Compare σέο δ' εἵνεκ' 'for your sake' with οὗ ἕνεκα στρατεύονται 'for the sake of which they go to war' in X. *Mem.* 3.2.1 .
[53] For examples and discussion see ch. 2, '*Laoi* in the *Odyssey*', pp. 102–26.
[54] *Il.* 2.24f., 61f.

AN EPIC IDEAL

What was implicit in the image of the shepherd is made explicit in these verses. According to Agamemnon's dream, being in charge of the people (λαοί) brings with it an obligation (χρή) to act responsibly. The nature of the task is summed up in language similar to Xenophon's.[55]

Socrates is not the only one who read his Homer carefully. Aristotle's statement discussed above[56] can be compared with the simile of the blameless king from *Odyssey* book 19:

> ὦ γύναι, οὐκ ἄν τίς σε βροτῶν ἐπ' ἀπείρονα γαῖαν
> νεικέοι· ἦ γάρ σευ κλέος οὐρανὸν εὐρὺν ἱκάνει,
> ὥς τέ τευ ἢ βασιλῆος ἀμύμονος, ὅς τε θεουδὴς
> ἀνδράσιν ἐν πολλοῖσι καὶ ἰφθίμοισιν ἀνάσσων   110
> εὐδικίας ἀνέχῃσι, φέρῃσι δὲ γαῖα μέλαινα
> πυροὺς καὶ κριθάς, βρίθῃσι δὲ δένδρεα καρπῷ,
> τίκτῃ δ' ἔμπεδα μῆλα, θάλασσα δὲ παρέχῃ ἰχθῦς
> ἐξ εὐηγεσίης, ἀρετῶσι δὲ λαοὶ ὑπ' αὐτοῦ.[57]

Lady, no mortal man on the endless earth could have cause
to find fault with you; your fame goes up into the wide heaven,
as of some king who, as a blameless man and god-fearing,
and ruling as lord over many powerful men,
upholds the way of good government, and the black earth yields
barley and wheat, the trees are heavy with fruit, the sheepflocks
continue to bear young, the sea gives fish, because of
his good leadership, and the people prosper under him.

In Homer, a normative thrust is less explicit than it is in Aristotle, but it can still be felt. The good king must act as he does so as to avoid blame (νεικεῖν). What his goodness amounts to is elaborated in a long list, at the end of which comes to stand the well-being of the people. This could have been the passage from which Aristotle developed his understanding of a leader's task. In each case he is called 'king' (βασιλεύς), and the Aristotelian glosses 'good' (ἀγαθός) and 'to fare well' (εὖ πράττειν) can easily be translated back into their Homeric counterparts 'blameless' (ἀμύμων) and 'to prosper' (ἀρετᾶν). One more example from Hesiod:

---

[55] Compare ἐπιμελεῖσθαι ('to see to it') and καὶ τόσσα μέμηλε ('with ... cares so numerous').
[56] Cf. p. 22.
[57] *Od.* 19.107–14.

τοὔνεκα γὰρ βασιλῆες ἐχέφρονες, οὕνεκα λαοῖς
βλαπτομένοις ἀγορῆφι μετάτροπα ἔργα τελεῦσι.[58]

> For this is why there are prudent kings: when the people
> are wronged in the assembly they make amends for them.

Hesiod once again stresses normative aspects. Line 88 in particular suggests that he, too, sees the leader of people as acting towards an end which is not his ('this is why ... because'). The people must be safe, and their welfare is ensured in an appropriate teleological narrative (μετάτροπα ἔργα τελεῦσι). Throughout the surviving texts of early Greek hexameter, single agents are assigned the task of guaranteeing the well-being of the people. The theme recurs with some insistence,[59] and, as we would expect, it finds expression at the level of formulaic language.[60] It is part of early Greek epic, even at its most traditional, that the single agent has to keep the people safe.

The failed ideal

Xenophon/Socrates and Aristotle were right to assume the guise of the Homeric interpreter. Like a shepherd, the single agent who leads *laoi* in early Greek epic takes on the task of saving the people. Having developed this first implication of the all-pervading formula 'shepherd of the people' at some length, I now turn to the second. The shepherd of epic, as we have seen earlier, is prone to fail. The same holds true for the single agent who leads *laoi*. Epic leaders typically lose or destroy their group,[61] and this is reflected in one of the largest

---

[58] Hes. *Th.* 88f.
[59] *Il.* 1.117, 4.184 (negative), 5.643 (negative), 8.246, 9.98f., 424, 681, 10.14–16, 13.47, *Od.* 11.136f., 22.54, 23.283f., Hes. *Th.* 84–7, Panyas. fr. 12.7f. (Davies), Callin. fr. 1.18 (West), Tyrt. fr. 11.13 (West).
[60] Cf. Appendix A.2; see also *Il.* 1.117, 8.246 and Ulf (1990) 99. These phrases occur in the *Iliad* only. For the special importance of the *laoi* in the *Iliad* see ch. 1, '"The people of the Achaeans"', and 2, '*Laoi* in the *Iliad*'.
[61] *Il.* 1.10, 117, 382f., 454, 2.115, 4.164f., 5.643, 758, 6.223, 327, 448f., 8.67, 246, 9.22, 118, 593 (as read by Arist. *Rh.* 1365a13), 11.85, 309, 764, 13.349, 675f., 15.319, 16.237, 778, 22.104, 107, *Od.* 3.305, 7.60, 9.265, 11.500, 518, 24.428, 528–30, Hes. *Op.* 243, perhaps fr. 30.16–19 (M–W) with schol. *Od.* 11.235, fr. 33(a).24 (M–W).

THE FAILED IDEAL

and most flexible formulaic clusters of the type *laos* + verb: 'he destroyed the people'. The following short list gives a sample of some relevant phrases:[62]

[‐∪∪‐∪∪‐∪∪‐∪∪] ὤλεσα λαόν	I destroyed the people (*Il.* 2.115, 9.22)
[‐∪∪‐∪∪‐∪∪‐∪∪] ὤλεσε λαόν	he destroyed the people (*Il.* 22.107)
[‐∪∪‐∪∪‐∪∪‐] ἀπὸ δ' ὤλεσε λαούς	and he destroyed the people[a] (*Od.* 24.428)
[‐∪∪‐∪∪‐∪∪‐] καὶ ἀπώλεσε λαούς	and he destroyed the people[b] (*Od.* 9.265)
[‐∪∪‐∪∪‐∪∪‐] ὀλέκοντο δὲ λαοί	and the people perished[a] (*Il.* 1.10)
[‐∪∪‐∪∪‐∪∪‐] ὤλλυντο δὲ λαοί	and the people perished[b] (Hes. fr. 33a.24 (M–W))
[‐∪∪‐∪∪‐∪] ἀποφθινύθουσι δὲ λαοί	and the people perish (*Il.* 5.643, Hes. *Op.* 243)

These phrases are evidently closely related. As indicated by the metrical patterns in square brackets, they occupy roughly the same metrical space at the end of a hexameter line; the translation is designed to highlight parallel phrasing.[63]

The list given here is by no means complete; there are many more ways of 'destroying the people' in early Greek hexameter poetry. Most of the relevant phrases are strongly standardised. As is shown by the examples quoted above, they tend to involve forms of the verbs ὄλλυμι, 'to lose/destroy' and ἀποφθινύθω, 'to perish',[64] characteristically found at line endings; but they may also be formed with different verbs and/or in different positions in the verse.[65] The detrimental role played by single leader figures is almost always clear from the context, if not from the phrases themselves: the people do not

---

[62] For full documentation of the Greek material see Appendix A.3.
[63] Letters are used where the differences between Greek phrases cannot easily be imitated in English.
[64] Forms of Greek ὄλλυμι are used both in the sense 'to destroy' and 'to perish'; for the inherently reciprocal nature of the word see Pazdernik (1995) and pp. 37–40 below; for (ἀπο)φθινύθω ('to perish') and plant growth see ch. 1, 'Society and the stone', n. 127.
[65] See Appendix A.3.

perish of their own accord; when they die, someone failed to save them. What exactly the individual involved actually did or intended to do in such cases is of little interest. Confronted with the needs of the people he simply has to function. As Agamemnon puts it in the *Iliad*, it is ἄμεινον, 'better', to save the people.[66]

I have argued for a close relationship between single agent and group in phrases of the type 'he destroyed the people', but this is not the only conclusion that can be drawn from what has been said. There is also a marked trend for such phrases to occur in direct speech only. This tendency is especially prominent in Homer.[67] Moreover, the people also tend to 'be destroyed' at important junctures in the texts. Again, this is particularly noteworthy in Homer. The fact that the *laoi* are almost always said to perish in direct speech would suggest that this is seen as a problem by the protagonists. Time and again Homeric characters feel the need to comment on what is happening around them. That phrases such as 'he destroyed the people' mark crucial points especially in Homeric narrative also suggests that they are of special interest to the Homeric narrator. Both points will be elaborated in chapter 2.[68]

No one in early Greek hexameter poetry ever doubts that the destruction of *laoi* is a terrible catastrophe and that those who cause it are to be blamed accordingly. Early epic as a genre carries in itself a strong and constant bias in favour of the people (*laos*), a bias which neither the Homeric narrator nor his characters ever question. Destroying the *laos* is unjustifiable, and even though disapproval is not always made equally explicit, there are enough passages for us to be quite certain. For instance, we hear in the *Iliad* that Apollo 'sent a bad plague, and the people were being destroyed'.[69] At the beginning of the narrative and in the words of the Homeric

---

[66] *Il.* 1.116f., already quoted and discussed by Taplin (1992) 50, Raaflaub (1997b) 17f.
[67] Hesiodic poetry seems to have no such restrictions.
[68] E.g. pp. 61f., 72f., 92–5, 107f.
[69] *Il.* 1.10; cf. *Il.* 1.382 (κακὸν βέλος, 'a bad missile') and 5.643 (κακός ... θυμός, 'bad spirit').

THE FAILED IDEAL

narrator himself the plague is 'bad' first and foremost because it destroys the *laoi*.[70] We note again the detrimental influence of the single agent in charge. The catastrophe happens, we are told, 'because the son of Atreus had dishonoured Chryses'.[71] Ironically, Agamemnon and Menelaus will be called 'marshals of the people' (κοσμήτορε λαῶν) shortly after.[72] There can be no doubt about how we are to view their failure.

A passage from Hesiod is even more explicit; here the fact that the single agent is 'bad' (κακός) and 'contrives evil' (ἀτάσθαλα μηχανάαται) is glossed – among other things – by the damage he does to the people:

> πολλάκι καὶ ξύμπασα πόλις κακοῦ ἀνδρὸς ἀπηύρα,
> ὅστις ἀλιτραίνῃ καὶ ἀτάσθαλα μηχανάαται.
> τοῖσιν δ' οὐρανόθεν μέγ' ἐπήγαγε πῆμα Κρονίων,
> λιμὸν ὁμοῦ καὶ λοιμόν, ἀποφθινύθουσι δὲ λαοί.[73]

> Often a whole city together suffers in consequence of a bad man
> who does wrong and contrives evil.
> From heaven Cronus' son brings disaster upon them,
> famine and with it plague, and the people perish.

There can be no doubt that the people of early Greek hexameter have the sympathy of texts and characters on their side. At the same time they do not usually survive for long, and, as in the case of the shepherd of flocks, this is felt to create a constant problem of leadership. The resulting tensions can be exploited at various levels. Speakers may use traditional phrases such as 'he destroyed the people' as a weapon against each other.[74] At the level of narration, the problem of a perishing *laos* can become a driving force in the making of the story. For example, in the *Iliad* the change of fortune in book 8 is introduced by a verse which later in the poem marks Agamemnon's *aristeia* and defeat (book 11),

---

[70] For the precise meaning of κακός ('bad', 'detrimental' etc.) see *LfgrE s.v.* with further literature.
[71] *Il.* 1.11f.
[72] *Il.* 1.16.
[73] Hes. *Op.* 240–3.
[74] See ch. 2 *passim*, esp. pp. 92–5, 107f.

Hector's break-through (book 15) and Patroclus' death (book 16):

τόφρα μάλ' ἀμφοτέρων βέλε' ἥπτετο, πῖπτε δὲ λαός.[75]

so long thrown weapons of both took hold and the people fell.

At four points in the Iliadic narrative the people are said to be falling on both sides. The narrative stagnates and progress is enforced, among other things, by the thematic scandal of a perishing *laos*.

I have argued that the metaphor of shepherd and people entails a potential narrative of individual obligation and communal salvation. However, failure of the leader and the destruction of the people are part of the same image. Unsuccessful shepherds populate the pastoral world of the *Iliad*, the *Odyssey*, Hesiod and the *Homeric hymns*. Similarly, death and destruction characterise life among the *laoi*. Drawing on and elaborating the paradigm of pastoral, the texts highlight the inherent weakness of the social model they describe. The shepherd is a failed ideal, exposing to scrutiny a social world without effective social structures. In the following section more will be said about what structures we find in early epic, how co-operation between leader and people is enacted and/or enforced, and why it fails so often.

Social structures

The metaphor of the 'shepherd of the people' suggested a model of social life which is fundamentally flawed. Shepherds are marginal to the epic world, and they cannot guarantee the permanent well-being of the flocks. If we ask what this tells us about the institutional organisation of life among the people, the metaphor of the shepherd can once again help our understanding. Like the flock of pastoral, the people of epic exist without institutional continuity. Institutions such as the

[75] *Il.* 8.67, 11.85, 15.319, 16.778.

SOCIAL STRUCTURES

assembly do exist, and I shall argue that the term *laos* has particularly close links with them.[76] However, such social formation is not on the whole depicted as successful. More importantly, it is not *permanent*, and this will prove a decisive point when we compare the results of chapter 1 with what we learn from non-hexameter texts.[77]

One of the most basic facts of social life in early Greek hexameter poetry is that the people need to be 'gathered'.[78] They do not assemble regularly or of their own accord. The well-known scandal of the Ithacan assembly is only one case among many:[79] without an individual taking the initiative, life among the *laoi* breaks down.[80] Once again an extensive formulaic system attests to the traditional nature of this idea. I quote some examples:[81]

[–∪∪–∪∪–∪∪–∪∪] λαὸν ἀγείρων	gathering the people (*Il.* 4.377)
[–∪∪–∪∪–∪∪–∪∪] λαὸν ἀγείρας	having gathered the people (*Il.* 2.664)
[–∪∪–∪∪–∪∪–∪∪] λαὸν ἄγειρεν	he gathered the people (*Il.* 11.716)
[–∪∪–∪∪–∪∪–∪∪] λαὸν ἀγείρω	I gather the people (*Il.* 16.129)
[–∪∪–∪∪–∪∪–∪∪] λαὸν ἄγειραν	they gathered the people (*Od.* 3.140, Hes. *Op.* 652)

The relationship between single agent and dependent group which is inherent in the formula 'shepherd of the people' re-

---

[76] As compared to, say, the concept of the 'hero' (ἥρως), for which see above Introduction, 'Between the omnipresent hero and the absent *polis*'.
[77] See ch. 3 *passim*, especially 'The founding people'.
[78] For this and the following I am indebted to Casewitz (1992) 194f. and Wyatt (1994–5); Martin (1997) discusses formulae of the type 'he gathered the people' (λαὸν ἄγειρεν).
[79] *Od.* 2.26f.
[80] See, for example, *Il.* 1.54, 313, 2.25, 62, 191, 280, 578, 580, 675, 708f., 817f., 4.90f. 201f., 287, 407, 430, 5.485f., 6.80, 433, 7.342, 9.338, 708, 10.79, 11.189, 204, 758, 796, 13.492, 495, 710, 833f., 14.93, 15.311 475, 506, 695, 723, 16.368f., 501, 551, 714, 17.250f, 19.139, 234, 23.156f., 258, 24.658, *Od.* 3.140, 155, 6.164, 24.530, *h.Cer.* 296f., Panyas. fr. 12.8 (Davies); *Il.* 24.788f. is only an apparent exception to the rule; see p. 97.
[81] For a fuller list of the Greek phrases see Appendix A.4.

mains substantially unchanged in such traditional phrases as 'gathering the people'. As becomes clear even from the small selection of formulae quoted here, the people of epic cannot stand outside the opposition of group and leader: they are the group which is led to the extent that they would not exist otherwise.

The institutions of the *laos* are not permanent. When the common enterprise is over, the people disperse or are dispersed.[82] Further, we note that epic *laoi* resist communal life for even a limited amount of time. This tendency is particularly marked in Homer, where assemblies break down or are dissolved by unsympathetic participants,[83] but as we shall see when comparing the findings of chapter 3, it is also characteristic of epic as a whole.

Once the people are gathered, single agents proceed to impose collective purpose. Although in this we find a clear sense of due process, we must once again rely on individual initiative. In the case of the assembly[84] and of public song,[85] the herald assists.[86] This figure carries in itself the promise of institutional progress, which becomes important in other (later) Greek literature.[87] In epic the herald remains relatively marginal.[88]

With the assembly (ἀγορή) settled and unwarranted initiative suppressed, figures of public standing suggest what further action needs to be taken. The leaders stir and contain, the people follow. Here as elsewhere we note the close interrelation of individual impulse and group action. Recurrent patterns on the leader's side are 'to encourage/stir' or 'hold back the people' (λαὸν ἀνώγειν, ὀτρύνειν, ὀρνύναι and λαὸν ἐρύκειν

---

[82] See Appendix A.5.
[83] See *Iliad* book 2 and *Odyssey* book 2.
[84] *Il.* 2.95–7, 99, 280, 438, 18.503–5; cf. also *Il.* 2.163f., *Od.* 3.155.
[85] *Od.* 8.471f.
[86] There is a small formulaic cluster to mark this; see Appendix A.7.
[87] As argued at length in ch. 3, '*Leos* ritual'.
[88] 'Relatively' is a crucial word here. While I am not suggesting that the heralds of epic are altogether unimportant, I do suggest that they are substantially less important than they are in other archaic and classical Greek texts and especially in ritual; for discussion see ch. 3, '*Leos* ritual'.

or ἐρυκακέειν). By comparison, the action of the people themselves is relatively uniform: they follow (ἕπεσθαι).[89]

From an analysis of the action in which *laoi* and their leaders typically engage, we begin to discern more institutionally stable elements. The battlefield and the assembly (ἀγορή) typically feature the gathered *laoi*.[90] Another form of gathering, the *agon*, which serves as a stage for public performances such as dancing and athletic competition, is also typically formed by *laoi*.[91] Finally, there are the public funerals, which again lie in the domain of the *laoi*.[92] On all these occasions the people interact with their leaders. The funeral marks the low point where the group is bereft of its shepherd. The *agon* re-establishes relations between group and single agents, serving, among other things, as a mustering-place for future leaders. The assembly, finally, opens a space in which the joint efforts of shepherd and group are co-ordinated with the aim of ensuring the success of social life.[93]

An incurable imbalance

From what has just been said, it becomes clearer just how much the *laoi* depend on their leaders. Interaction between group and single agents is not only important at the level of communal survival ('saving/destroying the people') and group identity ('gathering the people'). It is also essential for the more institutionally developed contexts of the assembly, the *agon*, the funeral and the battlefield. All these contexts depend on successful co-operation between the *laoi* and their leaders.

---

[89] See Appendix A.6.
[90] For the assembly (ἀγορή) see *Il.* 1.54, 2.95f., 191, 18.497, 502f., *Od.* 2.13, 41, 252, *h.Cer.* 296f., Hes. *Th.* 84f., 88f., 430; cf. also *Certamen* 281–3 (Allen); for the battlefield see e.g. *Il.* 18.509 and *passim*.
[91] *Il.* 23.258, 728, 881, 24.1f., *Od.* 8.125; cf. *Od.* 8.100; *Il.* 3.318–22 and 7.177f. are closely related.
[92] *Il.* 7.434, 23.156f., 162, 24.37f., 610f. (negative), 665, 777ff., 789–92, Hes. *Sc.* 472–5; cf. also *Il.* 24.740, Callin. fr. 1.18f. (West).
[93] It does not have to be assumed that all these events are reserved for the *laoi* alone, but they can be and in fact often are described in such terms; for a study of assembly scenes beyond the framework of the *laoi* see Bannert (1987).

Where co-operation breaks down, social life, too, comes to an end.

Now, we have seen already that the leader, while being crucial for the survival of the people, does not usually succeed in protecting them. If we ask what precisely it is that prevents him from acting as he should, we can point to phenomena we have seen already when studying the shepherd of flocks.[94] The single agent may simply be too weak, or he may be otherwise ill equipped for his task. But while these are potentially fatal problems, I would like to draw attention to a more specific one, where once again the paradigm of the epic shepherd can help us.

We have seen already that the herdsman of epic is not the owner of his flock and that therefore his collaboration must be bought at a price (μισθός).[95] The shepherd of the people, too, must be paid. In other words, there is a fundamental imbalance of interest – and hence loyalty – between the leader and the group as a *laos*. The people are emotionally attached to successful leaders. They 'long' for them when they are gone (the word is πόθος), and they feel 'grief' (ἄχος, ἄλγος) at their loss. For example, the people of Protesilaos in the *Iliad* 'miss' (πόθεον) Protesilaos, who was 'good' (ἐσθλός), although they have another leader.[96] A more immediate sense of bereavement is expressed when the leader dies. When Patroclus is mortally wounded and falls to the ground in *Iliad* 16, he is said to 'grieve very much' (μέγα ... ἤκαχε) the people of the Achaeans.[97] Priam says about Hector's imminent death:

> λαοῖσιν δ' ἄλλοισι μινυνθαδιώτερον ἄλγος
> ἔσσεται, ἢν μὴ καὶ σὺ θάνῃς Ἀχιλῆϊ δαμασθείς.[98]
>
> but for the rest of the people a sorrow that will be fleeting,
> as long as you are not killed by Achilles as well.

---

[94] See above ch. 1, '"Shepherd of the people"'.
[95] See ch. 1, 'Privilege and obligation'.
[96] *Il.* 2.708f.; cf. Callin. fr. 1.18 (West); see also Collins (1988) 98, who traces the theme of longing (πόθος) in connection with the king (βασιλεύς).
[97] *Il.* 16.822; for further discussion see ch. 2, '*Laoi* in the *Iliad*', pp. 78–81.
[98] *Il.* 22.54f., cf. also *Il.* 22.408f., 24.740, *Od.* 2.81; contrast *Od.* 2.233f.

No incentive is needed to mobilise the group. The fortunes of the people depend too directly on successful leadership for them to have a choice. Things look different for the single agent in charge. He does not 'miss' the group, and the *laoi* ensure his co-operation not by appealing to emotions such as 'longing' (πόθος) or 'grief' (ἄχος) but by assigning and withholding central tokens of social status such as, for example, 'fame', 'blame', 'honour' (e.g. κλέος,[99] νέμεσις,[100] τιμή[101]). This is typically done at the public occasions already discussed, assembly, *agon*, funeral and battlefield. Since the *laoi* have no monopoly over the tokens of social recognition just mentioned, co-operation regularly breaks down.

Negative reciprocity

I have argued that one reason why the 'shepherd of the people' does not deliver what is expected of him lies in a fundamental imbalance of interest, an imbalance which is built into the very structure that is meant to ensure the well-being of the group. The *laoi* are directly and emotionally attached to their leader; the leader in turn has to be bribed by tokens of social status such as 'fame' (κλέος) or 'honour' (τιμή) in order to take care of them. Outside early Greek hexameter poetry the solution to this problem is institutional progress.[102] In early epic the solution is the abortive one of negative reciprocity. Having destroyed the group first (ὤλεσε λαόν etc.), the leader suffers in turn.[103]

At critical moments the assumed ideal leader of early Greek hexameter dies for his group; but the 'actual' leader, more

---

[99] *Il.* 2.115 (negative), 9.22 (negative), 22.104–10, *Od.* 19.107–14, Panyas. fr. 12.8 (Davies); cf. also Hes. *Op.* 763f.
[100] *Il.* 5.757f., 6.325–7.
[101] *Il.* 23.728, 881, *Od.* 2.13, 7.71f., 8.382, 401, 472, 9.2, 11.355, 378, 12.28, 13.38, 17.64, Hes. *Th.* 84f., 430, Hes. *Sc.* 27 (here the word is κῦδος, 'status'); cf. also Hes. fr. 211.4 (M–W) (?) and *Il.* 17.251, where τιμή comes from Zeus.
[102] As discussed in ch. 3, 'The founding people'.
[103] For this and the following I am indebted to Pazdernik (1995).

often than not, makes the people die for himself. An example of the former can be found in the famous reverse simile of *Odyssey* 8.[104] Odysseus is there said to cry as a woman cries for her husband who has fallen in front of the city and the people. The reference to the city need not concern us here.[105] For the time being it is enough to note that the *laoi* are among those for whom a single agent is ideally, metaphorically, expected to give his life. If the assumed good leader of the Odyssean simile dies for his people, the leader of Iliadic 'reality' has them die in his place. Paris in particular reverses the Odyssean paradigm:

> τὸν δ' Ἕκτωρ νείκεσσεν ἰδὼν αἰσχροῖς ἐπέεσσι·   325
> "δαιμόνι', οὐ μὲν καλὰ χόλον τόνδ' ἔνθεο θυμῷ.
> λαοὶ μὲν φθινύθουσι περὶ πτόλιν αἰπύ τε τεῖχος
> μαρνάμενοι· σέο δ' εἵνεκ' ἀϋτή τε πτόλεμός τε
> ἄστυ τόδ' ἀμφιδέδηε..."[106]

> But Hector saw him and in words of shame he rebuked him:
> 'Strange man! It is not fair to keep in your heart this anger.
> The people are dying around the city and around the steep wall
> as they fight hard; and it is for you that this war with its clamour
> has flared up about our city...'

Hector detests such behaviour and threatens his brother with blame (νεικεῖν). The threat proves strong and Paris gives in, but things are not always so simple. In the previous section I suggested that the people have no monopoly over key items of social sanction such as 'fame' or 'blame' (κλέος, νεικεῖν), and that therefore they rarely succeed in preventing the worst. This does not mean that losing the people has no consequences at all. But punishment is only ever implicit; the people do not themselves take charge.[107] What is more, the unsuccessful leader of early epic suffers only after he has destroyed the group. Agamemnon in the *Iliad* may serve as an example: first he destroys the *laos*, then (ἐπεί ... ὤλεσα) he becomes 'infamous' (δυσκλεής).[108] Another interesting passage can be found in *Iliad* 11, where Nestor predicts that

---

[104] *Od.* 8.523-5. [105] For discussion see ch. 2, '*Laoi* in the *Iliad*', pp. 83-95.
[106] *Il.* 6.325-9. [107] Ulf (1990) 105. [108] *Il.* 9.21f.; cf. Taplin (1992) 50.

Achilles will have to cry (literally: 'after-cry', μετακλαύσεσθαι) once the people are destroyed (ἐπεί κε ... ὄληται).[109] The narrative of books 16–18 bears out what Nestor predicts. Achilles first expresses his satisfaction at having damaged the people before promptly being afflicted in turn.[110]

When I said that the people do not themselves take charge I must add that in extreme cases of individual failure the community of *laoi* may wish for the delinquent's death. Here I note the close echoes between Hector's speech in *Il.* 6.327 and the people's curse on Paris earlier in the poem.[111] The underlying relationship is strictly reciprocal. The same idea is expressed more tersely in the *Odyssey*:

> ἀλλ' ὁ μὲν ὤλεσε λαὸν ἀτάσθαλον, ὤλετο δ' αὐτός.[112]
>
> but he destroyed the reckless people and was himself destroyed.

After the people are destroyed by their leader (μέν), the leader himself is destroyed (δέ).[113] The reciprocal nature of their relationship is further stressed by the fact that the Greek for 'he was himself destroyed' (ὤλετο δ' αὐτός) takes the position in the verse which is traditionally occupied by the phrase 'he destroyed the people' (ὤλεσε λαόν). The leader, quite literally, follows in the footsteps of the people.[114]

Unsuccessful co-operation between leader and group triggers a process of negative reciprocity. Having destroyed the group the leader suffers in turn. The figure of Hector in the *Iliad* is particularly illuminating in this context. In his monologue outside Troy he deplores the fact that he has 'destroyed the people'.[115] The wording is traditional (ὤλεσα λαόν) but the metrical arrangement is not. The phrase is repeated three

---

[109] *Il.* 11.763f.
[110] See pp. 77ff.
[111] *Il.* 3.322, cf. 318. Note, however, that the *laoi* do not speak as a group. For the important aspect of collective restraint (εὐφημεῖν) see ch. 1, 'Social structures'. See also ch. 3, 'Ritual formulae', pp. 181f.
[112] *Od.* 7.60.
[113] See also the perceptive remarks in Pazdernik (1995) 357.
[114] Cf. Pazdernik (1995) 357f.
[115] *Il.* 22.104–10.

lines later, this time at the end of the verse, as is standard. It is this second judgement that determines Hector's decision to meet Achilles. The outcome is left open, but a marked echo between *Il.* 22.107 ('he destroyed the people' (ὤλεσε λαόν)) and *Il.* 22.110 ('or to be destroyed by him' (ἠέ κεν αὐτῷ ὀλέσθαι)) leaves little room for doubt: having lost the people Hector dies in turn.

Early epic depicts the relationship between the people and their leaders as flawed by an incurable imbalance. While the group is emotionally attached to the leader, he is often seen to neglect or abuse the group, bringing about the traditional narrative of destruction I have discussed above (ὤλεσε λαόν). Because they lack effective institutions, the *laoi* are unable to improve their situation once and for all. A solution is only offered in the abortive form of negative reciprocity; having destroyed the people, the leader suffers in turn.

Society and the stone

Life among epic *laoi* is in important ways marred. Their social structures are ineffective, and this leads to communal catastrophe caused by unsuccessful leaders (ὤλεσε λαόν), in extreme cases the death of a whole generation, otherwise conceptualised as the downfall of the heroes.[116] So far I have concentrated on the negative side of the issue and the results were bleak indeed. However, this is by no means all that can be said, and we should not turn to the Homeric texts before we have shed some light on a rather different aspect of the people in epic.

I start with the observation that *laoi* are socially inclusive. We have already seen that the image of shepherd and flock brings with it a strong element of social agreement – the group must be preserved. The consensual nature of this arrangement also finds expression in a number of other formulaic phrases,[117] some of which lend support to Taplin's view that

---

[116] Contrast *Il.* 6.223 (*laoi*) and Hes. *Op.* 156–65 ('heroes').
[117] See Appendix A.8; cf. also Wyatt (1994–5) 162 with n. 14.

laoi form a social whole which includes its own (potential) leaders.[118] The group is seen as inclusive also in its character as an audience,[119] especially an audience in dialogue with the divine. Weather signs, bird omens, plague or famine are often experienced by them, and the soothsayer (μάντις) as an expert reader of such divinely sent communications typically speaks to the gathered *laoi*.[120]

The fact that gods take a special interest in the *laoi* is in fact an important aspect of their existence. While they often lead or save them,[121] at times they may also destroy them.[122] Gods are even linked to the people by an epithet – λαοσσόος ('stirring/saving the people').[123] The group *vis-à-vis* the gods in turn becomes a prime factor in the well-being of a larger world of social life and social norm. As we have seen already, in the *Odyssey* the state of the people provides the climax in a vision of life under the good king.[124] Their well-being sums up growth and procreation in the animal world. Hesiod, in his version, changes the order of things and adds a political twist.[125] But the role he assigns to the *laoi* is similar:

---

[118] Taplin (1992) 50 with n. 7, against Ulf (1990) 108f.; it may also be relevant that the *laoi* are often said to be 'numerous'; cf. Appendix A.9.
[119] Cf. above 'Social structures'.
[120] *Il.* 2.163, 179, 279f., 450, 4.27f., 76f., 8.75–7, 11.758, 12.200–29, 13.822f., *Od.* 13.154–8, 15.244, Hes. fr. 25.34–6 (M–W), the last two with *Et. Gen. s.v.* λαοσσόος; for this epithet see n. 123.
[121] *Il.* 15.311 (Apollo), 694f. (Zeus), 18.516 (Athena and Ares), 21.458 (Poseidon about Apollo), *h.* 11.4 (Athena); modern lexicographers prefer to take λαοσσόος as 'stirring the people', but many ancient readers thought it to mean 'saving the people'; see n. 123.
[122] *Il.* 1.10 (Apollo), 312–17 (Apollo), 380–3 (Apollo), 454 (Apollo), 5.758 (Hera about Ares), 13.348f. (Zeus), 15.318f. (Apollo); perhaps Hes. fr. 30.15–19 (M–W) with schol. *Od.* 11.235 (Zeus).
[123] Typically of Athena; for passages and meaning see *LfgrE s.v.* The fact that Athena is worshipped as ἀγελείη may also be relevant (more often – and apparently with better reason – taken to mean 'of the booty' than 'she who leads the people'); see *Il.* 6.269, 279 and *LfgrE s.v.* for further passages and discussion. Λαοσσόος ('stirring/saving the people') often occurs in the narrative voice of heroic epic. By comparison, ῥυσίπτολις/ἐρυσίπτολις ('saving the city', only of Athena) occurs in an invocation (*Il.* 6.305) and in epicletic hymn openings (*h.* 11.1, *h.* 29.3).
[124] *Od.* 19.107–14; for discussion see p. 27; cf. *Il.* 1.313, *Od.* 11.134–7, 23.281–4 and perhaps *h. Ven.* 106; cf. also ch. 2, '*Laoi* in the *Odyssey*', pp. 118f.
[125] Hesiod's handling of the *laoi* would deserve its own full-scale treatment, which cannot be given here.

> οἳ δὲ δίκας ξείνοισι καὶ ἐνδήμοισι διδοῦσιν
> ἰθείας καὶ μή τι παρεκβαίνουσι δικαίου,
> τοῖσι τέθηλε πόλις, λαοὶ δ' ἀνθεῦσιν ἐν αὐτῇ.[126]

> But for those who give straight judgements to visitors and locals
> and do not deviate from what is just,
> their city flourishes and the people bloom in it.

Once again we have arrived at the fundamental level of vegetation and procreation. Hesiod's people are said to 'bloom' (ἀνθεῦσιν). The metaphorical language can be compared to the all-pervading metaphor 'shepherd of the people', from which we started. Both expressions, the former explicitly, the latter by implication, map processes of animal and plant life onto the realm of human interaction.[127] The more frequent image of the shepherd focuses on a basic social structure which aims to ensure the survival of a social world. The vision of the people we find expressed in the Hesiodic passage quoted last is even more fundamental. It is conceptualised most memorably in the myth of collective autochthonous birth, again mentioned in Hesiod:

> ἤτοι γὰρ Λοκρὸς Λελέγων ἡγήσατο λαῶν,
> τοὺς ῥά ποτε Κρονίδης Ζεὺς ἄφθιτα μήδεα εἰδὼς
> λεκτοὺς ἐκ γαίης ΛΑΟΥΣ πόρε Δευκαλίωνι.[128]

> Locrus led the Lelegan people
> whom Zeus, son of Cronus, who knows unwithering thoughts
> once gave to Deucalion as stones assembled from the earth.

Early epic *laoi*, in this version, are said to have been collected from the earth. The role of Zeus and Deucalion still implies a certain basic structure, but this is hardly the point here. Hesiod's people bring us down to the very basics of cultural pre-history – one cannot go back beyond the stone.[129] The autochthonous group exists at a level at which its existence *and nothing but its existence* is at issue. What once were stones

---

[126] Hes. *Op.* 225–7.
[127] The word φθίνω (or φθινύθω) may be relevant here; Nagy (1979) 176ff. argues for a primary meaning 'to wilt', Risch (1987) 4f. suggests 'versiegen' (of water).
[128] Hes. fr. 234 (M–W).
[129] For earlier attempts to interpret this etymology see Güntert (1932) 39f. and Specht (1944) 200; they are rightly criticised by Björck (1950) 327, n. 1.

are now people. Homeric texts do not explicitly mention the myth of autochthony, but the *Iliad*, too, alludes to it in a striking gesture of reversal:

... λαοὺς δὲ λίθους ποίησε Κρονίων.[130]

... for the son of Cronus turned the people into stones.

Carrying in themselves a memory of their non-existence (the stone), the *laoi* in early Greek hexameter are never far from the state from which they spring. This means, on the one hand, that we are left in close and threatening contact with non-being. Little is needed to bring about the decisive slip. On the other hand, the people who once were stones can make the strongest possible claim to survival. If indeed the stone begins where the *laoi* end, their well-being comes to include that of any other form of life.

The structural weakness of the epic group *laoi* is thus counterbalanced by an equally marked conceptual strength, which it derives from its tendency to subsume individual purpose under the overarching project of communal survival. As a mantic group, group under divine protection and autochthonous group, epic *laoi* make an undebatable claim to living. I next look at one particular aspect of the *laoi*'s conceptual strength which has generic implications. Our group, it will be argued, is closely linked with the most famous social world in Homer: Achaeans.

'The people of the Achaeans'

I have argued that epic *laoi* are cast as a social world at the fundamental level of collective survival, the level where the alternative would be stones. I conclude my overview by drawing attention to the recurrent phrase 'the people of the

---

[130] *Il.* 24.611; subsequent audiences must have understood the allusion, as is argued at length in ch. 3, 'Homer's people outside Homer'. Here it is enough to refer to schol. *Il.* 1.126 and Eust. 1 pp. 38.27–39.19 (van der Valk). In *Iliad* book 12 the similarity between λᾶας ('stone') and λαός ('people') resulted in a notorious textual crux: see schol. *Il.* 12.153a–d.

Achaeans' (λαός or λαὸν Ἀχαιῶν).[131] This may also serve to build a bridge to the second chapter. The phrase in question, although traditional in appearance, is not found outside the *Iliad*.

The expression 'people of the Achaeans' (λαός/λαὸν Ἀχαιῶν) occurs 23 times in the *Iliad*, where it also refers to the Theban war.[132] In its most canonical form it occupies the space after bucolic diaeresis; 5 times it is found after the second metron in the form 'people of the bronze-clad Achaeans' (λαὸν Ἀχαιῶν χαλκοχιτώνων). There is also a small system 'Achaic people' (λαὸς Ἀχαιϊκός) with a less definite metrical shape.[133]

Further formulaic analysis shows the relationship between 'Achaeans' and their *laos* to be particularly close. There are many alternatives to either *laos* or 'of the Achaeans' (Ἀχαιῶν) at the end of a Homeric verse, but we find no phrases such as 'race of the Achaeans' (*ἔθνος Ἀχαιῶν) or 'people = *demos* of the Achaeans' (*δῆμος Ἀχαιῶν), nor do we encounter the type 'people of the Epeians' (*λαὸς Ἐπειῶν etc.). More than any other word for 'group of people', the *laos* occurs in conjunction with the Achaeans.[134]

The name 'Achaeans' can refer to a tribe in Thessaly,[135] to the army outside Troy,[136] that of the Seven against Thebes,[137] the people of Ithaca,[138] Penelope's 'suitors'[139] or Odysseus and his companions.[140] Nagy has seen what unites all these seemingly disparate usages: where Achaeans are, there is Homeric poetry, song about the 'best of the Achaeans'

---

[131] Noted by Nagy (1979) 83f.
[132] *Il.* 6.223.
[133] See Appendix A.10.
[134] The expression λαὸς Μυρμιδόνων comes closest to being a real alternative; cf. *Il.* 11.796f., 16.39, without obvious connection to the formulaic phrases listed in Appendix A.10.
[135] *Il.* 2.684.
[136] *Il.* 1.2 and *passim*.
[137] *Il.* 4.384, 5.803, 6.223.
[138] *Od.* 2.7 and *passim*.
[139] *Od.* 22.46.
[140] *Od.* 9.259; the passage is discussed in ch. 2, '*Laoi* in the *Odyssey*', pp. 105ff.

in his various guises.[141] Compare what Hesiod says about the beginning of the Trojan war:

οὐ γάρ πώ ποτε νηὶ [γ'] ἐπέπλων εὐρέα πόντον,
εἰ μὴ ἐς Εὔβοιαν ἐξ Αὐλίδος, ᾗ ποτ' Ἀχαιοὶ
μείναντες χείμωνα πολὺν σὺν λαὸν ἄγειραν.[142]

For I have never yet sailed the broad sea in a ship
except to Euboea from Aulis, where once the Achaeans
waited through the winter and gathered many people.

The most Homeric of all undertakings, the siege of Troy, is undertaken by Achaeans – and we can now add with Hesiod: the *laos* plays its part from the beginning. Inherent in the formulaic combination 'people of the Achaeans' (λαός or λαὸν Ἀχαιῶν) is the claim that epic about the Achaeans is also about the *laos* and *vice versa*. Among the texts that survive, this claim is made most insistently in the *Iliad*, though the *laos* may have been prominent in now lost epics. The *Iliad* itself gives priority to the Theban cycle, suggesting that the people featured in songs about the Seven against Thebes.[143] The place of the 'people of the Achaeans' in larger formulaic patterns of the type 'destroying the people' further suggests that the combination is old.[144] In any case, we can say with confidence that, by virtue of being so closely attached to the name Achaeans, the *laos* also becomes attached to Homeric traditions of song more closely than to any other type of epic. *Laoi* as such are common to early Greek hexameter poetry as a whole. But as the 'people of the Achaeans' they are above all Homer's people.

Conclusion

In this chapter I set out to describe in rough outline the characteristics of the term *laos* as found in early Greek hexameter

---

[141] Nagy (1979) ch. 2; for the difference between Danaans and Achaeans see Pucci (1997) 172f.; for Argives see Drews (1979).
[142] Hes. *Op.* 650–2.
[143] *Il.* 6.223; cf. *Il.* 4.377, 407 with *Il.* 4.384, 5.803.
[144] See Appendix A.10.

poetry. Starting from the all-pervasive metaphor 'shepherd of the people' (ποιμένα/ποιμένι λαῶν), I argued that epic *laoi* form a social world for which a division into groups and leaders is fundamental. Two possible readings of the metaphor were singled out for discussion. On the one hand it was suggested that one could see the people in terms of their leader's status. This view is relatively rare and brings with it new responsibilities. By contrast, the shepherd's task was found to be central: the leader of early Greek epic must save the *laos*.

The genre of early Greek hexameter epic betrays a bias towards salvation of the *laoi* by single agents. At the same time it also dwells on the group's destruction as encapsulated in the powerful traditional phrase 'he destroyed the people' (ὤλεσε λαόν). Instead of saving his people and fulfilling his task, the leader of early Greek epic traditionally destroys them. This was taken to reflect the inherent structural weakness of the model, caused – at least in part – by an imbalance of interest between group and leader and further exacerbated by the absence of effective social structures. As a prime case of social interaction in the world of early epic, the fate of the *laoi* is characteristically bleak.

Having looked at how the relationship between leader and *laoi* is organised in early Greek epic, why it fails so often, and what consequences this has, I next discussed what I called their conceptual strength. I argued that their inclusiveness, their status as a group *vis-à-vis* the gods, a group of early social life and of autochthonous birth places them at the basis of any form of society. Where these people end the stone begins.

In a last step I argued for a close link between the *laoi* and the most famous social world of early Greek epic, 'Achaeans'. Where 'Achaeans' are, there is Homeric poetry, song about the 'best of the Achaeans' in his various guises. The fact that the *laos* of epic is typically 'Achaean' was taken to imply that this notion of the group is also central to Homer as song about the (best of the) Achaeans. *Laoi*, with all their peculiarities, with their strengths and their weaknesses, are thus above all Homer's people. I illustrate this claim in the second chapter.

2

HOMER'S PEOPLE

Having given an overview of what *laos* could mean in early Greek epic, I now turn to the Homeric texts. If I start with the *Iliad* before moving on to the *Odyssey,* this is partly dictated by convention – the *Iliad* is generally thought to be the earlier or more canonical of the two works. However, another consideration is more pertinent here. While the *Iliad* takes a constant and always open interest in the *laoi*, the case of the *Odyssey* is less clear-cut. In this poem, too, the *laoi* play an important role, but one that is overshadowed by two other groups: companions and suitors. In the section of this chapter headed '*Laoi* in the *Odyssey*' I argue that the *Odyssey* uses these two concepts to comment on and transform the view of Homer's people presented in the *Iliad*. So once again the *Iliad* has to come first.

Laoi in the *Iliad*

Of the surviving texts of early Greek hexameter poetry the *Iliad* presents itself as most interested in the *laoi*. The word occurs throughout the narrative,[1] and characteristic formulaic phrases such as 'shepherd of the people' are most frequent in this poem.[2] A generically relevant link between the Achaeans and their people is assumed in the *Iliad* and expressed in the formulaic phrase 'people of the Achaeans' (λαός or λαὸν Ἀχαιῶν).[3] The prominent place of the *laoi* in the language of the poem has its counterpart at a thematic level: the *Iliad*

---

[1] It appears 229 times.
[2] 'Shepherd of the people' (ποιμένα/ποιμένι λαῶν) occurs 44 times, 'he destroyed the people' (ὤλεσε λαόν) and related phrases are found 22 times, phrases expressing salvation of the people (σαώσετε λαόν) 5 times; see Appendix A.1–3.
[3] See above ch. 1, '"The people of the Achaeans"'.

begins and ends with the people, and throughout the narrative shows much interest in their plight.

In the following discussion I aim to develop in some detail what this could mean to our reading of the poem. In doing so, I follow roughly the order of events found in the text, concentrating on three leaders of the people – Agamemnon, Achilles, Hector. This structure deserves some explanation. First of all, it is of course traditional to focus on the main characters when reading the *Iliad*, and there are good reasons why this should be so. In many ways, the protagonists dominate the action of this poem, and it would hardly be wise to write them out of the text in an attempt to understand better the fortunes of the groups they lead. But there is also something more important to be said here. Groups in Homer cannot be understood without their leaders, and the term *laos* in particular constantly emphasises this point. Quite apart from any specific text, the problems of Homer's people are first and foremost problems of social structure. And that means, in a world without stable institutions, that they are problems of leadership.

There is no surviving text which takes this issue more seriously than the *Iliad*. Concentrating on three major leaders of the people, this text explores with increasing urgency the problems we have studied throughout chapter 1. Achilles is at the centre of this exploration. His wrath is thematic, and he alone knowingly destroys the *laoi* in order to recover his social position.[4] The central narrative of Achilles is framed by those of Agamemnon and Hector. They too destroy the people, but their actions are guided by an erroneous expectation: Agamemnon hopes, Hector fears that Troy will fall in the near future, whereas, at the end of our text, the city stands but the *laoi* have perished on both sides.

The theme

In the retrospective terms of the proem the *Iliad* does not introduce the *laoi* as being of particular interest. However, they come on stage as soon as the Muse takes over:

[4] As seen already by Nagy (1979) ch. 5.

Τίς τ' ἄρ σφωε θεῶν ἔριδι ξυνέηκε μάχεσθαι;
Λητοῦς καὶ Διὸς υἱός· ὁ γὰρ βασιλῆϊ χολωθεὶς
νοῦσον ἀνὰ στρατὸν ὦρσε κακήν, ὀλέκοντο δὲ λαοί.[5]

What god was it then set them together in bitter collision?
Zeus' son and Leto's, Apollo, who in anger at the king drove
the bad plague along the host, and the people perished.

In the proem we hear of Zeus, of Achaeans, and of heroes.[6] As we enter the narrative, we find a different god, Apollo, and a different thematic focus: not the heroes' death, not the Achaeans' suffering, but the people's catastrophe, expressed in highly formulaic language (ὀλέκοντο δὲ λαοί) and caused by a single agent. 'Marshals of the people' (κοσμήτορε λαῶν) is what the two Atreids are called in line 16 (in the proem Agamemnon had been a 'leader of men' (ἄναξ ἀνδρῶν)), and with this formulaic variant of the better-known 'shepherd of the people' we are reminded of the mechanisms that determine life among Homer's *laoi*.[7] In his account Achilles will later change the order of things. Having called the sons of Atreus 'marshals of the people' first (κοσμήτορε λαῶν), he then proceeds to recount Agamemnon's disastrous mistake.[8] If anything, this sharpens the contrast between Agamemnon's obligations and his actual behaviour even further.

Agamemnon is perhaps the most typical 'shepherd of the people' of early Greek hexameter,[9] and to have the narrative start with his shocking mistake sets the tone for much that is to come. Both the narrator and Achilles in his recapitulation call the opening plague 'detrimental' (κακός). There is no question as to how we are to view it. Indeed, as Agamemnon

---

[5] *Il.* 1.8–10.
[6] The retrospective word ἥρως ('hero') is typically used in proems, where it serves to introduce us to the world of epic; for discussion see Introduction, 'Between the omnipresent hero and the absent *polis*'.
[7] See above ch. 1, pp. 17–40. The words κοσμεῖν ('to marshal') and κοσμήτωρ ('marshal') are discussed by Collins (1988) 7.
[8] *Il.* 1.382f.
[9] This is what many ancient readers assume; see above ch. 1, 'Privilege and obligation'. The relevant Homeric passages are *Il.* 2.243, 254, 772, 4.413, 7.230, 10.3, 11.187, 202, 14.22, 19.35, 251, 24.654; *Od.* 3.156, 4.532, 14.497; cf. *Il.* 14.102 ὄρχαμε λαῶν ('leader of the people').

himself admits,[10] it is better, ἄμεινον, if the people are well. The only alternative (ἀπολέσθαι, 'to perish') echoes line 10 ('they perished') but is now envisaged by a character. The Homeric narrator steps back behind his protagonists. There will be no other place in the *Iliad* where a statement of the type 'he destroyed the people' (ὤλεσε λαόν) is uttered by the narrative voice. A hundred lines into the epic, the process of commenting and contesting has already begun.

From the beginning, the *Iliad* focuses on the innate problems of Homer's people specifically in terms of the interaction between groups and leaders. Agamemnon provides a starting-point, but he is not the only character to come into focus. Apollo's wrath foreshadows that of Achilles later in the poem.[11] Like its counterpart, it is called μῆνις,[12] and this has been shown to be the only thematic occurrence of the word which is not connected with Achilles.[13] Apollo's wrath is sweeping, but more specifically, it is lethal to the people. Apollo's reaction also shows how closely matters of 'honour' (τιμή) and general well-being are interwoven in the world of the *laoi*. This is how Chryses sums up what has happened towards the end of the episode:

τιμήσας μὲν ἐμέ, μέγα δ' ἴψαο λαὸν Ἀχαιῶν.[14]

you did me honour and smote strongly the people of the Achaeans.

The 'honour' (τιμή) of Chryses, and by implication Apollo's own, is restored through the damage inflicted on the *laos*. The line is ominous. It will recur much later in the epic, in Achilles' prayer to Zeus.[15]

Out of the singularly impersonal opening statement 'and the people were destroyed' (ὀλέκοντο δὲ λαοί) the *Iliad* devel-

---

[10] *Il.* 1.116f.; cf. Ulf (1990) 99, Taplin (1992) 50, Raaflaub (1997b) 17; the meaning of *Il.* 1.117 was debated in antiquity, sometimes with apologetic overtones (see schol. *ad loc*). For other attempts to improve Agamemnon's epic persona see Taplin (1990); see also schol. *Il.* 2.85b and here n. 34.
[11] Nagy (1979), Rabel (1990).
[12] *Il.* 1.75.
[13] Kahane (1994) 54f.
[14] *Il.* 1.454.
[15] *Il.* 16.237; cf. also *Il.* 9.118.

ops two versions of negative interaction between Homer's people and their leaders. One concerns the role of the 'shepherd': what is he supposed to do, and what happens if he neglects his duties? The other raises more complicated questions of who can expect what treatment and under what circumstances. Each one of these two narratives touches on problems of social interaction from a characteristically different angle. Taken together they converge in a larger vision of a social world without effective social structures.

The first book of the *Iliad* focuses closely on life among Homer's people. Problems of leadership are prominent from the outset, but that is not all. The fact that we start not with the people's war but with the plague that hits them and the animals around them should convince us that the issues involved are far-reaching indeed.[16] The phenomenon is familiar from chapter 1.[17] Different manifestations of animal life are threatened by a breach of social norm,[18] and when Homer's people are damaged as a consequence, they provide the measure for the well-being of a much larger system.[19] Their special role can be seen in the prayer of Chryses already quoted.[20] It is also implicit in the passage which describes the end of the plague:

λαοὺς δ' Ἀτρεΐδης ἀπολυμαίνεσθαι ἄνωγεν·
οἱ δ' ἀπελυμαίνοντο καὶ εἰς ἅλα λύματα βάλλον.[21]

Atreus' son told the people to wash off their defilement.
And they washed it away and threw the washings into the salt sea.

These lines are important for two reasons. First, the plague which affects all life outside Troy is cured with reference to Homer's people only. Thus we are reminded of their special

---

[16] On the paradigmatic nature of the plague – especially its status as a λοιγός (public catastrophe such as war, plague, etc.) – see Nagy (1979) 74–6, elaborated by Blickmann (1987).
[17] See ch. 1, 'Society and the stone'.
[18] *Il.* 1.50; the line caused problems for ancient readers from Aristotle onwards: *Po.* 1461a 9–12.
[19] Cf. *Od.* 11.134–7, 19.107–14, 23.281–4, Hes. *Op.* 225–7, 238–43, *h.Ven.* 103–6; perhaps also Hes. fr. 30.16, 19 (M–W) with schol. *Od.* 11.235.
[20] See above p. 50.
[21] *Il.* 1.313f.

status as a measure of general well-being. At the same time, however, attention is also drawn to the imbalance between group and leader discussed earlier.[22] It is ironic that Agamemnon who caused the plague in the first place is also the one who cures it.[23] Iliadic *laoi*, like the *laoi* in early Greek epic at large, are both strong and weak, all-inclusive and hopelessly dependent. Right from the start, the *Iliad* reflects on this inherent paradox. As we shall see, it never ceases to do so.

Agamemnon

Agamemnon's first mistake as a 'marshal of the people' is immediately followed by a second. Achilles draws attention to this by pointing out that it would not be right for the people to give back their share of the booty:

> λαοὺς δ' οὐκ ἐπέοικε παλίλλογα ταῦτ' ἐπαγείρειν.[24]
>
> it is unbecoming for the people to call back things once given.

We need not decide here what exactly the verse in question means, for this does not affect the role of the people in determining what is 'becoming' (ἐπέοικε).[25] The lack of respect Agamemnon shows for Achilles later in the story is already presented here as a lack of regard for the people. How pertinent Achilles' warning is becomes apparent as soon as Agamemnon has taken away Briseis.

In his answer, Agamemnon gives the quarrel a different direction, but the old issues soon surface again. Acting on the advice of Athena, Achilles accuses him of not joining in when the people go to war.[26] Not to join the *laos* is precisely what Achilles himself will do on purpose and polemically, later in the epic. Agamemnon's problems with the people closely foreshadow his own.

---

[22] See above ch. 1, 'An incurable imbalance'.
[23] Contrast *Il.* 1.10–12 and 313.
[24] *Il.* 1.126.
[25] Discussion in Leaf (1900–2) *ad loc.*, Ameis–Hentze–Cauer (1913) *ad loc.*, Kirk (1985) *ad loc.*
[26] *Il.* 1.225–8.

LAOI IN THE *ILIAD*

Agamemnon fulfils his role as a 'marshal' (*κοσμήτωρ) for the rest of book 1. He cleanses the people and gives Apollo his due. At the beginning of book 2, however, this picture of successful interaction is once again called into question.[27] We start with a dream which throws doubt on Agamemnon's qualities as a leader:

οὐ χρὴ παννύχιον εὕδειν βουληφόρον ἄνδρα,
ᾧ λαοί τ' ἐπιτετράφαται καὶ τόσσα μέμηλε.[28]

He should not sleep all night long who is a man burdened with counsels and responsibility for a people and cares so numerous.

The decisive lines are uttered twice, first by the dream in the guise of Nestor, then by Agamemnon himself. Renewed attention is drawn to his responsibility for the *laoi*, this time specified as those of a 'man of counsel' (βουληφόρος ἀνήρ). The dream takes up Achilles' warnings (οὐκ ἐπέοικε) earlier in the narrative,[29] pointing out that Agamemnon 'ought not' (οὐ χρή) to be sleeping all night long. Although Agamemnon reacts to the advice as any traditional leader of the people should, the speech with its scolding undertones suggests that something is amiss. The shepherd needs a guiding hand, and even if we cannot be sure what status the dream's suggestion has, there is a sense, with book 1 behind us and Zeus's deception beginning to work its effects, that Agamemnon's relationship with the *laoi* is heading toward crisis.

In response to the dream, Agamemnon summons the council near the ship of Nestor.[30] Announcing his plan,[31] he reports Nestor's precepts about how to manage the people,[32] and this part is then ratified by Nestor himself.[33] Nestor does not suggest deceiving the Achaeans. The so-called *peira* is Agamemnon's own contribution. It will appear from a close

---

[27] McGlew (1989) argues – against the *communis opinio* – that the Achaean assembly is a success for Agamemnon. As will soon become clear, I disagree.
[28] *Il.* 2.24f., cf. 2.61f.
[29] *Il.* 1.126.
[30] *Il.* 2.54.
[31] *Il.* 2.55.
[32] *Il.* 2.56–71.
[33] *Il.* 2.79–83.

reading of his speech why this is important; but first we need to look at Nestor in greater detail.

Agamemnon's dream, which reminds him of his responsibilities as a leader, takes the shape of Nestor, and it is no coincidence that Nestor himself later speaks with the authority of a 'shepherd of the people'.[34] Formulaic as it may be, this title does not remain innocently traditional in a context where the most traditional of shepherds is about to be humiliated. Later in the epic, we will repeatedly see Nestor step in for his colleague,[35] but at this point already he acts as Agamemnon's substitute. Nestor is the expert in matters concerning the *laoi*. Of course, this is not the only field in which he excels, just as Homer's people themselves only ever represent one possible aspect of Homer's world which competes with and complements others. There will be more examples of this as the investigation proceeds.[36]

Having summoned the council by appearing in the deceptive dream, Nestor also dismisses it. In response to his words Homer's people themselves enter the stage.[37] What follows, after the opening plague, is an elaborate description of social formation. The *laoi* storm to the assembly (ἀγορή) and gather.[38] They sit down noisily and chaotically[39] until they (again the word is *laoi*) are disciplined by heralds.[40] When order is restored, a single agent, here Agamemnon, stands up to speak.[41]

As is traditional in early Greek epic,[42] the people eventually form a space of communal restraint which is marked by the noise they make on arrival. Great care and energy go into

---

[34] *Il.* 2.85; the scholia *ad loc.* comment that the text 'refers to Agamemnon'. This cannot be meant, but the attempt to eradicate ambiguities is telling; for other attempts to improve Agamemnon's epic persona see above n. 10.
[35] *Il.* 2.362–6, 9.96–102, 10.73–9, 11.655ff., esp. 714–17, 754–8, 762–4, 769f., 796f.
[36] E.g. ch. 2, '*Laoi* in the *Iliad*', pp. 83–95, ch. 2, '*Laoi* in the *Odyssey*', pp. 104–25.
[37] *Il.* 2.84–6.
[38] *Il.* 2.94; the word is ἀγέροντο, 'they gathered'.
[39] *Il.* 2.95f.
[40] *Il.* 2.96–8.
[41] *Il.* 2.99–101.
[42] See above ch. 1, 'Social structures'.

organising the 'turmoil' (the word ὅμαδος is often used in battle descriptions[43]), but v. 99 also introduces an element of collective will. The change from unstructured to structured social life is made not without aetiological pathos. If anything, this is a beginning of communal action. We cannot, of course, say whether for an early Greek audience our scene would have been the most elaborate picture of gathering the people.[44] But certainly for an Iliadic audience it replays the 'original' assembly at the beginning of the Trojan war.

It comes as a shock that the assembly breaks down only a short while after it has been called. The man who is to blame is once again Agamemnon. His speech is complex, and since it is of some importance to our reading of the *Iliad*, let us take a closer look at what he says.

Agamemnon speaks with his sceptre in hand, passed on to him by Atreus, 'shepherd of the people'.[45] He starts by addressing 'heroes' (ἥρωες), not *laoi*.[46] Homer's people are very rarely addressed in early Greek hexameter poetry, and so this cannot in itself come as a surprise.[47] However, the opening 'heroes' does take on programmatic force when set against the lines that follow. There Agamemnon, in strikingly formulaic language, offers the following view of the Trojan war:

> Ζεύς με μέγα Κρονίδης ἄτῃ ἐνέδησε βαρείῃ,
> σχέτλιος, ὃς πρὶν μέν μοι ὑπέσχετο καὶ κατένευσεν
> Ἴλιον ἐκπέρσαντ' εὐτείχεον ἀπονέεσθαι,
> νῦν δὲ κακὴν ἀπάτην βουλεύσατο, καί με κελεύει
> δυσκλέα Ἄργος ἱκέσθαι, ἐπεὶ πολὺν ὤλεσα λαόν.[48]   115

Zeus son of Cronus has caught me fast in bitter futility.
He is hard; who before this time promised me and consented
that I might sack strong-walled Ilios and sail homeward.
Now he has devised a vile deception, and bids me go back
to Argos in dishonour having lost many people.

---

[43] *Il.* 7.307, 9.573, 12.471, 15.689, 16.295f., 17.380, 21.387 (variant παταγῳ).
[44] The *Cypria* and the *Thebais*, in particular, may have contained other such scenes.
[45] *Il.* 2.105.
[46] *Il.* 2.110.
[47] I have found only *Od.* 2.252; *Il.* 5.600f. is related, but note that Diomedes says 'friends' (φίλοι) in his direct address; see further p. 179.
[48] *Il.* 2.111–15.

What Agamemnon says here may bring to mind the nightmare situation of the Theban war with its concomitant destruction of the people.[49] But whether or not an allusion to the hapless Adrastus is implied, it is clear from everything the *Iliad* has shown us so far that Agamemnon's scenario is dangerously close at hand. Under such circumstances the blame falls entirely on him.

Agamemnon does not leave things there. As his address to the 'heroes' has already suggested, he goes on to convert his opening version of the Trojan campaign into something quite different. In what follows, Agamemnon turns a structured world of groups and leaders in which all the responsibility for success or defeat rests on him, the 'shepherd of the people', into a homogeneous social world of equally interested single agents who, *qua* 'heroes' (ἥρωες), cannot escape the role they must play in the drama of their own downfall. He does so in three steps.

After the opening lines with their terse exposition of communal catastrophe, a second section already suggests that things could be seen in a different light.[50] It is difficult to understand just what Agamemnon is trying to say here, but so much seems clear: he asks us to concentrate not on his own fame (κλέος) and the leader's traditional responsibilities, but rather on what reputation the people deserve. This is introduced as an additional explanation of Agamemnon's misfortune (ἄτη), but in effect it changes the issue. The catastrophe of the people is no longer due to the failure of their shepherd but to their own lack of success in their fight against Troy (ἄπρηκτον πόλεμον πολεμίζειν). The result is once again a bad reputation (αἰσχρὸν ... ἐσσομένοισι πυθέσθαι), but this time it affects the group.

Having threatened his group with blame, Agamemnon returns to his own role. This time we do not hear about the people any more.[51] Leader and group have parted company, and after the operation Agamemnon's failure is reduced to

---

[49] *Il.* 6.223 with Pi. *P.* 8.54; see above p. 45.   [50] *Il.* 2.119–22.
[51] *Il.* 2.132f.

the pathetic picture of someone who cannot get what he, personally, wants. No obligations any more, no questions of failure and social sanction. Agamemnon is 'thrown off course' (πλάζουσι) and prevented from fulfilling his wishes (οὐκ εἰῶσ' ἐθέλοντα). He has become a victim of higher might.

When Agamemnon eliminates Homer's people from Homer's war, this goes hand in hand with an attempt to redefine his fame exclusively through the capture of Troy. Not to save the *laoi* but to take the city is now the criterion for a successful epic career. Later in the text, Hector will similarly waver between the role of the city-saviour and that of a leader of the people.[52] Hector, too, privileges the city at the expense of the group. And he too will have to pay dearly.

Back in book 2, Agamemnon can now present himself as a single agent among others. This is the version of things which corresponds to the opening 'heroes' (ἥρωες):

   ... ἄμμι δὲ ἔργον
αὔτως ἀκράαντον, οὗ εἵνεκα δεῦρ' ἱκόμεσθα.[53]

... while still our work here
stays forever unfinished as it is, for whose sake we came hither.

Compare this passage with the ideal leader of the people in Xenophon, who had no personal agenda.[54] Agamemnon has turned the tables. The Greek adjective which I have translated 'unfinished' (ἀκράαντον) is formed from the stem *κραν-. In epic, this stem is often represented by the verb κραίνω, which is used of superior agents, most characteristically gods, who lend authority to a state of affairs suggested by a less powerful party.[55] In book 8, Agamemnon will pass this particular sort of competence on to Zeus; in *Iliad* 9 Nestor describes Agamemnon's own role in such terms.[56] The way in which the king employs a derivative of κραίνω here adds to the manipulative qualities of his speech: we have finally arrived at a

---

[52] See ch. 2, '*Laoi* in the *Iliad*', pp. 83–95.
[53] *Il.* 2.137f.
[54] See above pp. 21f.
[55] Benveniste (1973) 327–33, Collins (1988) 71, *LfgrE s.v.*
[56] See p. 63.

homogeneous social world without leaders and without social responsibilities. 'Getting things done' is everyone's business, and as such it concerns not a structure within, but an outside goal. The picture of Agamemnon, the frustrated fighter against Troy, is now made to include everyone else. The people's ambitions simply mirror his.

In his deceptive speech, then, Agamemnon simplifies his epic persona by narrowing it down to that of a fighter against Troy. The needs of Homer's people uncomfortably interfere with their leader's aspirations. In response, Agamemnon redefines the *laoi* and hence his own role as a 'shepherd' in such a way as to make no one look after anyone any more.[57] The trick, however, backfires, and Agamemnon is quickly overtaken by events. He cannot mobilise his group's interest in the capture of Troy. In the typical manner of Homer's people, they 'rush back' to their ships ((ἐπι-)σεύεσθαι),[58] and now that this is no longer channelled by the structures of life among the *laoi*, everything simply dissolves. It takes the intervention of Odysseus with the divine herald Athena at his side to restore order.[59] And once again it is the order of an assembled people (λαός).[60] Agamemnon's plan to mobilise a world of heroes has come to a quick and embarrassing end. Troy is not going to be taken without the people; the leader is thrown back on his dreaded task.

In the first book of the *Iliad*, Agamemnon's attempt at asserting an interest which interferes with his role as a 'marshal of the people' fails spectacularly. He causes a plague, the people perish, and as a result he has to admit personal defeat. In

---

[57] For a similar attempt at redefining Homer's people see *Il.* 13.108 and pp. 74f. below.
[58] Compare *Il.* 2.86 and 149f.
[59] *Il.* 2.278–80; cf. 2.163f., 179f. ἐρητύω ('hold back') is the word characteristically used of heralds in such contexts; see above p. 34 and Appendix A.7.
[60] This had been Odysseus' aim already in *Il.* 2.191; against Kirk (1968) 112 it should be noted that Thersites is not introduced as a member of the *laos*. For his association with the *demos*, see *Il.* 2.198f. and 211–69 and the discussion in Thalmann (1988) *passim*, esp. 11 with n. 26; cf. also Rose (1988), esp. 16. For the difference between *laos* and *demos* in Homer see *LfgrE s.vv.* and here n. 316 with further literature.

the second book Agamemnon's more subtle and far-reaching plan of redefining himself, his social surroundings, and with them our epic plot, is also thwarted. Instead of developing an interest in the capture of Troy, the Achaeans simply stampede. I have argued that this implies a silent vote for one model of social interaction as opposed to another. I would now add that it also implies a vote against the possible alternative *Iliad* envisaged by the deceptive dream and endorsed by Agamemnon. The dream, we recall, had promised the capture of the city within a day. We, the audience, knew from the start that this was not going to happen; and Agamemnon himself will have learned by the time we reach the end of the day in book 9.[61]

Death and unwarranted dissolution of the group are events that the traditional 'shepherd of the people' must help to avoid.[62] By book 2 of the *Iliad*, Agamemnon has already provoked both, and is thus hopelessly discredited. The poem does not suggest that Agamemnon can be replaced; but it does become clear that others would have done better: Achilles in book 1, Odysseus and Nestor in book 2. Odysseus with his courageous stand shows how to mobilise communal interest. And Nestor, the substitute shepherd, suggests how one might better control the people without creating chaos. The relevant section of his speech is carefully phrased.[63] At its beginning and end Nestor speaks of 'men' (ἄνδρες), while in the middle he refers to the people and the structures of leadership they rely on (ἡγεμόνες–λαοί).

Nestor's manœuvre reminds us of Agamemnon's speech earlier in the book. Their aims are similar – both Agamemnon and Nestor convert the *laoi* into something more like a gathering of single agents; but their strategies are fundamentally opposed. Nestor's suggestion, unlike Agamemnon's, does not aim at abolishing the people. Rather, he proposes to solve the

---

[61] The phenomenon is closely related to that of 'Homeric misdirection' as studied by Morrison (1992).
[62] See above ch. 1, especially pp. 28–35.
[63] *Il.* 2.362–6.

problems by creating new institutions (φρῆτραι, φῦλα).⁶⁴ The idea is hailed by Agamemnon, but we hear nothing about it later in the text. Institutional progress is not the *Iliad*'s prime interest. Instead, the assembly is dissolved and on the next day, once again with the help of heralds and Athena, the *laos* is gathered for fighting.⁶⁵

In the first two books of the *Iliad*, Agamemnon's traditional role as a leader of the people is exposed to merciless narrative scrutiny. Over the books that follow, his problems gradually develop towards their crisis in book 9. We start this development from an ominous high point in the *Catalogue of ships*. Agamemnon is singled out and glorified in a characteristic fashion:

> τῶν ἑκατὸν νηῶν ἦρχε κρείων Ἀγαμέμνων
> Ἀτρεΐδης· ἅμα τῷ γε πολὺ πλεῖστοι καὶ ἄριστοι
> λαοὶ ἕποντ'· ἐν δ' αὐτὸς ἐδύσετο νώροπα χαλκὸν
> κυδιόων, πᾶσιν δὲ μετέπρεπεν ἡρώεσσιν,
> οὕνεκ' ἄριστος ἔην, πολὺ δὲ πλείστους ἄγε λαούς.⁶⁶   580

of their hundred ships the leader was powerful Agamemnon,
Atreus' son, with whom followed by far the most and best
people; and among them he himself stood armoured in shining
bronze, glorying, conspicuous among the heroes,
since he was greatest and led by far the most people.

Nothing is said in these lines about Agamemnon's plans concerning Troy. Instead we are told twice how many people he leads. If the *Catalogue of ships* is anything to go by, Agamemnon's fame as a hero among other heroes (πᾶσιν δὲ μετέπρεπεν ἡρώεσσιν) depends on the *laoi* more than anything else.⁶⁷ He is 'greatest' only as long as they are 'most'. We can

---

⁶⁴ On phratries in Homer see Andrewes (1961); Ulf (1990) 145–9 argues that the army outside Troy is *de facto* organised in tribes (φῦλα) and phratries. If so, this does not bring the promised relief. On the close relationship between *laoi* and tribes outside epic see Nagy (1990b) 180 with n. 141; see also Hdt. 4.148.1, E. *Ion* 1575–9, *CEG II* 890 and, much later, *IG* 2(2) 3118.
⁶⁵ *Il.* 2.437f., 450f.; cf. 2.799.
⁶⁶ *Il.* 2.576–80.
⁶⁷ Cf. *Il.* 2.672–5 (Nireus), 708–10 (Protesilaos); Hector's entry in lines 816–18 is discussed on pp. 85f.; see also Ulf (1990) 95 with n. 24.

now see why any attempt on Agamemnon's part to ignore or sideline the people is doomed to fail.[68]

In the *Catalogue of ships*, then, Agamemnon's traditional heroic persona is presented as a function of his leading many people. We may wonder what has become of the tradition after the catastrophe of book 1 and the embarrassment of 2, but for the time being our attention shifts to other matters. Menelaus, Paris, Helen come and go. Diomedes struggles against epigonic unease. Hector enters and leaves his city. Homer's people are never far from the scene,[69] but their fate does not immediately concern that of Agamemnon.[70]

Book 8 brings a reminder of what is at stake, both for the people of the Achaeans and for their most prominent leader.[71] Agamemnon's prayer there is answered with a verse similar to one already known from book 1:

νεῦσε δέ οἱ λαὸν σόον ἔμμεναι οὐδ' ἀπολέσθαι.[72]

and he [Zeus] nodded approval that the people should stay alive,
and not perish.

Both in book 1 and in book 8 the final catastrophe is averted, but there are warning signs that the situation is deteriorating. In *Iliad* 1 it was Agamemnon's own choice to make the right decision – that is, to act in the interest of the people. By the time we arrive in book 8 he is more or less helpless. Zeus has to take over, but we know that in the long run Zeus has different plans. Agamemnon's tears prefigure those of books 9

---

[68] For a combination of Agamemnon's account (ὤλεσα λαόν, 'I destroyed the people') with the capture of Troy see *Od.* 9.265f. and the discussion on pp. 105–7.

[69] E.g. *Il.* 3.318–24, 4.27, 184, 377, 407, 5.643, 758, 6.223, 327, 7.177–80, 434.

[70] With the exception of *Il.* 4.184, which further exposes Agamemnon's weakness.

[71] *Il.* 8.66–72, 242–6; once again we note the shifting use of κραίνω ('to bring to pass'). In Agamemnon's own words in book 2, the word had referred to the capture of Troy and as such had been declared the task of everyone. In his prayer in book 8 Agamemnon takes a fresh approach. He acknowledges that the people cannot be expected to look after themselves in such a way; but the task of saving them is once more passed on, this time to Zeus. The delegation of responsibility ends with book 9.

[72] *Il.* 8.246; cf. 1.117.

and 10. The next point of crisis is not far away, and this time Zeus no longer steps in.

Agamemnon has his hour of reckoning at the end of the first day of fighting, when, contrary to the promise of the deceptive dream, Troy has not fallen and only the *laos* been lost.[73] As has often been remarked, Agamemnon repeats the opening of his speech in book 2.[74] However, the loss of people has now become 'infamous' (δυσκλεής) reality, a reality which rebounds on Agamemnon alone. The sections of the deceptive speech which transformed a world of leaders and people into one of equally responsible heroes are cut out in the recapitulation, and the grandiose appeal to world teleology that was suggested in the opening address (Troy must fall and many heroes die) has become a pathetic plea for help.

One may accuse Agamemnon of weakness in this difficult situation,[75] but that is hardly the point. We should rather remember that no less is at stake for him than the complete ruin of his epic fame. Agamemnon's good reputation, defined as it is to a large extent by his role as a leader of many people (πλείστους ἄγε λαούς), cannot possibly survive his destroying many (πολὺν ὤλεσα λαόν). Such behaviour may be damaging for anyone in early Greek hexameter poetry, but for Agamemnon alone is it directly and positively ruinous.

Nestor, the substitute 'shepherd', understands the problem and opens his answering speech by paying tribute to Agamemnon's traditional role:

Ἀτρεΐδη κύδιστε, ἄναξ ἀνδρῶν Ἀγάμεμνον,
ἐν σοὶ μὲν λήξω, σέο δ' ἄρξομαι, οὕνεκα πολλῶν
λαῶν ἐσσι ἄναξ καί τοι Ζεὺς ἐγγυάλιξε
σκῆπτρόν τ' ἠδὲ θέμιστας, ἵνα σφίσι βουλεύῃσθα.[76]

Son of Atreus, most lordly and master of men
with you I will end, with you I will make my beginning, since of many
people you are the master, and Zeus has given into your hand
the sceptre and rights of judgement, so that you may counsel them.

---

[73] *Il.* 9.18–22.
[74] E.g. Hainsworth (1993) *ad Il.* 9.18–28.
[75] E.g. Edwards (1987) 217.
[76] *Il.* 9.96–9; cf. Collins (1988) 79f., and Ulf (1990) 99, who reminds us that Nestor's speech highlights Agamemnon's obligations as well as his privilege.

Nestor speaks as if there had never been a problem. Agamemnon's privilege is to be 'master' (ἄναξ) over many people (λαοί) and his task is to counsel them. The task is slipped in as if it were part of the privilege. And even if there is more than a mere suggestion of disapproval in Nestor's words, it is glossed over by lavish, almost hymnic language.[77] Heightened glorification makes up for sinking repute.

In other ways, too, Nestor chooses his words carefully. He makes no direct appeal to the epic tradition of the 'shepherd', offering instead a transformation of the 'master of men' (ἄναξ ἀνδρῶν)[78] into a 'master of the people' (λαῶν ... ἄναξ),[79] who does not carry embarrassing overtones. Nestor goes some way toward re-inventing Agamemnon, but even he cannot or does not want to avoid complications. The man whose counsel (βουλή) 'had already appeared to be best'[80] reminds Agamemnon – in the council (βουλή) – that he is there to provide counsel (βουλή). Nestor twists and turns. From Agamemnon's double role as master and counsellor of the people he derives an obligation to listen as well as speak. In the end Agamemnon's persona is gently reworked as that of someone who authorises (again the verb is κραίνω) what others suggest.[81] Nestor's suggestions quickly follow.

As Nestor sees it, Agamemnon 'yielded to his great-hearted spirit' (θυμός) in putting down Achilles (ἀτιμάζειν). When Nestor advises him to make good his mistake with gifts and words, Agamemnon weighs his opponent's epic persona against his own. In *Il.* 9.97–9 Nestor had said of him:

... οὕνεκα πολλῶν
λαῶν ἐσσι ἄναξ καί τοι Ζεὺς ἐγγυάλιξε
σκῆπτρόν τ' ἠδὲ θέμιστας, ἵνα σφίσι βουλεύῃσθα.

---

[77] Leaf (1900–2) *ad* Hom. *Il.* 9.97, Hainsworth (1993) *ad* Hom. *Il.* 9.92–9.
[78] *Il.* 9.96.
[79] *Il.* 9.98; the phrase λαῶν ἄναξ ('master of the people') is not common in early Greek epic; cf., however, *Od.* 2.234 and perhaps Hes. fr. 33(a).2 (M–W). For the different models of the shepherd and the master (ἄναξ) see above ch. 1, '"Shepherd of the people"'.
[80] *Il.* 9.94.
[81] For the meaning of κραίνω ('to bring to pass') see above p. 57.

.... since of many
people you are the master and Zeus has given into your hand
the sceptre and rights of judgement, so that you may counsel them.

In 9.116f. Agamemnon says of Achilles:

... ἀντί νυ πολλῶν
λαῶν ἐστιν ἀνὴρ ὅν τε Ζεὺς κῆρι φιλήσῃ.

... worth many
people is a man whom Zeus in his heart loves.

Even with the liberties I have taken, the English translation cannot hope to capture the carefully wrought parallelism of the Greek. 'Since of many' echoes 'worth many' in sound and metre. In a similar way, 'master' and 'people' in the first passage prefigure 'man' and 'people' in the second. Finally, both passages are built around the name of Zeus, which stands in the same metrical position. In the light of the parallel phrasing the differences between the passages come out all the more drastically. Agamemnon's relationship with the people as seen by Nestor is inclusive. They enhance his status. For Achilles, as depicted by Agamemnon, it is exclusive. Achilles wins appreciation by allowing many people to die. He is quite literally 'instead of them', feeding on their demise.

By the time we reach book 9, the quarrel between Achilles and Agamemnon is firmly linked to the *laoi*. Agamemnon had hoped to avoid complications by ignoring the people and capturing Troy, but his failure to do so throws him back on his unwelcome responsibilities. In book 9 Agamemnon's fame (κλέος), his entire epic career, has gone to pieces together with his role as a 'shepherd of the people'. This role has been under scrutiny since the beginning of the poem, and the ensuing problems come to a crisis when Agamemnon has to acknowledge defeat. Achilles on the other hand recovers his honour (τιμή) and, by implication, his fame, precisely through that defeat. Once more in the words of Agamemnon:

ὡς νῦν τοῦτον [Achilles] ἔτεισε [sc. Zeus], δάμασσε δὲ λαὸν Ἀχαιῶν.[82]

[82] *Il.* 9.118.

> he [Zeus] has now honoured this man [Achilles] and broken the
> people of the Achaeans.

Achilles' social status derives from the destruction of the people. If Agamemnon's fame was implicated with their well-being, the same is true of him – but in the opposite sense.

Achilles is not often called a 'shepherd of the people'.[83] In this most obviously traditional sense he is not a man of the *laoi*. However, his wrath (μῆνις) as his prime characteristic, encapsulates a vision of social life which is also, this time negatively, bound up with Homer's people.[84] Muellner has argued convincingly that the wrath of Achilles must be seen as a function of his social world; and not as a mere emotion.[85] As such it can be described, more specifically, in its effects on the people. Apollo's divine anger (μῆνις) in *Il.* 1 was glossed in such terms from the beginning,[86] and Achilles' own wrath, too, is accomplished at the expense of the *laoi*. From now on this will be said or implied with some frequency.

Although Achilles is not a traditional 'shepherd' he takes a special interest in the *laoi*. So much so that he reacts to social upset in the same way as Apollo did: he becomes angry and seeks to restore his honour (τιμή) by causing damage to them. Like Apollo, Achilles can thus become both cause and indicator of the problems we have seen in chapter 1. His competence enables him not only to do more damage than others could, but also to pose deeper questions. For instance, when entreated to join battle in the embassy scene of book 9 he asks why the people have been gathered in the first place.[87] If the reasons are at all doubtful, should the group not be dissolved? Achilles is the only one outside Troy who asks this crucial

---

[83] He only acquires this role towards the end of the narrative, in *Il.* 16.2 and 19.386; cf. *Il* 21.221 (ὄρχαμε λαῶν – 'leader of the people').

[84] The modern etymology of Achilles as 'he who brings grief (ἄχος) to the people (λαός)' is particularly suggestive in this context; see above p. 2 with n. 11; however, the present argument does not depend on whether we believe it to be right or relevant.

[85] Muellner (1996) ch. 1, against Latacz (1996) 71.

[86] *Il.* 1.10, 117, 313, 382f., 454.

[87] *Il.* 9.337–9.

question,[88] thereby further exposing Agamemnon's vulnerability. He is even more brutal at the end of his speech:

> ... ἐπεὶ οὐκέτι δήετε τέκμωρ
> Ἰλίου αἰπεινῆς· μάλα γὰρ ἕθεν εὐρύοπα Ζεὺς
> χεῖρα ἑὴν ὑπερέσχε, τεθαρσήκασι δὲ λαοί. 420
> ἀλλ' ὑμεῖς μὲν ἰόντες ἀριστήεσσιν Ἀχαιῶν
> ἀγγελίην ἀπόφασθε – τὸ γὰρ γέρας ἐστὶ γερόντων –
> ὄφρ' ἄλλην φράζωνται ἐνὶ φρεσὶ μῆτιν ἀμείνω,
> ἥ κέ σφιν νῆάς τε σαῷ καὶ λαὸν Ἀχαιῶν.[89]

> ... since no longer shall you find any term set
> on the sheer city of Ilios, since Zeus of the wide brows has strongly
> held his hand over it, and its people have taken strength.
> Go back therefore to the great men of the Achaeans,
> and take this message, since such is the privilege of the princes:
> that they think out in their minds some other scheme that is better,
> which might rescue their ships and the people of the Achaeans.

Here is yet another passage which describes Achilles' wrath (his μῆνις) in relation to Homer's people. This time Achilles himself does it for us, and he does it in such a way as to make Agamemnon's involvement painfully clear.[90] The Trojan people fare as well as Agamemnon hopes the Achaean *laoi* would. Having presented Agamemnon with a picture of what he cannot achieve, Achilles goes on to send back a message which portends further destruction to the Achaean people. The message is duly reported.[91] And Odysseus, who acts as the messenger, concentrates entirely on the last sentences of Achilles' long speech, the lines concerning the *laos*. This is the important part; it contains Agamemnon's whole misery.

The situation in which Agamemnon is left in book 9 leads to desperation in book 10. Whatever one might think about

---

[88] For the unique character of these lines see Edwards (1987) 223; Ulf (1990) 157–64 sees a tension inherent in the Trojan war as a 'private' undertaking on a 'public' scale; cf. also Raaflaub (1997b). There are two reasons why this view should be resisted. First, to speak of 'public' and 'private' in the context of Homer's people is to obscure their specific character. Second, Ulf assigns to the Trojan expedition a special status which it does not have. The problems of motivation and co-ordination we see outside Troy are fundamentally the same for all undertakings of the *laoi*.
[89] *Il.* 9.418–24.
[90] Formulaic relatives of *Il.* 9.424 are listed in Appendix A.2; see also p. 28.
[91] *Il.* 9.676–87.

the *Doloneia*,⁹² in this respect it clearly develops the themes it inherits from book 9. Agamemnon had there wept over his loss of good fame caused by the loss of many people.⁹³ In book 10 the 'shepherd of the people'⁹⁴ is so devastated that he remains awake, just as the dream in the guise of Nestor in book 2 had recommended a leader of the *laoi* should do. There are more ironic echoes. When Agamemnon looks at the ships and people, towards the beginning of the episode, the narrative voice faithfully recalls the last line of Achilles' message.⁹⁵ Agamemnon is made to see Achilles' words come true. His problem could not be evoked in a more cutting way.

Nestor, the substitute leader of the people,⁹⁶ is summoned for help, and the night-raid he suggests brings temporary relief. As in book 2, Nestor cannot himself replace Agamemnon, but this time he finds others who can; and while Diomedes and Odysseus do not solve anything in the long run, they set the precedent for the second and decisive substitute: Patroclus.

Once the low point of Agamemnon's relationship with the people is reached, the *Iliad* loses interest in him. To be sure, he has his *aristeia* in book 11; but little is heard of him afterwards. When Agamemnon reappears in book 14 the old tensions soon surface again.⁹⁷ In response to his defiant speech, Odysseus asks Agamemnon to keep silent. The paradox of a leader who does not lead is summed up in the last line of his speech:

> ἔνθα κε σὴ βουλὴ δηλήσεται, ὄρχαμε λαῶν.⁹⁸
>
> there, O leader of the people, your plan will be ruin.

Agamemnon's counselling as a 'leader of the people' (*ὄρχαμος λαῶν) is so directly detrimental that he had better

---

[92] A recent analytical statement can be found in Danek (1988) with earlier literature; for a recent unitarian account see Stanley (1993) 118–28.
[93] *Il.* 9.14f. and 22.
[94] *Il.* 10.3.
[95] *Il.* 10.14–16; *Il.* 9.424, 681. Cf. Appendix A.2.
[96] *Il.* 10.73–9, cf. 10.170f.
[97] *Il.* 14.90–4; note the use of the term *laos*; cf. also Ulf (1990) 95, 100.
[98] *Il.* 14.102.

not counsel at all. The tone in which Odysseus speaks is new, but the substance of his argument is not. As a 'shepherd of the people' Agamemnon has long been beyond good and evil. Everything hinges now on Achilles.

Achilles

In book 9 the narrative emphasis shifts from Agamemnon to Achilles. As we have seen already, the embassy scene builds up an opposition which is of some importance to the story at large: Agamemnon's fame is exposed as depending not so much on the fall of Troy as on the well-being of the *laoi*.[99] By contrast, Achilles' wrath (μῆνις), and with it his social status, is for the first time explicitly linked to their destruction.[100] In books 1–9 of the *Iliad* Agamemnon's ambitions concerning Troy became more and more dubious, until his inability to save the people eclipsed all other concerns. In the following books Achilles' plans and actions will be scrutinised with similar insistence, focusing in particular on two issues.

On the one hand, the death of the *laoi* gradually builds up Achilles' fame as it is brought about by his anger (μῆνις). No-one is able to replace him, and the pressure of the people perishing weighs heavily on the Achaeans. On the other hand, the disaster of Homer's people has once more unforeseen consequences for the perpetrator. The events of book 11 represent a first and decisive stage in this twofold development. They will be discussed first. I then study Achilles' glorification, which culminates in his prayer to Zeus in book 16. In a third section I look at books 16ff., arguing that when Achilles loses his companion (ἑταῖρος) he comes to join the *laoi* in their suffering.

In book 9 Achilles had presented the situation of the people entirely as a problem of Agamemnon's and of the other Achaeans. The events of book 11 already complicate this view. Let us start by looking at the episode in which Machaon, the 'shepherd of the people' is wounded.[101] We note

---

[99] *Il.* 9.22.   [100] *Il.* 9.118.   [101] *Il.* 11.597–9, 602–4, cf. 11.506.

the insistence with which our metaphor recurs in this section of the epic. What attracts Achilles' attention is precisely the traditional role he has set out to undermine. At the same time, the wounded 'shepherd' highlights the theme of Achilles' own dissociation from Homer's people. This shepherd has to be Machaon because there was no Achilles.[102]

Machaon is the last in a long row of wounded leaders beginning with the most famous 'shepherd of the people', Agamemnon. He sums up the gradual bereavement of the Achaean people, and Achilles, as an onlooker, adds to the pathetic impact of the sequence. Here would be the point to go and step in once more; but he does not: he simply dispatches Patroclus to find out who the wounded warrior is. When Patroclus arrives on the scene Machaon is once more described as a 'shepherd', this time by Patroclus himself.[103] For those who come close enough no long narrative is necessary to understand what has happened. Instead of the story Patroclus does not need to be told any more, he is held back by Nestor to hear about the paradigmatic undertaking of the Pylians against the Epeians. It is the tale of a war of *laoi*, and here, in Nestor's words, a first warning is issued against the newly arisen destroyer of the people, Achilles.

Nestor's prophetic words open a narrative line which complements that of Achilles' self-contained glorification. The tale from which it springs is carefully told, and it is worth spending some time over it.[104] References to the *laos* appear at its beginning and end.[105] Homer's people open and close Nestor's war, providing the frame of reference within which martial activity is envisaged. Their role is sanctioned by the goddess who is most closely linked with them in early Greek hexameter, Athena. We may recall that Athena has a recurrent epithet that marks her out as a patron goddess of

---

[102] For parallels between Machaon and Achilles as healers see King (1987) 9f.; for the scene as a turning-point of the *Iliad* see Arieti (1983).
[103] *Il.* 11.649–51.
[104] For earlier discussion without reference to the *laoi* see Bölte (1934), Schadewaldt (1965a) ch. 3, Lohmann (1970) 70–5, Pedrick (1983); Raaflaub (1997b) 2f. discusses the process of escalation which leads to the war.
[105] *Il.* 11.714–17 and 11.756–61.

Homer's people (λαοσσόος, 'stirring/saving the people').[106] It is paraphrased in the *Homeric hymn* 11.[107] Together with Ares she leads the people on Achilles' shield,[108] and in book 2 of the *Iliad* she repeatedly helps to gather the *laos* of the Achaeans.[109] With Athena taking charge no-one steps out of line when the people (λαός) are assembled and put on armour. Father Neleus wrongly tries to prevent his son from joining in; but Nestor, who knows better, does not heed his advice.[110] Indeed, Nestor is in harmony with Athena and the people from the beginning to the end of the raid. He arms with everyone else, and he stops as soon as Athena stops the *laos*.[111]

The crux of Nestor's story is motivation. It is important that the Pylian people (λαός) are gathered in traditional language (ἐσσυμένους)[112] and not against their will (οὐκ ἀέκοντες).[113] We may remember that in book 9 Achilles had raised doubts about the reasons for assembling the Achaean *laos*. In Nestor's story, by contrast, the action taken by Athena is beyond doubt. As will be the case in the idealised world of Achilles' shield, a god replaces the human leader, whose motivations, as I have argued in chapter 1, are always problematic.[114]

At the turning-point of the *Iliad*, with Agamemnon and the other leaders wounded, Nestor's idealised vision of social action among the *laos* is held up against Achilles' own highly problematic one. As early as book 1 Achilles had suggested that co-operation between single agent and group can break down.[115] Of course, his insult to Agamemnon works on the

---

[106] See ch. 1, n. 123.
[107] *h.* 11.4.
[108] *Il.* 18.516–19.
[109] *Il.* 2.163, 179, 279f., 450f.
[110] *Il.* 11.720f.
[111] *Il.* 11.758f.
[112] *Il.* 11.717; cf. Ulf (1990) 157–64, who compares *Il.* 4.27f.; for criticism of his distinction between 'public' and 'private' see above n. 88.
[113] *Il.* 11.716.
[114] See above ch. 1, 'An incurable imbalance'; for discussion of the shield see pp. 81f.
[115] *Il.* 1.226.

assumption that the king ought to join, just as Nestor does in Pylos. But whether Achilles' situation is comparable may be less clear. Nestor would like us to believe so. The direct analogy is drawn shortly after, when Nestor recalls 'gathering the people' (λαὸν ἀγείρειν) with Odysseus.[116] These verses come as a reminder for Patroclus and his absent friend that they too are operating within the established framework of the *laos*. However, Nestor's story is pertinent only if we accept that the gatherings of the Pylians and the Achaeans are sufficiently similar. There is good reason not to.

Athena directly intervenes in Pylos, framing both the beginning and the end of group action. Nestor can only offer a beginning, and one that is marked by human messengers.[117] Even though the problematic Agamemnon does not feature at this point,[118] we may still wonder what legitimises the embassy described by Nestor and what action, precisely, it calls for. Father Peleus, unlike his counterpart, father Neleus, does not raise any objections. In book 1, Achilles had pointed out that no raid on his land, nor any other such problem, had stirred him into loyal action.[119] In Nestor's narrative there is no shortage of motives;[120] and Neleus, who still thinks them insufficient, is soon sidelined. Peleus, by contrast, insists that any occasion is good enough for his son. His motto is 'always to be best' (αἰὲν ἀριστεύειν).[121] Why Nestor would want to recall these words under the given circumstances is not, perhaps, too difficult to see. Having diagnosed the problem of the *laos* as one of motivation, he offers two ways of going about it. In Pylos the reasons for taking action are unproblematic and sanctioned by divine intervention, whereas for Achilles the problem of motivation is altogether abolished: he must be the best in all circumstances.

---

[116] *Il.* 11.769f.
[117] Note that this is not a matter of mythical 'fact', but of narrative choice; cf. *Il.* 4.27f.
[118] He may have in the *Cypria*: Proclus *Chrestomathia* p. 103 (Allen).
[119] *Il.* 1.154–7.
[120] *Il.* 11.701–4.
[121] *Il.* 11.783f.

Questions still remain. When does communal purpose begin? Is individual motivation always in harmony with collective interests when the *laoi* go to war? Neleus' reaction suggests that even in Pylos there is no guarantee for this. Further: when and why does the joint venture end? 'Always to be the best' gives an answer for Achilles which is too unspecific to solve his problem. Finally: can participation be enforced? In answer to this last, most sensitive question Gerenian Nestor, the substitute 'shepherd of the people' and chief ideologist of life among the *laoi*, raises his voice. Those who join and stay until the end are promised godlike fame.[122] But those who do not:

>   ... αὐτὰρ Ἀχιλλεὺς
> οἶος τῆς ἀρετῆς ἀπονήσεται· ἦ τέ μιν οἴω
> πολλὰ μετακλαύσεσθαι, ἐπεί κ' ἀπὸ λαὸς ὄληται.[123]
>
> ... but Achilles
> will enjoy his own valour in loneliness; indeed, I think
> he will weep much, too late, once the people have perished.

We have reached the climax of Nestor's story. Homeric speakers resort to formulaic language to make themselves understood at crucial points in the narrative.[124] The present crisis is such a point, and accordingly Nestor invokes one of the most common formulaic systems of early Greek hexameter: 'he destroyed the people'. Such phrases are not 'weak'. They do not, as so many modern scholars have thought with Aristarchus, 'repeat' what is perhaps expressed more appropriately elsewhere. On the contrary: as we have seen in ch. 1, Nestor's words resound through the echo-chambers of a whole poetic culture.[125] Speaking the genre, they come as an unmistakable warning: Achilles, the 'man equal to the *laoi*'[126] will pay for making his point.

Nestor's prophecy, as well as evoking an extensive for-

---

[122] *Il.* 11.761.
[123] *Il.* 11.762–4.
[124] For discussion see above ch. 1, 'The failed ideal'.
[125] See ch. 1, 'The failed ideal'; for the metaphor of echoing see Foley (1991) 7, Steiner (1996), from whom the phrasing is borrowed.
[126] See above p. 64.

mulaic system, also adapts traditional language to what is in many ways a unique situation. First, we may note that Nestor's warning is the only one of its kind. Homer's people are usually said to be perishing or, more often, to have perished already. Achilles alone is warned in advance. What is more, the (untranslatable) Greek particle *ke*, together with the subjunctive, marks Nestor's prophecy as only potential, indicating that while the people 'might be destroyed' it has not yet been decided beyond doubt that this will in fact happen. Finally, the Greek words λαός and ὄλλυμι which I have here translated 'the people' and '(they) have perished' have swapped places in the hexameter line. Such variations may seem minimal, but they do indicate tensions between the language of the genre and the exigencies of the narrative moment.

When Agamemnon and Hector are said to 'have destroyed the people' (ὤλεσε λαόν), they confront the issue themselves, in spectacular speeches in which they solemnly pronounce the most common version of the phrase: 'he/I destroyed the people'.[127] With Achilles, as ever, things are more complicated. Achilles does not accuse himself; nor does Nestor, who speaks out against him, use one of the standard forms of the phrase ὤλεσε λαόν. Above all, we may note a certain change of focus. Achilles, too, may be on the point of becoming a Hesiodic 'bad man'; but the emphasis has shifted from the plight of the people to the effect Achilles has on himself 'once (after) the people have perished'.[128] In this, as in so many other respects, Nestor turns out to be a sensitive reader. No one stands up towards the end of the *Iliad* declaring that Achilles 'trusted in his own strength and destroyed the people' (ἧφι βίηφι πιθήσας ὤλεσε λαόν).[129] His fate and that of the people will not be played out at the level of social task and social sanction. Rather, they will converge in shared grief.

Achilles' pain is developed from book 16 onwards. In the meantime the situation of the Achaean people continues to be

---

[127] *Il.* 2.115, 9.22, 22.104, 107.
[128] Note that the Greek for 'alone' at the beginning of the line is echoed by the Greek for 'I believe' at the end (οἶος–οἴω).
[129] *Il.* 22.107; for discussion see pp. 92–4.

of considerable concern. Machaon in book 11 pointed to the fact that a stronger 'shepherd' was now needed. Poseidon's intervention in books 13ff. suggests that help is indeed available. The god offers three ways of replacing Achilles.[130] First he declares the two Ajaxes substitute leaders. Then, in a more ambitious speech, he redefines the relationship between leader and group in a manner similar to Nestor's in book 2. Finally, Poseidon takes over himself. Here is the first of his measures:

> Αἴαντε, σφὼ μέν τε σαώσετε λαὸν Ἀχαιῶν.[131]
>
> Ajaxes, you two must save the people of the Achaeans.

Note the allusion to the theme formulated by Achilles in book 9 and echoed by the narrative voice in 10.[132] There is no escaping Achilles' words. The greater Ajax is the best warrior after Achilles and will later be the last resort for the Achaeans,[133] but even he is not able to save the people. In his next speech Poseidon takes up what Agamemnon and Nestor suggested in book 2. If there is no leader who can help, why not mobilise the collective's own resources? Poseidon analyses the problem thus:

> νῦν δὲ ἑκὰς πόλιος κοίλῃς ἐπὶ νηυσὶ μάχονται [the Trojans]
> ἡγεμόνος κακότητι μεθημοσύνῃσί τε λαῶν.[134]
>
> but now far from the city they fight by the hollow vessels
> through the badness of our leader and the slackness of the people.

Since Poseidon's last speech little has changed. The people are still dying, and this is caused, in his view, by the problem of finding a suitable leader (ἡγεμών). So far everything is as expected, but the second half of Poseidon's explanation is decidedly more enterprising. The *laoi* are not often scolded in

---

[130] In the following I concentrate on Poseidon's suggestions only in so far as they concern the *laoi*. For other aspects of his intervention in *Il.* 13 and 14 see Frazer (1985); for Poseidon's Iliadic role in general see Erbse (1986). Cf. also Schachermeyr (1950) and Simon (1985).
[131] *Il.* 13.47.
[132] *Il.* 9.424, 681; cf. 10.14f.
[133] *Il.* 2.768f., 15.674ff.
[134] *Il.* 13.107f.; what this speech tells us about Agamemnon's character is discussed in Taplin (1990) 74f.

early Greek hexameter poetry for their lack of initiative.[135] Nestor suggests in book 2 that Agamemnon should find out those among them who are 'bad' (κακοί), but no one ever comes back to this.[136] Poseidon takes things even further when he insinuates that the people are responsible for their own catastrophe – an awkward suggestion, which Poseidon's rhetoric does not make any more attractive. Would the *laoi* really prefer to die out of sheer slackness? Homer's people cannot be blamed for their own misfortunes. The attempt to do so merely exposes the lack of a real solution.

For the time being some progress is made, and by the end of book 13 it is Hector's people who are under threat.[137] Relief on one side results in problems for the other.[138] Although it is not said that the Achaean people are now safe, we seem to be getting closer to a solution. The solution, however, is abortive. No human being can replace Achilles; and the Achaeans do not fare better because the people have put an end to their 'slackness' either. It is true that with Poseidon we have finally been given a strong enough leader. But for all its advantages, there is an obvious problem with his third attempt at finding a substitute for Achilles. As a god Poseidon may be sufficiently strong to help, but he can only act successfully for a limited amount of time.

None of the major figures in the *Iliad* – Agamemnon and Achilles among them – can in fact provide the institutional continuity that would rescue the people permanently.[139] Poseidon makes no exception. He may not be weak in comparison with human agents, but he is too weak to prevent the progress of world teleology, which, at this stage, implies the destruction of Homer's people. To destroy the people, the *Iliad* assures us in book 13, is not itself the plan of Zeus, at least, not 'entirely' (οὐ πάμπαν).[140] But it is an integral part of that

---

[135] See above ch. 1, 'Social structures'.
[136] *Il.* 2.365; compare also what Agamemnon says in *Il.* 2.110ff. Both passages are discussed above on pp. 55ff.
[137] *Il.* 13.674–8.
[138] Cf. *Il.* 9.417–26, 680–7.
[139] Non-Homeric texts concentrate precisely on this – see ch. 3, pp. 163ff.
[140] *Il.* 13.345–50.

plan in so far as it guarantees Achilles' rehabilitation (the text has κῦδος, 'status').[141] Once again Achilles is seen to profit from the disaster which so damaged Agamemnon. He gains in stature (κῦδος) at the expense of everyone else around him.

The decisive stage of Achilles' glorification is reached when Poseidon leaves the people in book 15.[142] Apollo comes down to the battlefield to lead the Trojan *laoi*, *aegis* in hand.[143] Divine substitution on the Achaean side is answered by divine substitution on that of their enemy.[144] Battle is then held in equilibrium with a well-known verse:

> τόφρα μάλ' ἀμφοτέρων βέλε' ἥπτετο, πῖπτε δὲ λαός.[145]
>
> so long thrown weapons of both took hold and the people fell.

At four points in the *Iliad* a decisive turn of the narrative is marked by this line. We have seen two such passages, the Achaean defeat in book 8 and Agamemnon's abortive counter-attack in 11.[146] Patroclus' charge in book 16 will complete the sequence.[147] The verse in question combines the need for narrative action – the story has to go somewhere – with the people's need for protection – something has to be done. Something is done, in our case, by Apollo, and the ensuing slaughter is described in the telling image of the abandoned flock.[148]

Shortly thereafter Achilles' exaltation reaches its climax. In a prayer to Zeus he sums up the events of the preceding books. I have already quoted this verse, which is identical with that spoken by Chryses in his prayer to Apollo:

> τιμήσας μὲν ἐμέ, μέγα δ' ἴψαο λαὸν Ἀχαιῶν.[149]
>
> you did me honour and smote strongly the people of the Achaeans.

---

[141] *Il.* 13.345–50.
[142] *Il.* 15.218.
[143] *Il.* 15.311.
[144] Cf. also *Il.* 15.695.
[145] *Il.* 15.319.
[146] *Il.* 8.67, 11.85.
[147] *Il.* 16.778.
[148] *Il.* 15.323–6; for the world of pastoral as a dominant model of social life among Homer's people see above ch. 1, '"Shepherd of the people"'; for σημάντορες ('commanders') and *laoi* see *Il.* 4.430f.
[149] *Il.* 16.237; cf. 1.412, 505–10; the passage is also discussed in Nagy (1979) 82f.

The line shocked ancient and modern readers alike, who often reacted by marking it as spurious.[150] I see no reason to suppress it here – any more than there would be reason to suppress one or both of Agamemnon's speeches. Achilles' summary is crucial for our understanding of the *Iliad*. He finally agrees with Agamemnon's analysis in *Il.* 9.118. His 'honour' (τιμή), like that of Chryses in book 1, is restored through the damage that has been done to the people. For the priest this was the end of the story. For Achilles it opens a new chapter, as prophesied by Nestor and demanded by the logic of negative reciprocity: after 'the people have perished' the tears come.[151]

At this point our narrative takes another decisive turn. So far Achilles was seen as the exact counterpart of Agamemnon, the 'shepherd of the people', who had to learn that his epic persona depended to a large extent on the well-being of the *laoi*. Achilles, on the contrary, fed on their demise until in book 16 his honour – and by implication his fame – is fully asserted at their expense: 'as good as many people is the man ...'.[152] The change of fortunes comes abruptly. Achilles does not lose the status he has acquired throughout the poem. Negative reciprocity does not for him mean that he is socially degraded for failing to save a group whose 'shepherd' he has never been.[153] Rather, he is made to join them in their suffering. Through his 'companion' (ἑταῖρος), Achilles changes sides within the few lines of his prayer. The same Zeus who granted that the people of the Achaeans should suffer damage is now asked to protect his friend(s).[154] But this distinction cannot be upheld.

In response to the changed situation neither Achilles nor Zeus changes his behaviour in any substantial way. Achilles remains withdrawn. Zeus continues to destroy his social envi-

---

[150] It is athetised by Aristophanes/Aristarchus and omitted by Zenodotus (schol. *ad loc.*); Janko (1992) *ad loc.* summarises and refutes modern objections.
[151] Cf. *Il.* 11.764; for the principle of 'negative reciprocity' see above ch. 1, 'Negative reciprocity'.
[152] *Il.* 9.116f.
[153] See above p. 65 with n. 83.
[154] *Il.* 16.237–41 and 246–50.

ronment. Only the frame of reference has changed, from *laoi* to companion(s), and this shift brings about a radical turn in Achilles' fortunes.[155] From now on the unwilling leader finds himself on the side of the abandoned group. As a friend of his 'companion' (ἑταῖρος), he has to go through all the agony he has caused so far. Nestor was right. After destroying the people, Achilles suffers in turn. But how precisely this comes about cannot be understood unless we go back to the beginning of the epic one more time.

Ajax, in his short speech in book 9, addresses Achilles as a 'companion' (ἑταῖρος) in a last attempt to elicit the positive response the Achaeans are longing for.[156] Achilles' reaction to Ajax's speech is the most friendly of all, and that can hardly be a coincidence.[157] Achilles is the paradigmatic 'comrade' (ἑταῖρος) among the comrades of early Greek hexameter poetry. His most important partner is Patroclus. This has often been discussed in other contexts,[158] and for the purposes of the present argument it is enough to summarise some of the more important points.

Patroclus stays with Achilles at the low point of his career in book 1.[159] From then on the two form an alternative circle to the assembly, a circle which gives the impression of being self-contained precisely because Patroclus replaces Achilles' other social bonds. He acts out the wishes of his more powerful friend in books 1 and 9,[160] and he provides the link between Achilles and the people of the Achaeans later in book 11.[161] Achilles relies on his friend in order to isolate himself. But as he delegates to Patroclus his links with the *laoi*, he creates precisely the triangular situation in which the people's problems become his own.[162] In order to understand this

---

[155] For the complementary nature of epic 'companions' and *laoi* in general see ch. 2, '*Laoi* in the *Odyssey*', pp. 126–37.
[156] *Il.* 9.630.
[157] *Il.* 9.644f.
[158] E.g. Nagy (1979) ch. 6, Sinos (1980), Barrett (1981), Hooker (1989) 34.
[159] *Il.* 1.345–7.
[160] *Il.* 1.345–7, 9.190f., 201–8, 211–20, 620–2, 658–61.
[161] *Il.* 11.597–604, cf. 11.504–6.
[162] For this and the following see Nagy (1979) ch. 5.

process we must remember that Achilles' dependence on Patroclus is as directly emotional as is that of the people on their shepherd.[163] For Achilles as a friend of his 'companion' (ἑταῖρος), the incurable imbalance discussed in chapter 1 has been reversed.[164] He becomes as involved in the war and its toll on human life as the people (λαοί) have been all along. Patroclus' death provides the common denominator. First the people experience grief (ἄχος):

δούπησεν δὲ πεσών [Patroclus], μέγα δ' ἤκαχε λαὸν Ἀχαιῶν.[165]

he fell, thunderously, and greatly aggrieved the people of the Achaeans.

Then, Achilles does:

Ὣς φάτο, τὸν δ' [Achilles] ἄχεος νεφέλη ἐκάλυψε μέλαινα.[166]

He spoke, and the black cloud of grief closed on Achilles.

Achilles' special need for Patroclus is equal to the longing he (Patroclus) inspires in the people. And in so far as Patroclus has gone out to replace Achilles, it is equal to their special need for him. Achilles starts the Iliadic narrative as the most insistent protector of the people. It is he who calls the assembly in reaction to the plague,[167] and at this point he can even step into the protected metrical space of 'the people of the Achaeans' (λαὸν Ἀχαιῶν).[168] Later, in his quarrel with Agamemnon, Achilles is again portrayed as defending the interests of the people,[169] and as we have seen already he follows the narrator in calling the plague 'bad' (κακή), because it destroys them.[170]

As the narrative unfolds, Achilles' initial sympathy fades. The change of tone is marked by a passage just after the *Catalogue of ships* where the people of Achilles are described as

---

[163] Cf. *Il.* 2.708–10 and 19.315–21; for detailed discussion see ch. 2, '*Laoi* in the *Odyssey*', pp. 130f.
[164] See above ch. 1, 'An incurable imbalance'.
[165] *Il.* 16.822, cf. 22.52–5 with the scholion on *Il.* 22.54f.
[166] *Il.* 18.22.
[167] *Il.* 1.53f.
[168] The only other character to do so is Athena; cf. *Il.* 11.758.
[169] *Il.* 1.126; cf. 2.226.
[170] *Il.* 1.382f.; see above p. 49.

longing for their absent leader.[171] As early as book 2 Achilles' wrath against the 'shepherd of the people' Agamemnon overrules his former concerns. By the time we arrive in book 9 he can abuse the *laoi* in a more brutal way than his rival ever does, and although in book 11 there may be a hint of revived sympathy, it is only Patroclus who gets to hear Nestor's didactic parable. This first act of substitution is soon followed by a second one when Nestor asks Patroclus rather than Achilles to lead the people into battle.[172] Nestor's request is later repeated by Patroclus himself.[173]

When we arrive at book 16 the roles of a 'companion' (ἑταῖρος) and a 'shepherd of the people' (*ποιμὴν λαῶν) are on the point of being merged in the figure of Patroclus. Achilles himself is programmatically introduced as a 'shepherd of the people' (*ποιμὴν λαῶν) at the beginning of the episode,[174] and later in the same book he gathers the *laos* as a traditional 'shepherd' would.[175] From this it is clear that Achilles is about to take over from Agamemnon. But while it is Achilles who gathers the people, Patroclus is asked to put on his (Achilles') armour. As a symptom of the ensuing confusion I note that the same group that is called *laoi* in *Il.* 16.129 is called 'companions' (ἑταῖροι) only some forty lines later.[176] Achilles himself tries to gain clarity when he thanks Zeus for destroying the 'people of the Achaeans' (λαὸς Ἀχαιῶν)[177] and then asks for the safe return of his 'companion' (ἑταῖρος).[178] We can now see why this distinction is not easily upheld. Patroclus goes as a 'companion' (ἑταῖρος) and a leader of the people at the same time. Already in book 11 and more so in book 16 he mediates between the two worlds that Achilles

---

[171] *Il.* 2.771–9.
[172] *Il.* 11.796.
[173] *Il.* 16.38; see also Thetis' account in *Il.* 18.452.
[174] *Il.* 16.2.
[175] *Il.* 16.129.
[176] *Il.* 16.170; cf. also 16.248.
[177] *Il.* 16.237.
[178] *Il.* 16.240; cf. also 16.248. It is significant that Achilles ends on the word 'companions'.

plays off against one another. In the end he brings suffering to both.[179]

I have already suggested that the events of *Iliad* 16ff. can be read as a variation on the traditional structure of negative reciprocity which overshadows Achilles' Iliadic existence as a whole and which he so successfully turns against Agamemnon.[180] First the group suffers, then the leader. The story of Achilles and the people could have stopped here, as it does in the case of Agamemnon. Both are destroyed, and no traditional epic pattern reaches beyond this bleak state of unmitigated suffering. But, through the figure of Patroclus, who causes pain to everyone around him, the 'man' and the people are gradually reunited.[181]

A first implicit step in this direction is taken in book 18. Achilles' shield prominently features *laoi* in action. The relevant scenes are the two cities in peace and war. First – and tellingly so – we get a picture of Homer's people at peace.[182] On the occasion of a court case, a quarrel arises which is highly relevant to the Iliadic narrative, but which does not there involve the people. In the *Iliad* Achilles will be alone with Priam. On the shield Homer's people take a prominent part, providing a quasi-institutional frame for the debate.[183] Everything about this passage suggests a lively but controlled scene of social interaction. The *laoi* split into factions, but heralds (κήρυκες) prevent them from disintegrating. What had gone so wrong so often in the Iliadic world is reassuringly successful on the shield. Tensions between single agents are contained in the interest of the common good.

In the following vignette we see, once more, two sets of *laoi*,

---

[179] The second half of *Il.* 16.822 comes as an ironic echo of Achilles' prayer in *Il.* 16.237; cf. also 16.777–80, where Patroclus breaks the deadlock.
[180] On negative reciprocity see above ch. 1, 'Negative reciprocity'.
[181] It has often been argued that Achilles is re-integrated into his social environment towards the end of the poem; see e.g. Whitman (1958) 215 and 263, Segal (1971) 51–4, Dunkle (1981). Here I am concerned with this development only in so far as it affects Homer's people.
[182] *Il.* 18.497.
[183] *Il.* 18.502f.

this time at war. Again the scene chosen is highly relevant to the *Iliad*,[184] and once again the crucial theme of interaction between group and single agent appears in a harmonised form. Ares and Athena function as ideal substitutes,[185] perpetuating Apollo's and Poseidon's temporary role in the narrative. They, too, are beyond the complicated and potentially disruptive negotiations between the people and their shepherds; only that this time there is no end to their help. As human leaders of *laoi* we see the harmless 'watchmen' (σκοποί) who do not fight and seem to have little to win or lose.[186]

After he has received his armour, Achilles summons the assembly.[187] Allusions to the people are rare at this stage (Achilles, tellingly, calls an assembly of 'heroes' (ἥρωες)), but the references to the people we do get should be noted. Finally handing over the remains of his own role as a leader of the people, Agamemnon instructs Achilles on the duties attached to it.[188] The language in which he does so is as traditional as the task.[189] With different emphasis, Odysseus, too, in his two speeches, asks Achilles to act as his newly acquired role demands.[190] As so often, he recommends the exact opposite of Agamemnon: dissolving instead of stirring. Language and ideas are again traditional. To dissolve the people at the right moment is as important as stirring them into battle. The leader who knows that, Odysseus goes on to point out in his second speech, can expect to be obeyed by the group.[191] With characteristic rhetorical skill, Odysseus confirms the transition of power which has taken place. There will now be no other 'exhortation' (ὀτρυντύς) than that of Achilles. The man who has so long relied on the destruction of the people must now act on their behalf.

---

[184] Becker (1995) 114; for the relevance of the shield see also Reinhardt (1961) 401–11, Schadewaldt (1965b) 352–74, Andersen (1976), Taplin (1980), Vilatte (1988), Lynn-George (1988) 183–5.
[185] *Il.* 18.516–19.
[186] *Il.* 18.523f.
[187] *Il.* 19.34, 40f.
[188] *Il.* 19.139.
[189] For further examples and discussion see ch. 1, 'Social structures'.
[190] *Il.* 19.171f., 233f.
[191] *Il.* 19.233f.

Agamemnon and Odysseus, each in his own way, pronounce Achilles the new leader of the people. As in the case of the shield, Achilles himself does not take much notice. In the end he does go out as a 'shepherd of the people',[192] but a tense moment in book 22 reminds us that his priorities are still elsewhere.[193] The coincidence of grief is not complete at this point. Achilles acts above all out of anger and longing for revenge. These are impulses a single agent can experience and act upon in early Greek epic; but they do not motivate the *laoi*.[194] Only in the feelings of pain and grief can their emotions coincide with those of their new leader; therefore it is only after Achilles has had his revenge that he and the people are properly reconciled. Meanwhile, we witness the catastrophe of Hector and with it the dramatic high point of life among Homer's people.

Hector

Achilles must be at the centre of any study of the *Iliad*, and ours is no exception. He embodies the crucial narrative experiment in which the value of a single man is weighed against that of Homer's people. While others also fail to co-operate, only Achilles, the non-shepherd, turns the destruction of the group into a means of asserting his social position and epic fame. Agamemnon and Hector dramatise the fundamental narrative decision this implies. Agamemnon hopes to destroy the city but destroys his own *laos*. Hector makes a similar mistake on the other side. He fears that Troy might fall and does everything to prevent it – until in the end the city stands and the people are lost. Of course the city will fall soon after. But with his death Hector draws the line between what is Iliadic and what is not.

Why the obligation to save one's city should interfere with that of saving the people is not, perhaps, intuitively clear to a

---

[192] *Il.* 19.386, for the last time in the poem.
[193] *Il.* 22.205–7.
[194] Homeric *laoi* are never said to be 'angry', 'vengeful', etc. The point deserves closer study than can be undertaken here.

modern audience. Indeed, earlier audiences, too, may have been surprised to find that the *Iliad* does not allow for a straightforward alliance between the two. I have already looked at the ideal picture drawn in *Odyssey* 8.[195] Dying for the city in this passage also means to die for the people. Although the city comes first, hierarchies of obligation do not create any serious problem there. The scenario of a man who gives his life for the city and (therefore also) for his people could have summed up Hector's epic fame in a song about the fall of Troy, as he himself implies in book 6 of the *Iliad*:

> ἔσσεται ἦμαρ ὅτ' ἄν ποτ' ὀλώλῃ Ἴλιος ἰρὴ
> καὶ Πρίαμος καὶ λαὸς ἐϋμμελίω Πριάμοιο.[196]

> there will come a day when sacred Ilios shall perish,
> and Priam, and the people of Priam of the strong ash spear.

In these lines, the needs of the city are made to include those of the people. Priam stands for them both. The city, Priam in the city, and Priam's people with him may give us a reassuringly simple scenario. However, the *Iliad* insists that things are not so straightforward. As we have seen already when studying Agamemnon, the text presents as problematic the relationship between Troy and Homer's people. I have suggested that this is at least partly due to a thematic shift away from the sack of Troy, a shift which is closely associated with the central Iliadic character, Achilles. When Agamemnon tries to write Homer's people out of the story and endorses an abortive narrative of the capture of Troy, Achilles reminds him of what text he is in. Hector suffers from a similar self-deception, but because he is on the other side the issue becomes rather more complicated.

Hector's responsibilities to his city are documented in numerous passages, from the puns on his own name[197] to the more explicit pun on that of his son.[198] Hector is the cornerstone of Troy's defence.[199] He is the 'holder'. Yet, in order to

---

[195] *Od.* 8.523–5; see above p. 38.   [196] *Il.* 6.448f.; cf. 4.47, 164f.
[197] Taplin (1992) 116.   [198] *Il.* 6.402f.
[199] E.g. Redfield (1975) *passim*, esp. 123, Ulf (1990) 101.

fulfil this role, he needs others. Sarpedon, who fights far from home but close to his people, reminds us of this important point.[200] He does so specifically by confronting the 'sole' defender of Troy[201] with the fact that *laoi* are involved in the task.[202] Like Nestor on the other side, Sarpedon acts as an expert advisor. He is a 'bulwark of the city' of Troy (ἕρμα πόληος) because many *laoi* follow him.[203]

Hector's need for the people brings with it a set of responsibilities which are not automatically included in those he has towards his family and city. As a result, tension develops between Hector 'the holder' and Hector the shepherd. Much of his story in the *Iliad* focuses on this problem. It is already in evidence at the beginning of the text. When Iris instructs Hector to lead out the Trojans in the guise of Priam's son Polites, she calls them *polietai*, 'citizens'.[204] However, when they rush out of the doors to face the countless *laoi* of the enemy,[205] they also become *laoi*.[206]

Hector's entry in the *Catalogue of the Trojans* continues this trend. It reads like an abbreviated version of Agamemnon's entry in the *Catalogue of ships*:

> Τρωσὶ μὲν ἡγεμόνευε μέγας κορυθαίολος Ἕκτωρ
> Πριαμίδης· ἅμα τῷ γε πολὺ πλεῖστοι καὶ ἄριστοι
> λαοὶ θωρήσσοντο μεμαότες ἐγχείῃσι.[207]

> Tall Hector of the shining helm was leader of the Trojans,
> Priam's son; and with him by far the most numerous and best
> people were armed and eager to fight with the spear's edge.

Hector's relationship with the people is brought to our attention at the expense of his relationship with the city. As in the case of Agamemnon, this seems quite deliberate. No other

---

[200] *Il.* 5.472–4; cf. Ulf (1990) 101.
[201] Cf. 'alone' (οἶος) in *Il.* 6.403 and 'alone' (οἶος) in *Il.* 5.474.
[202] The roles of 'kinsmen' (γαμβροί) and 'people' (λαοί) are contrasted to illustrate this point.
[203] *Il.* 16.549–51; for Sarpedon's concern with the people see also his last words in *Il.* 16.501.
[204] *Il.* 2.791, 806.
[205] *Il.* 2.799.
[206] *Il.* 2.809.
[207] *Il.* 2.816–18; cf. also 2.809.

Trojan ally, not even Sarpedon, is seen leading *laoi* in this context. Hector may be 'the holder', but from now on he is also the 'shepherd of the people' *par excellence* on the Trojan side.[208]

Hector guarantees the welfare of the Trojan *laoi*. He stirs, defends, attacks. His positive role is set against his brother's, who unites the people on both sides in a communal curse.[209] Hector's speech in book 6 can be read as a comment on this extraordinary speech act.[210] He knows what is right and wrong for the people and acts accordingly. At times of crisis he is able to formulate principles of behaviour in traditional language. I have already drawn attention to the corresponding lines *Il.* 3.322 and 6.327.[211] Implied in both passages is the obligation of a leader of the people not to harm his group and, if necessary, to die in their defence. This could have been Hector's fate, as it was that of the ideal husband and defender of the city in the *Odyssey*.[212] In fact, Hector's vision of things is even more extreme: the leader must die even after his people have perished. Nothing like this is ever proposed on the Achaean side.

Paris is set up as a negative model of the man who sits in his city and lets the people die around it. More than for Paris, however, this motif becomes crucial for Hector himself. It is already implied in book 5 when Ares scolds the sons of Priam.[213] His attack can be read as a precursor of Hector's criticism of Paris. Interestingly, though, it is not directed against Paris alone. Ares suggests a deeper-running tension between Priam's sons and the people; as if a Priamid is always suspected of putting the concerns of the people second to those of the city. Ares urges that the *laos* should not be allowed to die as long as the city is safe. Not long afterwards,

---

[208] *Il.* 10.406, 14.423, 15.262, 20.110, 22.277.
[209] *Il.* 3.318–22; cf. 24.27f.
[210] *Il.* 6.325–9.
[211] See above ch. 1, 'Negative reciprocity'.
[212] See above p. 84.
[213] *Il.* 5.464–6; cf. Ulf (1990) 101.

Sarpedon openly turns against Hector, thus taking us to the heart of his problem:

ἔνθ' αὖ Σαρπηδὼν μάλα νείκεσεν Ἕκτορα δῖον·
'"Ἕκτορ, πῇ δή τοι μένος οἴχεται ὃ πρὶν ἔχεσκες;
φῆς που ἄτερ λαῶν πόλιν ἑξέμεν ἠδ' ἐπικούρων
οἶος, σὺν γαμβροῖσι κασιγνήτοισί τε σοῖσι."[214]

Then Sarpedon spoke in abuse to brilliant Hector:
'Where now, Hector, has gone that strength that was yours?
  You said once
that without people and without allies you could hold this city
alone, with only your brothers and brothers-in-law.'

As a Priamid, as 'the holder' of Troy and father of Astyanax, Hector is a man of the city. But Hector's Troy relies on the welfare of the people. So, even if only in order to save his city, Hector must think of the *laoi* first. Towards the end of his speech in book 5 Sarpedon comes back to this point.[215] Someone who defends the people, according to Sarpedon, also defends his women and city. When they are ranked like this there is no conflict between the different tasks. It is when we change the order of things that the problems begin.

Paradoxically, then, the well-being of the city in the *Iliad* cannot be achieved by putting the city first. We can now rephrase in terms of narrative priorities what Sarpedon sees in terms of social responsibility. Both the city and the people are important in the *Iliad*, and in the long run both perish. The matter is not one of absolute choice. However, it is not therefore of any lesser importance, for the fact that the *Iliad* concentrates on the people is reflected in its decision not to sing about the fall of Troy at all.[216] We can now see why for Hector, the 'holder', this must become a problem.

When the prince enters Troy, his difficulties are again obvious. I start with Helenus' speech in book 6. Once again both the people and the city play their part:

---

[214] *Il.* 5.471–4.
[215] *Il.* 5.485–9.
[216] For the related phenomenon of 'Homeric misdirection' see Morrison (1992).

Αἰνεία τε καὶ Ἕκτορ, ἐπεὶ πόνος ὔμμι μάλιστα
Τρώων καὶ Λυκίων ἐγκέκλιται ...
...
στῆτ' αὐτοῦ, καὶ λαὸν ἐρυκάκετε πρὸ πυλάων   80
πάντῃ ἐποιχόμενοι, πρὶν αὖτ' ἐν χερσὶ γυναικῶν
φεύγοντας πεσέειν ...[217]

Hector and Aeneas, on you beyond others is leaning
the battle-work of Trojans and Lycians ...
...
stand your ground here; hold the people fast by the gates,
visiting them everywhere, before they fall into the women's
arms in flight ...

Helenus warns that the Trojans might fall 'into the women's arms' unless the *laos* is rallied first. Note the order of things: 'first' (πρίν) come the people. Having looked after them Hector is allowed to enter his city.[218]

Everything is done to avoid the impression that Hector leaves the battlefield at the expense of the *laos*. He goes on request, and Helenus who asks him to go is perhaps the most authoritative speaker available.[219] At a surface level Helenus smooths out any possible tensions between Hector's role as leader of the people and the needs of the city. However, Hector's adventures later in the book bring to the fore the old conflict with renewed urgency.

Having restored the people outside the city walls, Hector enters Troy. On arrival he meets his mother, then Helen and Andromache. 'Falling into the arms of women': everyone he encounters wants to keep Hector from going away again. Hector himself finds this unacceptable. Paris who has already fallen into the arms of Helen is hardly a model.[220] But when Andromache suggests that Hector, too, should leave the fighting to the people, this comes as a more serious variation on the theme:

ἀλλ' ἄγε νῦν ἐλέαιρε καὶ αὐτοῦ μίμν' ἐπὶ πύργῳ,
μὴ παῖδ' ὀρφανικὸν θήῃς χήρην τε γυναῖκα·

---

[217] *Il.* 6.77f. and 80–2.
[218] *Il.* 6.86.
[219] *Il.* 6.76 with Aristarchus' variant reading as reported in the scholia *ad loc.*
[220] *Il.* 6.325–9; for discussion see above pp. 26, 38.

λαὸν δὲ στῆσον παρ' ἐρινεόν, ἔνθα μάλιστα
ἀμβατός ἐστι πόλις καὶ ἐπίδρομον ἔπλετο τεῖχος.[221]

> Please take pity on me then, stay here on the rampart,
> that you may not leave your child an orphan, your wife a widow,
> but draw the people up by the fig tree, there where the city
> is openest to attack, and where the wall may be mounted.

As a representative of city life Andromache is concerned about Hector's child and herself, his wife. They are protected by the city and its walls which, Andromache suggests, should be defended by the people. We need not decide how precisely this would have worked 'in practice'.[222] Let us rather note the following two points. First, Andromache's scenario is less questionable than what Paris is already doing, for it implies that Hector does not completely leave the fighting – and dying – to the *laos*, but rather that he leads them from afar. Second, it is equally questionable in terms of social and narrative priorities for, very much like Paris, Andromache is prepared to put the city first. This, I have argued, runs counter to what the *Iliad* presents as its narrative project. As Hector himself points out to her in the same context, the city will eventually perish, and with it Priam and his people.[223] But that lies in the future, is literally 'a different story'.[224] And so Hector resumes battle.

As the Trojans get the upper hand in the following books Hector's dilemma fades, but it never disappears. In book 8, for example, he shows himself concerned that the city might be conquered in the absence of the people:

μὴ λόχος εἰσέλθῃσι πόλιν λαῶν ἀπεόντων.[225]

> lest a sudden attack get into the town when the people have left it.

---

[221] *Il.* 6.431–4; contrast *Il.* 6.80; the lines *Il.* 6.433–9 are athetised by the Alexandrians on the ground that Andromache 'takes charge against Hector' (ἀντιστρατηγεῖ ... τῷ Ἕκτορι) – see schol. *Il.* 6.433–9, followed by Lohmann (1988) 35; schol. *Il.* 6.433 defeats any such attempts.
[222] Do the people stand inside or outside the city walls? 'By the fig tree' (παρ' ἐρινεόν) may suggest the latter, but the question cannot be decided beyond doubt.
[223] *Il.* 6.448f.; cf. 4.47, 165, 24.27f.
[224] Recounted in such epics as the *Sack of Troy* and the *Little Iliad*.
[225] *Il.* 8.522.

Hector continues to worry about Troy. Might it be captured while the *laoi* are not there? What does not come to his mind is the security of the people themselves. The second camp outside Troy will decide the fate of the city not because it is captured in an ambush, but because the people are destroyed. The problem is familiar from Agamemnon's story. Once again we are invited to see it not in terms of an absolute alternative. Both city and people are important, and they are both under threat. Hector does not go wrong in principle, but he fails to see basic social and narrative priorities. The well-being of the *laoi* includes that of the city of the Priamids, but the reverse is not true; not at this stage of the war.[226]

In book 11 Hector takes over from Agamemnon as the most important leader of *laoi* on the battlefield.[227] At this point in the narrative we find a strong emphasis on his role as a 'shepherd of the people'. After all we have seen, this must strike an ominous note. And in fact we get a fresh reminder of possible complications as early as book 12. Reading the bird omen sent by Zeus, Polydamas determines its position relative to that of the people.[228] He does not explicitly present the impending catastrophe as one of the *laoi* and Hector does not dismiss it as such; but the end of the scene is once more indicative of his mistake. Polydamas claims to be speaking 'like a seer who is trusted by the people'.[229] Hector does not obey. His priority is the 'fatherland' (πάτρη).[230]

In the following books Hector's relationship with the people continues to fluctuate. In book 13 his diligence is vindicated against the odds,[231] and not long afterwards Hector appears reunited with the *laos*.[232] Their co-operation is fur-

---

[226] Troy will of course eventually be sacked in an 'ambush' (λόχος); see *Odyssey* 4.277, 8.515, 11.525.
[227] *Il.* 11.186–90; cf. 11.201–5.
[228] *Il.* 12.218f.
[229] *Il.* 12.228f.
[230] *Il.* 12.243.
[231] *Il.* 13.674–6.
[232] *Il.* 13.833f.

ther emphasised in Zeus's speech after the deception[233] and the grandiose image of him pushing Hector and the *laos* along with his hand.[234] Another critical point is reached in book 16,[235] where the short phrase 'and he left the people' (λεῖπε δὲ λαόν) brings back to mind all the anxieties that had been latent since books 5 and 6. Leaving the *laos* in the moment of their distress is something that the epic shepherd should avoid: in this form the phrase occurs nowhere else in early Greek hexameter.[236] Although Hector's relationship with the people is by no means catastrophically bad at this point, we are given another reminder of how complicated it has become.

The books that follow lead up to the second Trojan camp and to the final crisis of leadership in the *Iliad*. In Hector's case, as opposed to Agamemnon's, the events are not presented in terms of open disregard; moreover, contrary to what we see in the case of Achilles, they do not speak of deliberate manipulation. Rather, Hector's conflict between serving the city and serving the people gradually deepens. In book 17 we hear that he 'wears out the people' for the sake of Trojan family life.[237] This comes suspiciously close to what Paris was accused of doing in book 6. And yet, Hector is vindicated by a passage which occurs shortly after.[238] Hector never entirely forgets his people. Even when he is about to destroy them, he pays exceptional attention to their needs. This leader does not just remember that the group has to be dispersed at the end of a fighting day – he also feeds them at public expense.

Hector does not openly turn against the people. Even when his problems reach their climax and solution in *Iliad* 22, he remains sympathetic to their cause. In this important respect, he is the opposite of Agamemnon. Hector tries harder and often does better. And yet, like Agamemnon he struggles with a basic fact of his Iliadic existence. The fall of Troy is Agamemnon's primary concern, but it is not the primary concern of the *Iliad*. And so it is with Hector; only that this time the

---

[233] *Il.* 15.15.　　[234] *Il.* 15.694f.　　[235] *Il.* 16.367–9.
[236] Cf., however, Poseidon in *Il.* 15.218.　　[237] *Il.* 17.220–6.　　[238] *Il.* 18.300–2.

point is made with unmistakable, brutal, closing force. When the Trojan people have perished, Hector, too, must die. The end of their story is also the end of his.

We begin with Priam's speech before the duel between Hector and Achilles. The old man in his anguish suggests that familial ties and the needs of the 'other *laoi*' demand that Hector retreat into the city.

> εἰ δ' ἤδη τεθνᾶσι καὶ εἰν Ἀΐδαο δόμοισιν,
> ἄλγος ἐμῷ θυμῷ καὶ μητέρι, τοὶ τεκόμεσθα·
> λαοῖσιν δ' ἄλλοισι μινυνθαδιώτερον ἄλγος
> ἔσσεται, ἢν μὴ καὶ σὺ θάνῃς Ἀχιλῆϊ δαμασθείς.[239]

> But if they [Lycaon and Polydorus] are dead already and gone
>   down to the house of Hades,
> it is sorrow to our hearts, who bore them, myself and their mother,
> but for the rest of the people a sorrow that will be fleeting,
> as long as you are not killed by Achilles as well.

As so often, Hector's role is contrasted with that of his brothers, who are firmly located in a political and family framework. Their death may cause grief to their closest relatives, but they are not missed by the people. Only Hector stands between the two sides. Priam acknowledges his special status but suggests a way out. In his words the 'people' become 'other people', a mere appendix to what Hector's relatives want anyway. Both groups would react with grief (ἄλγος) to his death.[240]

Priam does not mention the destruction of the *laoi* for the sake of Troy. He simply reasserts the old harmony of *Il.* 6 as if nothing had happened. But Hector disagrees: for him the catastrophe of the people is a *fait accompli*, and there is no escaping the mechanisms of negative reciprocity. Here are the decisive lines:

> νῦν δ' ἐπεὶ ὤλεσα λαὸν ἀτασθαλίῃσιν ἐμῇσιν,
> αἰδέομαι Τρῶας καὶ Τρῳάδας ἑλκεσιπέπλους,   105
> μή ποτέ τις εἴπῃσι κακώτερος ἄλλος ἐμεῖο·
> '"Ἕκτωρ ἧφι βίηφι πιθήσας ὤλεσε λαόν."
> ὣς ἐρέουσιν· ἐμοὶ δὲ τότ' ἂν πολὺ κέρδιον εἴη

[239] *Il.* 22.52–5.   [240] Compare *Il.* 22.53 and 54.

ἄντην ἢ Ἀχιλῆα κατακτείναντα νέεσθαι,
ἠέ κεν αὐτῷ ὀλέσθαι ἐϋκλειῶς πρὸ πόληος.[241]

> But now, since by my own recklessness I have ruined the people,
> I feel shame before the Trojans and Trojan women with trailing robes,
> that someone who is less of a man than I will say of me:
> 'Hector believed in his own strength and ruined the people.'
> Thus they will speak; and as for me, it would be much better
> at that time, to go against Achilles, and slay him, and come back,
> or else be killed by him in glory in front of the city.

Hector's self-accusation is part of a larger speech. It furnishes only one reason among others why he decides to stay outside the city gates, yet it is certainly an important one. This section can be divided into three parts: first Hector's own analysis of the situation, then the public verdict imagined by him, and finally his response to it.

Hector acknowledges the catastrophe of the *laos* without qualifications such as Agamemnon's 'many people' (πολύν ... λαόν); and, unlike Agamemnon, he does not attempt to excuse himself. On the contrary, everything is done to read what has happened to his disadvantage; there is no reference to any outside force. 'My reckless folly' (ἀτασθαλίαι ἐμαί) throws back all the responsibility on the leader.[242]

Hector accuses himself of destroying the people in a phrase which, for the time being, is displaced from its formulaic locale and does not yet take its most characteristic form, the third person singular.[243] The crucial transposition is performed by an anonymous voice (τις) who says, or rather might say, what one plausibly would under such circumstances. It does not take an actual speech to activate the traditional theme. 'Someone' (τις) 'some time' (ποτε) might say: 'he destroyed the people' (ὤλεσε λαόν), and the possibility alone is enough to force a decision.

What Hector says differs in some ways from what 'one' (τις) might say. Hector diagnoses 'recklessness' (ἀτασθαλίαι); his faceless opponent suggests surrender to his might, βίη. This speaker is generic in more than one way, for apart from his

---

[241] *Il.* 22.104–10.   [242] *LfgrE s.v.* (B).
[243] See above ch. 1, 'The failed ideal'.

skilled handling of the language of *laos*, he also echoes a number of other epic passages in which a group perishes through the excessive self-assertion of its leader. For the purpose of the present argument we may compare Nestor's analysis of Agamemnon in *Iliad* 9.[244] The context there was similar to ours here. In book 9, too, excessive behaviour had caused a problem between the people and their leader. The city is not the only competitor for the attention claimed by the *laos*. Individual ambition can always be mobilised as an alternative code.

The conclusion Hector draws from the impending verdict in book 22 is that he must fight Achilles, thereby restoring the situation of might against might, which, according to his imaginary opponent, misled him in the first place. Two possible outcomes are left open, but I have already argued that one of them is more prominent.[245] Greek ὀλέσθαι, 'to perish', in line 110 recalls ὤλεσα/ὤλεσε, 'I have/he has destroyed', earlier in Hector's speech. The idea of dying for the city finally coincides with that of dying for the people, thus combining the two strands of Hector's responsibility. However, they are not combined on an entirely equal footing; for the echo between lines 107 and 110 suggests that Hector has understood, at last, that the people (have) come first.

Let us consider, one more time, the Odyssean simile so often mentioned in this chapter. Here is the text:

ὡς δὲ γυνὴ κλαίῃσι φίλον πόσιν ἀμφιπεσοῦσα,
ὅς τε ἑῆς πρόσθεν πόλιος λαῶν τε πέσῃσιν,
ἄστεϊ καὶ τεκέεσσιν ἀμύνων νηλεὲς ἦμαρ.[246]

As a woman weeps lying over the body
of her dear husband, who fell fighting for her city and the people
as he tried to beat off the pitiless day from city and children.

The husband falls, under the eyes of his crying wife, first and foremost in front of his city and then (also) his people. Line 525 is glossed with reference to city (ἄστυ) and children

---

[244] *Il.* 9.109–11.   [245] See above p. 40.
[246] *Od.* 8.523–5; see above pp. 84 and 86.

(τέκη), a further hint at what is already expressed by the choice of the word 'husband' (πόσις), the mediating onlooker and the order of things: first the city, then the people. This arrangement may reflect an Odyssean bias, but if it does, it also draws renewed attention to Hector's dilemma. As Hector, the lonesome 'holder', he must fight for Ilios. As a 'shepherd of the people' he must die for the *laoi*.

The expression 'outside the city' (πρόσθεν πόλιος) in *Odyssey* 8 has a counterpart in the *Iliad* (πρὸ πόληος, 'outside the city'). Hector dies for his city. However, only the people are already destroyed; Hector dies for them. Dying for one's city is the beginning of a new story – the un-Iliadic fall of Troy. Dying for the people is the end of an old one – the Iliadic tale of Homer's people. One last time the *Iliad* reaffirms its interest in the *laos* at the expense of a powerful competitor. Troy will fall, but outside the text. Hector, who closes the text, atones for what has happened to the people in it.

The people at the end

The *Iliad* has often been seen as a ring composition in which book 1 corresponds to 24, book 2 to 23.[247] This is a helpful way of looking at a variety of themes, including Homer's people. Here, as in so many other respects, we can see a contrast between suffering and strife in the early books and reconciliation in books 23–4. Against the bleak image of the plague in book 1 and the assembly in 2 are set two equally impressive tableaux of gathered people in books 23 and 24: the funeral of Patroclus and that of Hector. This time the proceedings are not disrupted. What is more, the funerals unite those who have been apart for so long. Patroclus' funeral involves both the people of the Achaeans and his comrades. When Hector is buried by the *laoi* this also includes the members of Priam's city, represented by Hector's mother, wife and sister-in-law, and by his brothers and friends.

---

[247] E.g. Lynn-George (1996) 23–6, Stanley (1993) chs. 1 and 4, introduction to Macleod (1982), section 3, Sheppard (1922) 208f.

This new harmony has to be achieved in stages. As late as book 22 there are still tensions between Achilles and the people, threatening the fragile coincidence of grief (ἄχος) which draws them together.[248] By the time we reach book 23 this has changed and Achilles offers the sympathetic understanding which he displayed in book 1.[249] He now brings together the two concepts that have been played off against one another for a long time. Differences between the worlds of Achilles' comrades and Homer's people can still be seen. The *laoi* dissolve after the pyre is lit;[250] whereas the mourning of the companions for their friend Patroclus lasts all night long.[251] But although they do not act in the same way, the two groups are held together by their shared grief. Achilles, who embodies the suffering of both, naturally takes the lead. His special status as companion and leader finally becomes a token of his powers of integration.

When the burial is over, Achilles organises the final public event on the Achaean side. Once again we note the double status of the occasion: it is held for 'companions' (ἑταῖροι) and *laoi*. Patroclus, the friend, is never far from the scene; yet the people, too, are mentioned as they gather and dissolve; and also as spectators.[252] The funeral games offer no lasting solution to life among Homer's people. But they heal at least some of the disruptions we have seen earlier. When at the beginning of book 24 the people disperse, there is a sense in which relief has been only temporary; but, in striking contrast with book 2, the end of communal action happens peacefully and in harmony with both major leaders: Agamemnon and Achilles.

From now on Achilles travels his own path, a path which eventually leads to Hector's burial and with it the last gathering of Homer's people.[253] The *laoi* receive the returning

---

[248] *Il.* 22.205–7.
[249] *Il.* 23.156–63.
[250] *Il.* 23.162.
[251] *Il.* 23.218–25.
[252] *Il.* 23.257f., *Il.* 24.1f., *Il.* 23.728, 881.
[253] Note, however, that in *Il.* 24.611 Achilles mentions the people around Niobe, on whom see above p. 43. In *Il.* 24.658 Achilles promises to 'hold back' the *laos*.

Priam at the city gates.[254] The highly emotional character of the scene echoes Priam's speech in book 22 (ἄλγος).[255] At the end of a narrative which has seen so much grief caused by misguided shepherds, the group finally gathers in grief for its dead leader.

Tensions between Hector's two tasks – fighting for the city and saving the people – are visible after his death as they were before. When social life (and the narrative with it) threatens to come to a standstill outside the city gates, Priam makes way by asserting Hector's place in the house and suggesting that lament take place there. Indeed, the political–familial part of the funeral is held inside, but we do hear that the *laoi* 'around the city' join in.[256] When the women's lament is over and the burial itself takes its course, it is organised, one last time, as an assembly of the people. First the preparations:

> λαοῖσιν δ' ὁ γέρων Πρίαμος μετὰ μῦθον ἔειπεν.[257]

Now Priam the aged king spoke forth his word to the people.

then the burial:

> Ἦμος δ' ἠριγένεια φάνη ῥοδοδάκτυλος Ἠώς,
> τῆμος ἄρ' ἀμφὶ πυρὴν κλυτοῦ Ἕκτορος ἔγρετο λαός.[258]

But when the young dawn showed again with her rosy fingers, the people gathered around the pyre of illustrious Hector.

The people mourn their dead leader. Note that the Trojan *laos* gathers without any individual taking the initiative – or rather, Hector's initiative survives his death. The final assembly is not exclusive. After the uncertainties at the city gates we are left with a picture of the accommodating powers of Homer's people. 'Brothers' (κασίγνητοι) were specific to Hector's story, 'companions' (ἑταῖροι) to Achilles'. Both can play their role within the framework of the gathered *laoi*.[259]

---

[254] *Il.* 24.713–17.
[255] *Il.* 22.54.
[256] *Il.* 24.740.
[257] *Il.* 24.777.
[258] *Il.* 24.788f.
[259] *Il.* 24.793f.; for the notion of inclusiveness see above ch. 1, 'Society and the stone'.

Conclusion

Implicit in the treatment of the *laos* in the *Iliad* is a vivid interest in matters of communal life, expressed mainly through Achilles. In a text which stands somewhat uncomfortably between singing the fame of some (κλέα ἀνδρῶν) and deploring the fate of others (ὤλεσε λαόν), Achilles, who destroys the people for the sake of his own fame, bridges the gap by making the very devastation he wreaks the basis of his glory (κῦδος). Like Achilles himself, the *Iliad* at large is as keenly aware of the *laoi* and their needs as it is of individual aspiration. This double interest can be seen to motivate a fundamental narrative decision. Notoriously, the *Iliad* as the most canonical Homeric epic about Troy does not sing about the fall of the city. I have argued that this choice coincides with a less well-known one, namely, to tell the story of Homer's people. If we, the Iliadic audience, expect with Agamemnon and Hector what we might feel entitled to expect from a narrative about the Trojan war, we shall be disappointed. Troy will eventually fall, but not for us. What we see instead is the destruction of the people on both sides. The end of their story is also the end of ours.

In the first chapter I argued that the *laoi* represent an important Homeric concept of the group. This was first illustrated with reference to the *Iliad*. They open and close the text, and they are important throughout. In chapter 1 we also saw that the *laoi* of epic are a group with a leader. This group is never allowed to be aggressively exploited as a commodity. On the contrary, the single agent of early Greek hexameter poetry is expected to save those entrusted to him. The *Iliad* dramatises this fundamental tenet of the genre in terms of a struggle between communal obligation and individual ambition. Agamemnon comes to stand between his need to save the *laos* and his wish to capture Troy. He has to learn that the former cannot be subsumed under the latter. Achilles instrumentalises the people to reassert his honour (τιμή) and, by implication, his fame (κλέος). Through the death of his companion Patroclus, however, he comes to join the people in their grief. Hector, finally, is caught between the overlapping but separate worlds of the city and the *laoi*. As was the case with Agamemnon and Achilles, his dilemma results first in the destruction of the people, then of himself.

The Iliadic leader of the people tends to destroy them (ὤλεσε λαόν) as he does elsewhere in early Greek epic; but there is no other text which focuses on this aspect with quite the insistence and subtlety which the *Iliad* displays. The bias of the genre in favour of the people is mirrored in a large number of passages as well as in the overall structure of the text. The *Iliad* progresses along the traditional lines of negative reciprocity – from destroying the group to destroying the leader. The way in which this is arranged suggests a more and more immediate retaliation. Agamemnon loses face, Achilles his dearest friend, Hector his life. In this we may discern a programme. The *Iliad* does not tell us how the people could have solved their problems. But it does explore with increasing urgency what the nature of these problems is.

In chapter 1 I argued that the *laoi* of early Greek epic allow us an inside view of the social world without effective social structures. The resulting picture in the *Iliad* is pessimistic, even aporetic. However, I also argued that the structural weakness of Homer's people has a counterpart in an equally marked conceptual strength. This too is an important aspect of what the *Iliad* tells us. Its opening and closing scenes can be taken as programmatic in this respect. Both depict Homer's people as inclusive and precious; but while the first two books show a world in disarray, the end brings together various groups in a framework of undisturbed communal activity. The burial of Patroclus involves 'companions' (ἑταῖροι) as well as *laoi*; and when the people stand around Hector's tomb in book 24 they come to embrace and accommodate many of the social forces that have been important in the narrative: self-assertion, friendship among comrades, political and family ties. Thus, the bleak narrative of communal catastrophe is balanced by an increasing sense of social cohesion.

The peace and cohesion achieved at the end of the *Iliad* is at least partly owed to the fact that after the people themselves have died for so long, leaders on both sides have finally died for them. Although we know that the Trojan war and its concomitant suffering are merely suspended in books 23 and 24, within the logic of the *Iliad* as a text, there is a sense of almost aetiological advance at the end. This epic cannot – or at any rate does not – offer us the permanent ritual structures which we find in the texts of the archaic and classical era discussed in chapter 3;[260] and yet, there are glimpses of a more permanent solution. Pindar's hero who is 'venerated by the people' (ἥρως λαοσεβής) has become thinkable.[261] In the following section we will see that the *Odyssey*, which situates itself closer to the end of the epic world, can also promise something closer to a permanent solution.

Laoi in the *Odyssey*

The *Iliad* is in many ways the model text for our understanding of Homer's people. The *laoi* feature prominently from beginning to end, and their problems are central to the narrative. With the *Odyssey* we enter a different world. Here, too, the people play an important role; but standing in the shadow of the more prominent 'companions' (ἑταῖροι) and 'suitors' (μνηστῆρες), they become the object of narrative scrutiny in a different way. We get a first impression of this when looking at Teiresias' version of the plot in his underworld exchange with Odysseus.

> ... αὐτὸς δ' εἴ πέρ κεν ἀλύξῃς
> ὀψὲ κακῶς νεῖαι, ὀλέσας ἄπο πάντας ἑταίρους
> ... δήεις δ' ἐν πήματα οἴκῳ,   115
> ἄνδρας ὑπερφιάλους, οἵ τοι βίοτον κατέδουσι
> μνώμενοι ἀντιθέην ἄλοχον ...
> ...
> αὐτὰρ ἐπὴν μνηστῆρας ἐνὶ μεγάροισι τεοῖσι
> κτείνῃς ἠὲ δόλῳ ἢ ἀμφαδὸν ὀξέϊ χαλκῷ,   120
> ἔρχεσθαι δὴ ἔπειτα ...
> ...

---

[260] See especially ch. 3, '*Leos* ritual' and 'Ritual formulae'.
[261] Pi. *P.* 5.94f.; for discussion see p. 163.

>   ... θάνατος δέ τοι ἐξ ἁλὸς αὐτῷ
> ἀβληχρὸς μάλα τοῖος ἐλεύσεται, ὅς κέ σε πέφνῃ
> γήρᾳ ὕπο λιπαρῷ ἀρημένον· ἀμφὶ δὲ <u>λαοὶ</u>
> ὄλβιοι ἔσσονται· τὰ δέ τοι νημερτέα εἴρω.[262]

> ... but if you yourself get clear,
> you will come home in bad case, having lost all your *companions*,
> ... and you will find troubles in your household,
> insolent men who are eating away your livelihood
> and courting your godlike wife ...
> ...
> But after you have killed the *suitors* in your own palace,
> either by treachery, or openly with the sharp bronze,
> then you must go ...
> ...
> Death will come to you from the sea, in
> some altogether unwarlike way, and it will end you
> in the ebbing time of a sleek old age; and the *people*
> about you will be prosperous. All this is true that I tell you.

Here, in Teiresias' 'true' (νημερτής) account of the *Odyssey*, three groups around Odysseus are singled out and lined up in a characteristic succession: first 'companions' (ἑταῖροι), then 'suitors' (μνηστῆρες), finally *laoi*. In the *Iliad* we found that the *laoi* dominated from the beginning. Their need to be saved is assumed throughout in a narrative which constantly focuses on problems of leadership. Teiresias suggests that in the *Odyssey* things are different. For him the single agent is the given, and the changing role and identity of the world around him comes into much sharper focus. Once again, *laoi* stand at the end of the story, but this time they are missing from its beginning. As we shall see, this has important implications for the teleology of our text.

Odysseus' groups differ in what they do and suffer. On Teiresias' account his 'companions' (ἑταῖροι) are with their leader until they are lost or destroyed (ὀλέσας). The suitors are first encountered, then 'killed' (κτείνειν). Only the *laoi* who do not meet Odysseus at all survive him. This raises a number of

---

[262] *Od.* 11.113f., 115–17, 119–21, 134–7 (cf. 23.281–4); the long middle section which is not quoted here concerns Odysseus' travels without a group; it is discussed in Dornseiff (1937), Hansen (1977).

questions: why do some groups perish and others not? Why are only the groups who die allowed a place in the narrative proper? And what, precisely, is the role of the *laoi* at the end of the narrative? The following discussion attempts to answer some of these questions, using Teiresias' prophecy as a starting-point.

The theme

In one respect Teiresias is obviously right. The *Odyssey* is not primarily concerned with *laoi*. The word occurs less frequently than it does in the *Iliad*.[263] Characteristic formulae such as 'shepherd of the people' are rare,[264] and no strong link between the Achaeans and the *laos* is assumed.[265] In the proem we hear about 'companions' (ἑταῖροι). Later in book 1 'suitors' (μνηστῆρες) play an important role. It is only in the second book that the *laoi* make their first appearance.[266]

Like Teiresias in his prophecy, the *Odyssey* at large plays down the role of the people. However, it also provides some of the most unequivocal examples of what we might call *laos*-ideology. Consider, for example, the passage that celebrates the blameless king, already discussed earlier in this study.[267] Much of what has been said in chapter 1 is expressed in these few lines: the people function as a touchstone for the well-being of a larger world of vegetation and procreation; they depend on a single agent – the 'blameless king' (βασιλεὺς ἀμύμων) – who is bribed into co-operation with such tokens of social esteem as 'fame' (κλέος) and 'blame' (νεικεῖν).[268] All this is more explicit than anything we find in the *Iliad*. As a pas-

---

[263] Altogether 65 times against 229 times in the *Iliad*; cf. Wyatt (1994–5) 167, who also draws attention to the fact that most occurrences of the term *laos* in the *Odyssey* are in books 2–4.
[264] 'Shepherd of the people' (ποιμένα/ποιμένι λαῶν) appears 13 times; 'he destroyed the people' (ὤλεσε λαόν) and similar phrases 6 times.
[265] The phrase 'people of the Achaians' (λαὸς Ἀχαιῶν) does not occur in the *Odyssey*; examples and discussion in ch. 1, '"The people of the Achaeans"'.
[266] *Od.* 2.13.
[267] *Od.* 19.107–14; see above ch. 1, 'An epic ideal'.
[268] *Od.* 19.108.

LAOI IN THE ODYSSEY

sage from book 6 makes clear, the Odyssean narrator is also familiar with the formula 'he destroyed the people' (ὤλεσε λαόν) and the principle of negative reciprocity attached to it.[269] That the *Odyssey* transposes 'recklessness', ἀτασθαλίαι, from the leader to the people comes as a characteristic departure from the model established in chapter 1.[270] However, not only does the principle of negative reciprocity as such remain unchanged but it is also summarised more succinctly than it ever is in the *Iliad*. As a last example of how the *Odyssey* employs the language of *laos* one may consider the reverse simile from book 8 which I have discussed already.[271] This time the term *laoi* is glossed by the political–familial terms that were so important for Hector in the *Iliad*.[272] And again, what was there a complex set of overlapping obligations is stated with paradigmatic simplicity in the *Odyssey*. The man of the simile dies for his city and the people.

The Odyssean narrator is as aware of Homer's people as is the narrator of the *Iliad*. What is new is that his people are kept largely in the background. For all their explicitness, the passages I have adduced so far can be taken as symptomatic of this. Two of them are similes; situations which do not 'actually' involve the people.[273] The passage from book 7 is removed from the main narrative in another sense. With or without *laoi*, giants are certainly not central to the Homeric world.[274] In each case the result is a curious mixture of narrative awareness and narrative distance. What this means becomes clear when we turn to the people of Ithaca.

The *laoi* in Ithaca are first introduced in book 2.[275] They are traditional in appearance. Relations between single agent and the people are negotiated in the Odyssean assembly as they are in the assemblies of the *Iliad*.[276] The relevant proce-

---

[269] *Od.* 7.58–60; see above ch. 1, 'Negative reciprocity'.
[270] Cf. *Il.* 22.104 with analogous shape; see above ch. 1, 'The failed ideal'.
[271] *Od.* 8.523–5.
[272] See above ch. 2, '*Laoi* in the *Iliad*', pp. 83–95.
[273] Homer's people do not feature in similes outside the *Odyssey*.
[274] For a reading of the passage as mock-Iliadic see p. 115.
[275] *Od.* 2.13, 41.
[276] *Od.* 2.13, 41, 81, 234, 252.

dures are equally familiar.[277] New, however, is the fact that Odysseus, as the obvious 'shepherd of the people',[278] is absent from the beginning of the text almost to its end. As far as the *Odyssey* is about the people in Ithaca it is hardly a story at all. While this does not make them wholly insignificant, it is certainly true that their role is very different from that in the *Iliad*. *Laoi* in the *Odyssey* are the curious case of a group which is at the same time thematic and marginal.

Laoi *and companions*

I have argued that in the *Odyssey* the *laoi* are seen either as remote in time and space (Teiresias' prophecy, the giants), or situated at a different narrative level (the similes), or remote simply because they do not take an active part in the plot (the people of Ithaca). However, this is not to say that they are unimportant. Just as the end of Teiresias' prophecy is an integral part of it, the *laoi* in the *Odyssey* function as a constant point of reference without which the main narrative cannot be told or understood. I hope to show this in the following two sections.

I start by looking at the relationship between the *laoi* and Odysseus' companions. For Teiresias in his prophecy the companions around Odysseus are a given. They are there when the prophetic narrative starts, and they are clearly separate from the *laoi*, whom we see when it ends. However, elsewhere in the text this arrangement does not stand unquestioned. Note, for instance, that Odysseus' companions have been *laoi* in the past. The decisive lines occur in Nestor's account of the departure from Troy. As long as the Achaeans are on shore they are consistently referred to as *laoi*.[279]

---

[277] E.g. 'to gather the people' (λαὸν ἀγείρειν) in *Od.* 2.41, 'to disperse the people' (λαὸν σκεδαννύναι) in *Od.* 2.252.
[278] *Od.* 18.70, 20.106, 24.368; cf. 10.538 (ὄρχαμε λαῶν, 'leader of the people'), other leaders of the people are Agamemnon in *Od.* 3.156, 4.532, 14.497; Nestor in *Od.* 3.469, 15.151, 17.109; Menelaus in *Od.* 4.24; cf. 4.156, 291, 316, 15.64, 87 (ὄρχαμε λαῶν, 'leader of the people'); Mentor in *Od.* 24.456, Aegisthus in *Od.* 4.528; cf. Amphinomus in *Od.* 18.152 (κοσμήτορι λαῶν, 'marshal of the people').
[279] *Od.* 3.140, 144, 155-7.

However, as soon as the return journey starts, we hear of 'companions'.[280]

Nestor creates two narrative realms, one of *laoi* and one of 'companions'. These realms are not unconnected. Rather, the shift from 'people' to 'companions' is one of perspective, mapped as it is onto the difference between Troy and *nostos*.[281] For Nestor this difference has a quasi-generic significance, but even for him it cannot be complete. *Nostos* is post-Homeric, not un-Homeric. The return stories always belong to the larger undertaking against Troy, and where the *Odyssey* is seen as part of the larger whole, 'companions' revert to being *laoi*. For example:

> Ἡμεῖς τοι Τροίηθεν ἀποπλαγχθέντες Ἀχαιοὶ
> παντοίοις ἀνέμοισιν ὑπὲρ μέγα λαῖτμα θαλάσσης,   260
> οἴκαδε ἰέμενοι, ἄλλην ὁδόν, ἄλλα κέλευθα
> ἤλθομεν· οὕτω που Ζεὺς ἤθελε μητίσασθαι.
> λαοὶ δ' Ἀτρεΐδεω Ἀγαμέμνονος εὐχόμεθ' εἶναι,
> τοῦ δὴ νῦν γε μέγιστον ὑπουράνιον κλέος ἐστί·
> τόσσην γὰρ διέπερσε πόλιν καὶ ἀπώλεσε λαοὺς   265
> πολλούς ...[282]

> We are Achaeans coming from Troy, beaten off our true course
> by winds from every direction across the great gulf of the open
> sea, making for home, by the wrong way, on the wrong courses.
> So we have come. So it has pleased Zeus to arrange it.
> We claim we are the people of the son of Atreus,
> Agamemnon, whose fame now is the greatest thing under heaven,
> such a city it was that he sacked and destroyed the people,
> many of them ...

As Nestor does in his tales and the Muse in the epic at large, Odysseus usually emphasises the gap between Troy and *nostos* by referring to his group as 'companions' (ἑταῖροι) rather than *laoi*.[283] But the gap can be closed. Odysseus himself and Odysseus' men have not only started off as Homer's people in

---
[280] *Od.* 3.167, 181, 191, 4.367, 374, 408, 433, 11.412, (23.324 ?).
[281] *Od.* 14.245–50 is parallel. For the generic implications of the term *laos* see also ch. 1, '"The people of the Achaeans"'.
[282] *Od.* 9.259–66.
[283] The word is used of Odysseus' army 102 times; the only other place where *laos* is used instead (*Od.* 24.426–8) is discussed on pp. 107f. below.

the distant past, but also become *laoi* once more in the cave of the Cyclops.

Teiresias' juxtaposition of well-defined Odyssean groups, 'companions' – 'suitors' – *laoi*, has become rather more complicated: Odysseus' companions are of course not 'in fact' *laoi* because they once were. Rather, under certain circumstances they can be seen as such. While Nestor indicates an important, quasi-generic convention when he switches from one term to the other on entering the realm of *nostos*, Odysseus' own redefinition during his travels warns us not to assume any straightforward correlation. Since *nostos* is post-Homeric, not un-Homeric, there are always at least two possible ways of looking at what remains fundamentally one and the same group.

What I have suggested last can be understood better if we study more closely the circumstances under which Odysseus' redefinition occurs. Shortly after the beginning of his travels the protagonist has arrived at an important point of his career, for it can be argued that the Cyclops-adventure marks the departure into the wilderness more drastically than any other episode before or after, not only because the Cyclops is a singularly bizarre creature and the confrontation with him especially new and surprising,[284] but also because Polyphemus articulates the adventures to come. His curse, quite literally, sets Odysseus on his Odyssean path.[285]

In the cave of the Cyclops we have reached an important point of transition, a point where Odysseus is about to begin his journey through the wilderness. This is marked by a stark juxtaposition of Trojan and non-Trojan elements. Odysseus himself takes one side by building a network of belonging: in his introduction he mentions in one breath Troy, Achaeans, Agamemnon the famous. It is in this context of narrative signposting that he also calls himself and his men *laoi*. Polyphemus takes the other side and, as the true exponent of the post-Trojan wilderness, answers back in terms of 'companions'

---

[284] Mondi (1983) 27.   [285] *Od.* 9.526–36.

(ἑταῖροι).²⁸⁶ From now on Odysseus' men will always be called by that name.

When Odysseus presents himself and his men as Agamemnon's 'people' (λαοί), he claims that there is continuity between Troy and his own emerging world of Märchen and monsters.²⁸⁷ However, the term *laos*, once evoked, brings with it certain complications: the phrase 'he destroyed the people' (ὤλεσε λαόν), in particular, carries uncomfortable overtones.²⁸⁸ As we have seen, Agamemnon in the *Iliad* destroys not the Trojan *laos* but his own, and the fame (κλέος) he derives from this is appropriately bad (δυσκλεής). According to Odysseus' version, Agamemnon destroys Troy and many Trojan *laoi*; but the language is fraught with ambiguity.²⁸⁹ Quite apart from Agamemnon's problems in the *Iliad*, 'destroying the people' is not something on which any character in early Greek hexameter would want to build his fame.²⁹⁰

There is more than a mere suggestion, then, that Odysseus, as well as claiming Agamemnon's fame for himself and his group, also evokes some of its less welcome aspects. These aspects – all too well-known from the *Iliad* – allow Odysseus an intertextual jibe at his famous counterpart in a situation where his own place in the world of epic fame is painfully uncertain. However, that is not where the story ends. The echoes and resonances of formulaic language do not end at this point any more than they could be reduced to a straightforward appropriation of an unambiguously positive Iliadic model. Odysseus' *double entendre* turns against himself towards the end of the epic, when Eupeithes denounces him:

---

[286] *Od.* 9.278.
[287] For Märchen and the *Odyssey* see Petersmann (1981), Hölscher (1989), Peradotto (1990).
[288] See Pazdernik (1995) 365 with perceptive remarks on what he calls the 'jarring' effect of the Odyssean scene.
[289] Pazdernik (1995) 365 offers a wide range of possible readings from a conscious strategy on the part of Odysseus to a complicated echoing effect at the level of narration.
[290] See above ch. 1, especially 'The failed ideal' and 'Negative reciprocity'.

> ὢ φίλοι, ἦ μέγα ἔργον ἀνὴρ ὅδε μήσατ᾽ Ἀχαιούς·
> τοὺς μὲν ἐνὶ νήεσσιν ἄγων πολέας τε καὶ ἐσθλοὺς
> ὤλεσε μὲν νῆας γλαφυράς, ἀπὸ δ᾽ ὤλεσε λαούς.[291]
>
> Friends, this man's will worked great evil upon the Achaeans.
> First he took many excellent men away in the vessels
> with him, and lost the hollow ships and destroyed the people.

A misunderstanding of the 'misunderstanding' promoted by Odysseus in the Cyclops' cave results in this devastating account of his travels: 'he destroyed the people' (ὤλεσε λαούς). Odysseus' speech in book 9, 'rightly' understood, precludes such a reading, since Agamemnon is there the leader of the people, among whom Odysseus cunningly includes himself. Odysseus *is* the people. But there remains a problem. Whatever he may tell the Cyclops, Odysseus does act as the leader of his men during his travels, and in this as in so many other respects it is not difficult to see certain parallels between him and Agamemnon.[292] Eupeithes' version of the events is by no means absurd. Rather, it articulates a highly plausible, forcefully traditional alternative to the official version, an alternative which needs to be rejected precisely because it sounds so convincing. It is hardly a coincidence that the speaker who puts forward this anti-Odyssean *Odyssey* is called 'he who persuades well'. Indeed, the effect he has on his audience in the text shows just how persuasive it is.[293] The epic cannot be closed before this point is clarified. It is closed at the expense of Eupeithes, who is promptly killed together with his story.[294] The triumphant 'true' tale is then complete.[295]

---

[291] *Od.* 24.426–8; cf. Ulf (1990) 103 with n. 42, but note that 'Laoi = Hetairoi' is precisely what *cannot* be assumed. Here as elsewhere Ulf's argument is marred by imprecise glossing; see above ch. 1, n. 2.

[292] In other respects the paradigmatic status of Agamemnon's return has long been acknowledged; see for example Hommel (1955), Skiadas (1980), Goldhill (1986) 147–50, Hölscher (1989) 300–5, Cook (1995) 21–4, Ahl and Roisman (1996) ch. 1, esp. 28.

[293] *Od.* 24.438, 464f.

[294] *Od.* 24.523–5.

[295] We need not here rehearse the age-old analyst–unitarian debate about the end of the *Odyssey*, which goes back to schol. *Od.* 23.296, Eust. II p. 308.24–34 (Stallbaum); for recent contributions see Page (1955) ch. 5, Erbse (1972) ch. B 3,

A search for the boundaries between Odysseus' 'companions' (ἑταῖροι) and Homer's people quickly exposes considerable overlap between the two, especially at points of crisis such as the beginning and end of travel. On the one hand, the *Odyssey* places itself in a tradition of story-telling about the *laoi*, a tradition which is treated with half-mocking deference. On the other hand, it insists on telling a tale of lost companions. While we may be encouraged to identify the two groups for the sake of generic continuity and/or jokes at the expense of the Iliadic Agamemnon, any further similarities are rejected with some insistence. This balancing-act is never unproblematic. To illustrate the amount of potential slippage, I return to Teiresias' prophecy.

The text as given in the vulgate tells us that Odysseus dies among prosperous people at the end of a long life of travel.[296] This is a characteristically Odyssean way of casting the *laoi*.[297] Eupeithes tries to muddy the waters by suggesting that Odysseus has destroyed them (ὤλεσε λαούς). Such a version can only serve to reopen the story, as indeed Eupeithes himself points out. For Teiresias, narrative closure is achieved in a harmonious restoration of the norm: the leader dies among the people who (therefore?) move into a brighter future. This picture is comfortable enough, but it did not remain unchallenged. After all that has been argued so far, we can perhaps understand why Eustathius or someone before him felt provoked to replace 'the people' in line 136 with 'companions'.[298] Teiresias' version of the *Odyssey* may be the ultimate attempt to control the ambiguities of the main narrative. But even his account does not remain stable beyond doubt.

Moulton (1974), Stössel (1975), Wender (1978), Postlethwaite (1981), Dawe (1993) 823–5 and Seaford (1994) 38–42; the end of the *Odyssey* as we have it is vital for the present argument and I see no reason why we should not include it in our discussion.

[296] *Od.* 11.134–7 *vulg.*; cf. 23.281–4.
[297] Cf., however, *h.Ven.* 103–6; for further examples and discussion see above ch. 1, 'Society and the stone'.
[298] Eust. 1 p. 402.37 (Stallbaum).

Laoi *and suitors*

In the *Odyssey* the *laoi* are rarely in the foreground. And yet, located as they are at the end of Odyssean travel they function as a point of constant reference. Starting from the overlap between Odyssean 'companions' (ἑταῖροι) and the *laoi* we have seen how the *Odyssey* explores the possibilities and struggles with the problems that ensue. While we are encouraged to see Homer's people in the marginal space of the Cyclops' cave, any attempts to generalise are violently repressed. This dichotomy is also operative in the tale of Odysseus and the suitors. Here, too, we find ourselves standing between two conflicting tendencies.[299] The interplay between them is not always equally clear-cut, and the following investigation can only hope to bring out some of its more salient features.

Uncertainty about the status of Penelope's suitors goes back to the second book, which brings a programmatic exposition of the people gathered in the assembly (ἀγορή).[300] It is here that we witness the first and most elaborate debate over the relationship between suitors and *laoi* in the *Odyssey*, and from then on the issue never entirely disappears from the narrative agenda. The presence of *laoi* as an audience is established at the very beginning of the episode:

τὸν δ' ἄρα πάντες λαοὶ ἐπερχόμενον θηεῦντο.[301]

and all the people had their eyes on him as he came forward.

Two things emerge from this verse which will be important for the further development of the *Odyssey*. First, the *laoi* provide the backdrop against which we are invited to view the struggle between Odysseus' house and the suitors. They will not always be present as an audience (most of the narrative is set inside Odysseus' house), but their judgement will be invoked, contested and manipulated throughout.

---

[299] For further parallels between companions and suitors see Nagler (1990) *passim*, esp. 340–5, Cook (1995) 26f.
[300] *Od.* 2.13, 41, 81, 252.
[301] *Od.* 2.13.

The second point to note is that the people depend on what happens in Odysseus' house. Telemachus not only commands their admiration and respect but also unites an otherwise sporadic social world: 'and *all* the people had their eyes on him'. Notoriously, the assembly of Ithacan people has not been summoned for years.[302] Telemachus ends this state of affairs for his own reasons, but he also appears as a benefactor of communal life. In his reply to Aegyptius his own private concerns and those of the *laos* are closely linked.[303] Voicing his personal agenda, Telemachus *creates* a gathered people. By contrast, the suitors resist social formation.[304] We are left with a party which is interested in gathered *laoi* and another which works towards dispersal and individuation (ἕκαστος).

This impression is further enhanced by the response which Telemachus' outburst elicits: it unites the *laos*.[305] No comparable reaction is reported to the suitors' various speeches, and although the assembly is in the end ineffective, much has been done to convince us that Telemachus has won the day.

What has been offered so far is a rather cursory reading of the assembly in *Odyssey* 2. Telemachus gathers the *laoi* and is greeted with admiration (πάντες λαοὶ ... θηεῦντο) and sympathy (οἶκτος δ' ἕλε λαὸν ἅπαντα). The suitors who disperse them can count on no such response. Odysseus' house thus defines and monopolises life among Homer's people. However, that is not all there is to say. Like Odysseus in book 9, Telemachus and his helpers, too, struggle to play down certain aspects of early epic *laoi* which are not altogether welcome. Mentor's speech is interesting in this context:

μή τις ἔτι πρόφρων ἀγανὸς καὶ ἤπιος ἔστω   230
σκηπτοῦχος βασιλεύς, μηδὲ φρεσὶν αἴσιμα εἰδώς,
ἀλλ' αἰεὶ χαλεπός τ' εἴη καὶ αἴσυλα ῥέζοι,
ὡς οὔ τις μέμνηται Ὀδυσσῆος θείοιο
λαῶν οἷσιν ἄνασσε, πατὴρ δ' ὡς ἤπιος ἦεν.

---

[302] *Od.* 2.25–7.
[303] *Od.* 2.40f.; for discussion of the metrical and thematic anomalies of line 41 see Martin (1997) 269–71.
[304] *Od.* 2.252.
[305] *Od.* 2.80f.

ἀλλ' ἦ τοι μνηστῆρας ἀγήνορας οὔ τι μεγαίρω
ἔρδειν ἔργα βίαια κακορραφίῃσι νόοιο.[306]

> No longer now let one who is a sceptred king be eager
> to be gentle and kind, be one whose thought is schooled in justice,
> but let him always rather be harsh, and act severely,
> seeing the way no one of the people [*laoi*] he was lord over
> remembers godlike Odysseus, and he was kind, like a father.
> Now it is not so much the proud suitors I resent
> for doing their violent acts by their minds' evil devising.

This speech, set in the 'actual' world of the Odyssean story, forms a remarkable counterpart to some of the idealising scenarios of *laoi* and leader discussed at the beginning of this chapter.[307] Mentor sees the situation as one of tacit compliance between the people and the suitors. He reacts by arguing that the people at least should behave differently. Part of his point seems to be that the *laoi* lose their distinctive character when they side with the suitors. They themselves become something like suitors and as a result can no longer claim the sympathies and privileges (μή ... ἔτι) that they usually command.

Mentor's argument entails a remarkable narrative manipulation. In his view, Homer's people have brought themselves into a position where they become liable to being abused. As part of this rearrangement of traditional features, Odysseus is placed before the needs of his group. For Mentor it is not the *laoi* who oblige their leader, but the leader who obliges them.[308] This idea is explained in terms of family ties (πατὴρ δ' ὣς ἤπιος ἦεν).[309] A father is emotionally attached to his children, whereas we recall that the shepherd of the people is not. More importantly, the father's emotional attachment is inextricably bound up with his privileged position of having been – and acted – first. Whereas the flock is prior to the shepherd, the father is prior to the child.

In Mentor's speech the *laoi* and the suitors show a close affinity. The two groups seem ready to merge at any point,

---

[306] *Od.* 2.230–6. [307] See pp. 102–4.
[308] *Od.* 2.233f. [309] *Od.* 2.234; cf. 2.47.

and keeping them separate takes some imaginative effort. From open threat[310] to blame[311] and subtle redefinitions[312], Mentor's rhetorical manœuvres are hardly less complex than those employed by Agamemnon in *Iliad* 2. Taken together, they form a remarkably aggressive argument: either the *laoi* actively participate in the story – in which case Mentor suggests they should lose their claims to constructive leadership – or they remain *laoi* properly speaking, endowed with their traditional epic character, in which case there is no story to be told about them. One version wants to have Homer's people on stage. The other insists on an Odyssean choice not to sing about them. Together, they sketch out the complex position of Homer's people within the narrative project of the *Odyssey*.

The uncertainties which the assembly at large plays down are exposed by Mentor's speech and stay with us for the rest of the epic. While an affinity between suitors and *laoi* is often assumed or asserted, outright identification of the two groups is violently rejected. Consider the following passage in book 3:

εἰπέ μοι ἠὲ ἑκὼν ὑποδάμνασαι, ἦ σέ γε λαοί
ἐχθαίρουσ' ἀνὰ δῆμον, ἐπισπόμενοι θεοῦ ὀμφῇ.[313]

Tell me, are you willingly put down, or are the people
who live about you swayed by some divine voice, and hate you?

Nestor, the Iliadic expert in matters concerning the people,[314] assumes that Telemachus either willingly succumbs (ἑκών) or has the *laoi* against him. The fact that the first alternative is self-defeating[315] makes the second seem all the more likely: Telemachus is regarded as an enemy (ἐχθαίρουσιν) by the people. Two things may be noted here. Homer's people are associated by a third party with the suitors, not with Odysseus' house. Secondly, the *laoi* in Ithaca are assumed to reflect the will of the gods. Their partisanship alone determines the power-struggle in Odysseus' house.

[310] *Od.* 2.230–2.
[311] *Od.* 2.239.
[312] *Od.* 2.233f.
[313] *Od.* 3.214f.
[314] See above ch. 2, '*Laoi* in the *Iliad*', especially pp. 54, 59f., 69–72.
[315] Cf. *Od.* 3.213.

Telemachus neither accepts nor denies Nestor's allegations,[316] but the apparent ease with which they are put forward supports the link between the suitors and the *laoi* which was implied by Mentor; it is further emphasised by Penelope in book 4.[317] Although Penelope does not claim that the *laoi* are, as a group, identical with the suitors, she accuses them of 'destroying her and Odysseus' offspring', which is precisely what the suitors are plotting to do.[318] We might decide not to trust Penelope on this point, but she is not the first nor will she be the last to see things in such a light. While Penelope thus further narrows the gap between the suitors and the *laos*, her words can also be read in a different way. Being accused of co-operating with the enemy of the house, the people are placed outside its boundaries (one has to contact them 'outside', ἐξελθών). Somewhere behind Penelope's words there is an inkling that the people could play the role of a third party who watches and judges from a distance.

Nestor in book 3 and Penelope in 4, each in their own way, add to the complex picture of Odyssean *laoi* drawn by Mentor. Mentor's speech is then repeated by Athena in book 5.[319] The anxieties over the people's role on Ithaca do not cease. Indeed, they are felt to be so pressing that they penetrate the Olympian stage at a point where Odysseus' return is finally brought into effect. Once again the issue is raised by an expert. Athena is the god of Homer's people.[320]

In books 2–5 our theme is gradually built up and explored in its complexities and contradictions. *Laoi*, the people, are introduced as a powerful third party which watches over the struggle in Odysseus' house and holds the key to its outcome.

---

[316] The fact that he answers in terms of *demos* may be compared with Mentor's speech in *Od.* 2.230–6; Donlan (1989) 15 uses the passage to argue that the two words are usually equivalent. I disagree. For the difference between *laos* and *demos* in Homer see Casewitz (1992), Taplin (1992) 49 with n. 6, Wyatt (1994–5) 169; see further ch. 3, n. 140 below.
[317] *Od.* 4.739–41.
[318] *Od.* 4.669–72, 700f.; cf. schol. *Od.* 4.740: 'She will weep among the suitors [!] and they will take pity and not kill Telemachus' (ἐν τοῖς μνηστῆρσι [!] κλαύσει καὶ οἰκτειρήσουσι τοῦ μὴ κτεῖναι Τηλέμαχον).
[319] *Od.* 5.7–12.
[320] See above pp. 69f.

Whose side they are on has not yet been established beyond doubt. Much is done to link them with Odysseus' family, but I have also suggested that there are strong affinities between them and the suitors. The opening assembly in particular is important here, but the picture is fleshed out in speeches by Nestor in book 3, Penelope in 4 and Athena in 5. More and more, as the story proceeds, the *laoi* become a crucial narrative force – and as they become more important, they also become more ambivalent, less easy to control.

The uncertainties I have been tracing do not disappear when the narrative moves on to Odysseus' travels. Scherie, too, although ostensibly unproblematic in its depiction of the *laoi*, cannot but keep the old issues fresh in our minds. We start with a fanfare in book 7.[321] I have already argued that the story of Eurymedon, king of the giants, is similar to what we find in the *Iliad*. Communal catastrophe is caused by a leader (ὤλεσε λαόν) who is destroyed in turn (ὤλετο δ' αὐτός).[322] However, given the character of this particular leader and his people, the story is mock-Iliadic at best. Moreover, the traditional narrative of negative reciprocity is compromised by the fact that the people, not the leader, are here called 'reckless', ἀτάσθαλος.[323] Through this caricature of Achaean epic we approach the *laoi* on Scherie themselves.

The opening picture proves telling – though not in any straightforward way. There is no violent disruption on Scherie. The people of the Phaeacians do not commit 'reckless' deeds, in fact, they do not seem to commit much at all. In striking contrast with their overgrown, pseudo-Iliadic relatives, the *laoi* of Scherie have sunk into blissful stagnation.

The formulaic address to Alcinous as 'famous among all the people' (πάντων ἀριδείκετε λαῶν) may serve as a case in point.[324] Elsewhere in early Greek hexameter poetry, a leader has to earn the support of his people by acting on their

---

[321] *Od.* 7.58–60.
[322] See above pp. 102f.
[323] Cf. *Il.* 22.104–10.
[324] First introduced in an elaborated form in *Od.* 7.69–72; then taken up in *Od.* 8.382, 401, 9.2, 11.355, 378, 13.38.

behalf.[325] There is no such work to be done here. Alcinous is an acceptable and accepted leader by poetic default; he monopolises the support of his people to the extent that it becomes frozen in a traditional epithet. It is the only epithet of its kind. What it implies is elaborated elsewhere in the text, for example, when Odysseus bids farewell to Arete:

> αὐτὰρ ἐγὼ νέομαι· σὺ δὲ τέρπεο τῷδ' ἐνὶ οἴκῳ
> παισί τε καὶ λαοῖσι καὶ Ἀλκινόῳ βασιλῆϊ.[326]
>
> Now I am on my way; but have joy here in your household,
> in your children and your people, and in the king, Alcinous.

For once we are justified in translating 'your people' where the Greek simply has *laoi*. Reduced to keeping their queen happy, the *laoi* of Scherie have become part of her household. The idea goes back to book 4,[327] where Menelaus offers Odysseus a new home. 'All the people' follow Odysseus when he moves house. They belong to his furniture and are as such unproblematic, a mere appendix. Importantly, the resettlement à la Scherie which is envisaged in *Odyssey* 4 remains a mere possibility. On the island of the Phaeacians it has long become reality.

Scherie as a model of life among Homer's people is not untraditional. Rather, out of the parameters common to all early Greek hexameter poetry, it builds a vision of peaceful coexistence. Clytoneus' foot-race furnishes an example of how familiar motifs may be reinterpreted.[328] Victory in the race is achieved among *laoi* and relative to them. The idea itself is traditional, but that alone means little. In the *Iliad* the *laoi* actively participate in contests whose outcome determines the group's social structure and future well-being. The main contestant on Scherie has little to do with the people, and his victory cannot mean much to them. They function as a mere yardstick.

The same trivialising tendency can be seen in many other parts of the episode. For example, the people of Scherie wit-

---

[325] See above ch. 1, 'An incurable imbalance'. [326] *Od.* 13.61f.
[327] *Od.* 4.174–7. [328] *Od.* 8.124f., cf. also 8.471f., 13.27f.

ness the treaty between Poseidon and Alcinous. Again their role is potentially important, but again its impact is minimised by a hasty gloss.[329] When the Phaeacian ship is turned into stone, an event which marks the beginning of a new era in the history of Scherie, this is ratified by 'all the *laoi*'. But the following line already speaks of 'all human beings' (ἅπαντες ἄνθρωποι), thus shifting attention to a far less specific – and rather more characteristically Odyssean – frame of reference.

Parallels between books 4 and 6–8 of the *Odyssey* suggest that the people of the Phaeacians furnish us with an idealised version of their troubled counterpart in Ithaca. In both cases the *laoi* show the potential for being a powerful social force, but in Scherie their links with the household of Alcinous effectively domesticate their power. The formula from which we started sums up the process: instead of the Iliadic 'shepherd', who has to earn his recognition, we see here a leader who has secured his standing once and for all. Any possible problems have been left to Eurymedon and his giants. The people in Scherie are still a force to be reckoned with. They are named,[330] they form the audience of public song and sport,[331] they ratify divine aetiologies[332] and mark out the boundaries of the world.[333] But all this they do without ever making any demands on their leaders. If this is the model for Ithaca, we can see why there is no story to be told about it.

Back in Ithaca the old problems soon resurface. In book 14 the opposition between the *laos* and 'companions' becomes visible once more.[334] A passage in book 16 recalls Nestor's speech from book 3,[335] and again it raises the same uncertainties. The episode on Scherie notwithstanding, the *Odyssey* keeps skirting around the eternally unsolved problem of Homer's people. Later in book 16, Antinous remarks on behalf of the suitors at large that the people are 'no longer in favour of them'.[336] In some ways this can be seen as a step away from Nestor's speech in 3 and Odysseus' in 16. Once

---

[329] *Od.* 13.154–8. [330] *Od.* 6.194. [331] See above n. 328.
[332] See above n. 329. [333] *Od.* 7.322f. [334] *Od.* 14.245–50.
[335] *Od.* 16.91–6. [336] *Od.* 16.375.

again the people are seen as a powerful judge, but this time to the disadvantage of the suitors. It would, however, be misleading to extract from this a linear development. Clarification at the surface creates further complication in depth. To say that the *laoi* no longer approve of the suitors makes them two separate entities. However, we are also invited to believe that they used to be closer in the past ('no longer' – οὐκέτι) and could perhaps be close again; which, indeed is exactly what happens.

In book 17, Telemachus returns home after a long absence. On the threshold he meets Eurycleia and Penelope. Having greeted them both he enters the house, at which point we hear that 'all the people marvelled at him'.[337] The line is known from book 2, where it describes Telemachus' appearance in the assembly. It is of course perfectly normal to expect the people in a Homeric *agore*, but what are they now doing in a house? Could it be that someone else is meant? The text hastens to quench any such questions by introducing the suitors in the following line.[338] Awkward as it is, the manœuvre can tell us much about the Odyssean predicament. Our epic is eager to have the people standing on the sideline, watching and cheering (θηεῦντο). *Laoi* must be in the story, if only to show that they are not (really) *in* it. Having been allowed to enter Odysseus' house, they are immediately sidelined by the suitors, who take over and act out the drama of book 22.

Before turning to that episode, however, we must consider what is arguably the most spectacular piece of *laos* ideology in the whole of early hexameter poetry.[339] I have already discussed the simile of the blameless king at some length,[340] but what needs to be pointed out here is that it once more draws attention to the curious tension – characteristic of the *Odyssey* – between a narrative background with the people in it and a foreground without them. Penelope is in fact surrounded by suitors, not *laoi*. But being where she is and what she is, she *looks very much like* the blameless king who rules over the

---

[337] *Od.* 17.64.   [338] *Od.* 17.65.
[339] *Od.* 19.107–14.   [340] See above p. 27.

people.³⁴¹ As in Teiresias' prophecy, the ideal world of Odyssean story-telling – ideal also in the teleological sense of a narrative goal – is one of the *laoi* thriving under their leader. But this world can only ever be hinted at, never *narrated*. Without suitors Penelope would not be who she is, Odysseus could not do what he does, and the *Odyssey* would be an altogether different text (or no text at all).

There is hardly a place in the *Odyssey* where this last point can be seen more clearly than at the crucial moment of recognition in book 22. Odysseus has dropped his disguise, stepped onto the threshold and begun to slaughter his enemies. At this point, the problems of definition we have been tracing for so long erupt in the most spectacular manner. Let us look at Eurymachus' speech, which suggests a second, collective recognition scene:

> εἰ μὲν δὴ 'Οδυσεὺς 'Ιθακήσιος εἰλήλουθας, 45
> ταῦτα μὲν αἴσιμα εἶπας, ὅσα ῥέζεσκον Ἀχαιοί,
> πολλὰ μὲν ἐν μεγάροισιν ἀτάσθαλα, πολλὰ δ' ἐπ' ἀγροῦ.
> ἀλλ' ὁ μὲν ἤδη κεῖται ὃς αἴτιος ἔπλετο πάντων,
> Ἀντίνοος· ...
> ...
> νῦν δ' ὁ μὲν ἐν μοίρῃ πέφαται, σὺ δὲ φείδεο λαῶν
> σῶν ...³⁴²   55

> If in truth you are Odysseus of Ithaca, come home,
> what you have said is fair about all the wickedness done you
> by the Achaeans, much in your house and much in the country.
> But now the man is down who was responsible for all
> this, Antinous ...
> ...
> Now he has perished by his own fate. Then spare the people,
> your own ones ...

For Eurymachus, the group that has always 'officially' been called 'Penelope's suitors' has now turned into Odysseus' *laoi* and deserves to be spared.³⁴³

---

³⁴¹ *Od.* 19.114 may suggest a hierarchy which is not normally found in conjunction with Homer's people; see above ch. 1, 'Society and the stone', but compare also *Od.* 3.305 (of Aegisthus).
³⁴² *Od.* 22.45–9, 54f.
³⁴³ For a first attempt at interpreting this change see Casewitz (1992).

I have argued earlier that to see Odyssean 'companions' (ἑταῖροι) as *laoi* can mean different things. On the one hand, their appearance in a post-Trojan environment may help to close an unsettling gap between the journeys of the *Odyssey* and the Achaeans outside Troy. On the other hand, they bring with them a set of ideas which are potentially unwelcome: if Odysseus' companions are 'in fact' *laoi*, their leader should have saved them. Similar complications are at work in the case of the suitors. They, too, often come close to turning into *laoi*, and there is always a residue of ambiguity as to what, precisely, their relationship to Odysseus should be.

Eurymachus' speech aims to ensure the survival of his group.[344] In order to save his own life and that of his peers he has recourse to a term which helps him make his point. The *laoi* must be saved; and since there is a deep-rooted ambiguity in the *Odyssey* as to how the suitors differ from 'the people', Eurymachus simply pushes to its extremes a theme that pervades the text. Implied in this gesture is something very much like the anti-*Odyssey* which Eupeithes outlines in book 24. Once again the alternative is close at hand. And again it has to be superseded in order to conclude the narrative.

In his answer Odysseus sets one definition against the other.[345] With 'suitors' instead of *laoi* the slaughter can take its course, and the narrative of revenge (ἀποτίνειν) is brought to a 'complete' end (πᾶσαν ὑπερβασίην). Retaining control over the identity of the group around him, Odysseus ensures that their actions can continue to be evaluated as 'transgression' (ὑπερβασίη). As a result he secures the possibility of narrative closure. Suitors are suitors; they, together with the story, can be finished off accordingly.

Eurymachus' speech, like Eupeithes', confronts an actual *Odyssey* with a 'potential' counterpart at a point of high narrative crisis. In these two extreme cases of anxiety the *laoi* are cast as an obstacle to the narrative process. Only if 'companions' (ἑταῖροι) really are companions and 'suitors' (μνηστῆρες) remain suitors (μνηστῆρες) at all times can the

---

[344] *Od.* 22.54. [345] *Od.* 22.61–4.

story take its course. Yet, suitors in the *Odyssey* are never just suitors and from time to time companions are *laoi*. Far from solving the uncertainties it has accumulated over thousands of hexameter lines, the *Odyssey* continues on its ever more ambivalent path.

Eurymachus makes no exception. Misguided as he may seem, his speech is still part of the same play with possibilities. Consider, for example, its opening lines. In Eurymachus' words Odysseus is called 'Ithacan' ('Ιθακήσιος), the suitors are 'Achaeans'.[346] As Odysseus himself did in the cave of the Cyclops, Eurymachus plays out the generic ambiguities of a post-Iliadic existence. Without 'Achaeans' the man from Ithaca becomes a potentially marginal figure.[347] If the suitors are Achaeans and Odysseus allows them to be, he can hope to recover the world of epic song, which he has left behind.

Antinous tried too hard to take over on Ithaca.[348] Accordingly, he is handed over to be sentenced. Eurymachus, by contrast, apart from offering an Achaean frame to an action set in Ithaca, insinuates further privileges for the future: 'your people' (λαῶν σῶν) suggests that Odysseus might win for himself the renown of a leader of the people, a renown which is all the more desirable because it is built on the opposite of Agamemnon's infamous 'I destroyed the people'. A new Alcinous is in the making.

I have already suggested that the change of Odysseus' persona cannot but affect everyone around him. 'Suitors' can be the suitors of a woman, here Penelope; but they cannot be the 'suitors of Odysseus'. At the moment where the narrative focus shifts from Penelope to Odysseus, when the woman on display is no longer available, but becomes herself a function of the protagonist, the group's identity is radically destabilised. Alcinous on Scherie was 'famous among all the people', not (of course) 'all the suitors'. Odysseus as a leader can be

---

[346] *Od.* 22.45f.
[347] There is no phrase of the form 'people of the Ithacans' (*λαὸς 'Ιθακησίων). The combination 'suitors of the Achaeans' (μνηστῆρες 'Αχαιῶν) occurs only in *Od.* 2.87.
[348] *Od.* 22.52.

'blameless' (ἀμύμων) or 'reckless' (ἀτάσθαλος) among his *laoi*. But it is hard to see how he can be anything among 'suitors'.

The word 'σῶν' ('your') in Eurymachus' speech, placed in heavy enjambment,[349] gives a typically Odyssean twist to this last point. We have seen in chapter 1 that Homer's people are not usually owned by anyone, at least not in the sense in which commodities such as sheep can be owned and consumed.[350] Rather, the single agent who interacts with *laoi* takes on a task, as does a shepherd of flocks (the owner is not the shepherd but the master). The *Odyssey* on the whole respects this. But while it takes on board traditional language and ideas it also shifts the vantage point from group to leader. Mentor in book 2, the giants in book 7, Alcinous among his people, all testify to the same tendency. Seen in the light of Iliadic usage, Eurymachus' speech implies a threat: if he and his peers are Odysseus' people, he has all the more reason to respect their impunity. For the Odyssean reader it entails a promise: if Odysseus spares these people, they will be his. The traditional epic model of the *ποιμὴν λαῶν (the shepherd) has finally been converted into that of a master, ἄναξ λαῶν.

In her discussion of this episode, Murnaghan remarks that '[Odysseus] does not enter negotiations with the suitors but begins to attack them at once'.[351] I have argued for a rather more complicated scenario. Eurymachus threatens and pleads. He pays tribute to a changed social context. He is the 'weak spot' where generic anxieties come to the fore. Without claiming to have exhausted the passage, I would like to close my discussion by looking at one final issue. If Odysseus were to accept Eurymachus' suggestion, the result would be something like the picture of the *laoi* we have seen so often throughout the epic: peaceful stagnation. This is perhaps the ultimate threat behind the crisis in book 22. Odysseus might turn out to be a leader of people too soon. He might not be able to do what only a man among suitors can do. Eupeithes

---

[349] The term 'enjambment' needs to be qualified; see Bakker (1990). What is meant here is a striking case of 'runover adjective' as described by Edwards (1966) 140–3.
[350] See above ch. 1, ' "Shepherd of the people" ' and 'Privilege and obligation'.
[351] Murnaghan (1987) 56.

later in the narrative threatens to prevent the Odyssean story of companions from being closed. Similarly, Eurymachus threatens that the story of return and revenge prematurely collapses into silence. The prophecy of Teiresias can remind us how much this runs counter to the *Odyssey*'s narrative plans. Odysseus must die before Homer's people are finally allowed to take over.[352]

The *laoi* are never far from the narrative surface of the *Odyssey*, and they also stay with us in the last phase of the suitors' unfortunate career. They are never again explicitly equated with Homer's people; but, under the leadership of Agelaos, 'he who leads the *laos*',[353] they very narrowly are. Agelaos has his moment of glory when the three former leaders of the suitors, Antinous, Eurymachus and Amphinomus, have been killed. After their death the battle takes an Iliadic turn.[354] It is at this point that Agelaos (here in the Attic/Ionic form Ἀγέλεως) delivers his first speech:

> ὦ φίλοι, οὐκ ἂν δή τις ἀν' ὀρσοθύρην ἀναβαίη
> καὶ εἴποι λαοῖσι, βοὴ δ' ὤκιστα γένοιτο;
> τῷ κε τάχ' οὗτος ἀνὴρ νῦν ὕστατα τοξάσσαιτο.[355]

> Dear friends, could not one man slip away, through the side door,
> and tell the people? So the hue and cry could be most quickly
> raised, and perhaps this man will now have shot for the last time.

The first thing Agelaos tries to do in his new role as a leader of the suitors is to call in the people. By now we know that this is misguided, and it will not surprise us to find that the attempt is thwarted in due course. The narrative route towards the *laoi* is quite literally blocked.[356] After this necessary clarification,

---

[352] See above pp. 101f.
[353] *LfgrE s.v.*; von Kamptz (1982) 36f. suggests that the name bears no significance ('nicht sprechend'). However, we may safely assume that the allusion to the *laoi* was understood at least from the fifth century onward; cf. A. *Pers.* 297 and fr. 406 (Radt), Ar. *Eq.* 163f., Call. *Lav. Pall.* 130, Hesch. *s.v.* Ἀγεσίλαος; *Et. Gen. s.v.* Ἀγησίλαος καὶ Ἀγεσίλαος; Homeric passages such as *Il.* 2.580 (ἄγε λαούς, 'he led the people') suggest that the same is true for epic audiences; there may be a play on Agelaos' name in *Od.* 22.299 (ἀγελαῖαι, 'in a herd').
[354] *Od.* 22.101ff.
[355] *Od.* 22.132–4.
[356] *Od.* 22.136–8.

the narrator adorns the ensuing battle with allusions to the *laoi* wherever it seems opportune. Agelaos himself and the way he acts,[357] Odysseus' identification of Athena as 'stirring/ saving the people' (λαοσσόος),[358] and, finally, the scene in which the king kills his last opponent with the sword of Agelaos all contribute to this general impression.

The last suitor to be killed is Leiodes. Much could be said about his status as a would-be soothsayer, the pair which he forms with Phemius the bard, etc. For now let us concentrate on the circumstances of his death.[359] As is the case earlier in the epic, the possibility of closure, of finally completing the homecoming and the revenge, is once again at the forefront of narrative concern. Leiodes' name has most convincingly been explained by modern etymologists as 'he who pleases the *laos*'.[360] No such suggestion has survived from antiquity, and it is possible that the name was not connected with Homer's people at an early stage; yet, given that Leiodes comes last in a row of two other, clearly relevant figures,[361] it is tempting to think that his name should be significant, too. But be that as it may, he is certainly killed in a telling way.

Eurymachus, Eupeithes and Agelaos denied Odysseus the right to close his story by destroying the groups around him. In doing so they invoked the right of the Homeric *laos* to live. Leiodes interferes with Odyssean narrative teleology (τέλος νόστοιο) at an even more fundamental level.[362] Odysseus himself suggests that, as far as Leiodes is concerned, he would have been lost. His *nostos* would have ended 'far away' (τηλοῦ), it would have spun no narrative thread between Troy and Ithaca. Against this most fundamental suspicion that might occur to an Odyssean audience, the suspicion that Odysseus should never have made it home – against this voice

---

[357] E.g. ὄτρυνε ('he stirred') *Od.* 22.241.
[358] *Od.* 22.210; for meaning and parallels see above ch. 1, n. 123.
[359] *Od.* 22.326–9.
[360] Fick–Bechtel 2 (1894) 397, von Kamptz (1982) 76, 107, 206, *LfgrE s.v.*
[361] Agelaos in *Od.* 22.293 (here referred to by his patronymic), Leocritus in *Od.* 22.294.
[362] *Od.* 22.322f.

that never stops,[363] the protagonist draws the sword of Agelaos, 'he who leads the *laos*'.

I hesitate to spell out the implications of this extraordinary gesture. First, and most obviously, we have found a new 'leader of the people' (*agelaos*); a man, whose links with the people are characterised by the sword he uses against his opponents; a leader who cuts throats. More to the point, perhaps, we have found a new people amidst the bodies of those who only some 300 lines earlier claimed to be precisely that, Odysseus' *laoi*. But none of this captures the breathtaking violence of the event. One needs to reread the texts of early Greek epic many times in order to appreciate what it means for such a text to draw 'the sword of *agelaos*'. And even then the worst is yet to come. We cannot be appalled by what we hear without feeling relieved.

The people at the end

We have reached a climactic moment in Odysseus' dealings with Homer's people. In an unprecedented gesture of social and narrative violence, Odysseus has drawn the sword of Agelaos. Companions and suitors are now gone and only the people left. There has been growing unrest towards the end of the epic as to what status, precisely, we are to assign to the groups involved. The redefinition of the 'suitors' as *laoi* in book 22 is repeated for 'companions' in book 24. In each case the proposition is rejected by authorised speakers and the proponent is killed. Both passages represent a 'misreading' of large parts of the *Odyssey* – traditional to the genre and therefore easy to believe, but 'misreadings' none the less. When Odysseus gets ready for his final battle no such clarification is offered any longer.

Under the leadership of Eupeithes, the Ithacans have decided to attack Odysseus and his supporters.[364] The two

---

[363] *Od.* 22.329.
[364] For the question whether or not we should read the end of the *Odyssey* see above n. 295.

armies meet outside the hut of Eumaeus, Eupeithes is killed by Laertes, and a general slaughter ensues. At this point Athena intervenes:

> καί νύ κε δὴ πάντας ὄλεσαν καὶ ἔθηκαν ἀνόστους,
> εἰ μὴ Ἀθηναίη, κούρη Διὸς αἰγιόχοιο,
> ἤϋσεν φωνῇ, κατὰ δ' ἔσχεθε λαὸν ἅπαντα.[365]
>
> And now they would have killed them all, and given none of them homecoming, had not Athena, daughter of Zeus of the aegis, cried out in a great voice and held back all the people.

Our scene is parallel to that in which Eurymachus redefined his group. A leader has been killed, and we are waiting for the final showdown. At this point Athena comes *ex machina* to stop the slaughter, and she does so by holding back 'all the people'.[366] The *laos* finally enters the narrative foreground. What Eurymachus, Agelaos and Eupeithes had so often suggested in vain is now reality. Yet, the entry is abortive, the *laoi* come on stage only to be arrested. Note that it is them, not Odysseus and his men, who are first 'held back'. After some problems with stopping Odysseus on the other side, peace is made and the text collapses into silence. I have argued that the crisis of redefinition in book 22 threatens precisely that at a premature point. We have now reached the moment where silence is allowed to take over.

The group dies for its leader

Following the *Odyssey* as it steers between *laoi* on the one hand and 'companions/suitors' on the other, it has become clearer just how crucial the former are to the making of this text. In a sense the same had already been true for the *Iliad*, but the phenomenon takes on rather different implications in the *Odyssey*. Here Homer's people function as a point of reference against which the main actors are defined. Being primarily about suitors and companions, the epic constantly hints at and moves toward that other group, whose presence

---
[365] *Od.* 24.528–30.
[366] Cf. *Il.* 11.758 and the discussion in ch. 2, '*Laoi* in the *Iliad*', pp. 84–7.

in turn becomes a source of narrative anxiety. We have seen some of the forces that are at work in this curious balancing-act. Without the *laoi*, generic continuities break down and narrative goals are lost sight of. On the other hand, the very term *laos* has implications which are unwelcome and need to be rejected.

Having so far approached the *Odyssey* mainly in connection with Homer's people, I would now like to have a closer look at the suitors and companions who supersede them. Why do they become the Odyssean groups *par excellence*? In Teiresias' prophecy, 'companions' (ἑταῖροι) and 'suitors' (μνηστῆρες) perish while Odysseus survives. *Laoi*, by contrast, survive the protagonist. One conclusion to be drawn from this is that the Odyssean Odysseus and the *laoi* of epic exclude one another. Anchises in the *Homeric hymn to Aphrodite* prays to grow old among prospering *laoi*.[367] The Odyssean version of the same scenario is characteristically exclusive: the people prosper at the moment of Odysseus' death.

For the *Odyssey*, as for any other text of early Greek hexameter, the formulaic narrative that above all characterises the people is 'he destroyed the people' (ὤλεσε λαόν). If Odysseus is the eternal survivor who must forever defy the constraints of negative reciprocity, he and the *laoi* cannot easily coexist. But Odysseus in the *Odyssey* is not merely the given in the trivial sense that the epic sings his fame and cannot therefore also sing his blame. Rather, in telling the tale of his survival, the text transforms epic preoccupations with the *laos* into someting quite different. Its main means of doing so are precisely the two concepts which I intend to study for the rest of this chapter: ἑταῖροι, 'companions', and μνηστῆρες, 'suitors'.

The *laoi* of early epic are in constant conflict with the single agent's need to assert himself and his fame. By making Homer's characters part of a social project – and in a way which exposes their shortcomings – the all-pervasive concept of the 'shepherd of the people' almost inevitably exposes them to blame (νέμεσις, νεικεῖν). We have seen how this problem was

---

[367] *h. Ven.* 103–6.

addressed by the Iliadic Achilles. Odysseus takes a different approach. He too turns on its head a traditional pattern. Like Achilles, Odysseus feeds on collective disaster; but, unlike Achilles, he does not pay for it. Odysseus' social violence is 'clean'. His slaughter of two generations of Ithacans not only brings him personal fame but is also presented as socially uplifting; in the end the people around him flourish. For this arrangement to be successful, the *Odyssey* needs groups that are less protected and more teleologically dynamic than the *laoi*. It needs, in short, groups that die for the sake of the protagonist. This is true in different ways for both companions and suitors. In order to see the full implications of the concepts in question, we need to take a short detour into the early epic usage. Once again I start with Odysseus' companions.[368]

The formulaic systems surrounding the epic word 'companion' are not as extensive as are those that cluster around the term *laos*, but they are nevertheless telling. The phrase 'staunch [?] companion' (ἐρίηρος ἑταῖρος) is the most common,[369] followed by 'trustworthy' or 'good companion' (πιστός/ἐσθλὸς ἑταῖρος) and others.[370] The epithet which I have translated 'staunch [?]' (ἐρίηρος) is almost exclusively used to qualify 'companions'.[371] Unfortunately its meaning is slightly obscure,[372] so that we will have to rely on 'trustworthy' and 'good' (πιστός/ἐσθλός) for semantic analysis. This is an inconvenience which does not, however, seriously impede the task.

Both 'trustworthy' (πιστός) and 'good' (ἐσθλός) are qualifying adjectives. They are among a number of other such words that occur together with the epic term for 'companion', and it is natural to assume that ἐρίηρος, whatever its precise meaning, belongs to the same category. We have hit upon a first

---

[368] For discussion of the companion in epic see Pinsent (1983) to whom this section is particularly indebted; see also Stagakis (1966), (1971), (1975), Ulf (1990) ch. 4.1, *LfgrE s.v.* with further literature. The overview offered here is tailored to the needs of the present discussion. It is not meant to be complete.
[369] It occurs 17 times in Homer.
[370] Each one of them occurs 9 times in Homer, including forms in the accusative and the nominative plural; taken together the two words form a metrical system.
[371] With the exception of ἐρίηρος ἀοιδός ('excellent [?] singer') in *Od.* 1.346, 8.62.
[372] *LfgrE s.v.*

difference between *laoi* and companions. Whereas the *laoi* are often quantified, but rarely qualified, it is inherent in the formulaic language of epic that 'companions' (ἑταῖροι) are constantly under judgement.[373] Another observation can be added. The plural form ἑταῖροι ('companions'), like the plural of *laos*, denotes a group of people. The singular ἑταῖρος ('companion'), unlike *laos*, does not. Singular and plural illuminate each other, and it is important never to forget their complementarity. Sometimes the texts play on it, as for example in *Od.* 8.581–6, where we, the audience, know from the proem that Odysseus has not lost 'a (one) companion' (ἑταῖρος, sing.) but many (ἑταῖροι, pl.). The sentimental thrust of the passage rests precisely on the tendency of 'companions' to refer to a group as a gathering of individuals. Whereas the Greek for 'people' (λαός or λαοί) can only refer to a group, the Greek for 'companion' (ἑταῖρος), even if used in the plural, focuses our attention on individuals. What this means becomes clearer when we look at the issue of naming.

Homeric companions are not named as a group. Instead we are often told their individual names. Homer's people on the other hand cannot be broken down in such a way. Where they are reduced to individual members we are left with 'someone' (τις) without a name.[374] As a group, then, 'companions' (ἑταῖροι) do not have a strong identity. Instead they are seen as a function of their superiors,[375] whom they are expected to support:[376]

σχέτλι', ἐπεὶ Σαρπηδόν' ἅμα ξεῖνον καὶ ἑταῖρον
κάλλιπες Ἀργείοισιν ἕλωρ καὶ κύρμα γενέσθαι,
ὅς τοι πόλλ' ὄφελος γένετο πτόλεΐ τε καὶ αὐτῷ.[377]

Terrible man, for you have left Sarpedon who is a guest and a comrade
to fall prey to the Argives and become their spoil,
He was a great support to the city and to you yourself.

[373] Cf. Pinsent (1983) 317, Ulf (1990) 128. In *Il.* 2.708f. the leader of *laoi* is judged 'good' (ἐσθλός).
[374] De Jong (1987a) collects and discusses the relevant passages.
[375] E.g. *Od.* 3.180–2; cf. Pinsent (1983) 316f. against Stagakis (1966) 415; see also Ulf (1990) 128, *LfgrE s.v.*
[376] This and pp. 130f. are indebted to Pinsent (1983).
[377] *Il.* 17.150–2.

Although Glaucus in this passage from the *Iliad* stresses Hector's obligation to help, his speech implies that the 'companion' (ἑταῖρος) commends himself because he proved useful in the first place. Idomeneus, too, when reminded of his duties, promises to be 'a staunch [?] companion' (ἐρίηρος ἑταῖρος) as originally agreed.[378] If a companion is judged 'staunch [?]' (ἐρίηρος), 'trustworthy' (πιστός) or 'good' (ἐσθλός), this is because he proves to be of continuous use to his superior friend. Often the qualifying adjective is further elaborated.[379] The question of perspective (of who sees whom) is particularly important here. While in a context of *laoi* we tend to look from the group to the single agent, in a context of companions we look at the group – as consisting of single agents – from the point of view of their superior.[380] Because the relationship between a leader and 'his' companions focuses on the needs and wishes not of the group but of the leader, any crisis of the group is seen in terms of the 'anger' or 'grief' (χόλος/ἄχος) the leader experiences.[381] 'Grief' (ἄχος) as a reaction to bereavement leads to πόθος/ποθή, the wish to regain what has been lost. I have already mentioned the use of ποθεῖν ('to long for') in connection with the people,[382] and I compared it with the 'longing' (ποθή) that overcomes Achilles at the death of Patroclus.[383] Just as suffering was assigned to the group where we refer to it as *laoi* and to its leader in a context of 'companions',[384] the longing for support (ποθεῖν, ποθή) changes sides according to context.

The loss of a companion who is 'good' (ἐσθλός) brings 'grief' (ἄχος) and 'longing' (ποθή) to his superior friend. The

---

[378] *Il.* 4.266f.
[379] E.g. *Il.* 9.584-6, 23.6.
[380] This may be reformulated in terms of spatial arrangement; note the recurrent phrases ἀμφὶ δ' ἑταῖροι ('around him the companions', 7 times in Homer) and πολέες/φίλοι δ' ἀμφ' αὐτὸν ἑταῖροι ('but around him many/dear companions', 7 times in Homer); see also the related passage in *Il.* 16.290.
[381] E.g. *Il.* 16.584f. for 'anger' and *Il.* 16.581 for 'grief'.
[382] *Il.* 2.708f.; see above ch. 1, 'An incurable imbalance'.
[383] *Il.* 19.315f., 319-21; see above n. 382.
[384] The disease in *Il.* 1.10, which is 'bad' (κακή) because it destroys the *laoi*, should be compared with Achilles' outburst in *Il.* 19.321f.

loss of a leader does the same to the *laoi*.[385] In both cases dependence of one side on the other is balanced by payment for good service. The currency is honour and material wealth. Like the successful leader of people, the successful companion can hope for τιμή ('honour').[386] This, of course, is once again an individualising factor in the making of the group, for it is in the very nature of Homeric honour that it cannot be equal for all.[387] Different companions develop different relationships to their superior friends, individual comrades stand out, and the group inevitably breaks up into its members.

Honour can be won by individual companions depending on how useful they prove to be; but it is also a means of reminding of his duties a companion who shows less enthusiasm than might be desirable.[388] As a 'shepherd of the people' the leader must do what is demanded of him. The 'staunch companion' is in a similar situation. The difference between the two can be summed up as one of focalising bias:[389] we find ourselves on the side of the leader in one instance and on that of the group in the other. This is perhaps the most essential difference between a context of *laoi* and one of 'companions' (ἑταῖροι).

Companions, like *laoi*, gather around single leader-figures. But the leader of companions is not, as he would be among *laoi*, subject to the group's needs. There is no 'shepherd of the companions' in early Greek hexameter poetry. In such contexts rewards for good service are not distributed from the group to the single companion but rather handed from the leading companion to the members of the group.[390] In response to the honour they receive, companions support their leaders in a way which is analogous to the shepherd who

---

[385] See above ch. 1, 'An incurable imbalance'.
[386] E.g. *Il.* 18.81.
[387] On the competitive nature of honour (τιμή) in Homer see e.g. Adkins (1960b), Yamagata (1994) ch. 8, esp. 131–3, where she also discusses relationships among companions (ἑταῖροι); see also Ulf (1990) 134.
[388] E.g. *Il.* 4.257–64 with the answer in *Il.* 4.266f.
[389] The concept is borrowed from de Jong (1987b).
[390] For this point see also above ch. 2, '*Laoi* in the *Iliad*', pp. 78–81.

looks after his people. Failure of the joint enterprise is typically blamed on the members of the group.

After this brief excursus we are now ready to return to the main argument. When choosing to tell a tale of companions rather than *laoi* the Odyssean narrator sets up a competing model of social interaction to the one which we have seen to dominate in the *Iliad*. In his universe, the leader is not there for his group, but the group for its leader. In this respect as in so many others, the *Odyssey* draws on a framework of already existing language and ideas. The *Iliad*, too, knows of relationships among companions; however, only in the *Odyssey* does the word compete with *laos*, only there is it employed to redress our view of social interaction on a large scale. Achilles was drawn back into the world of Homer's people precisely *because* he had companions. For Odysseus, 'companions' become a way of replacing them.

This is seen most strikingly in the proem. The epic, notoriously, opens with a sharp programmatic statement about groups and leaders.[391] In it Odysseus' men are characterised as 'companions', who are brought down by their own, misguided initiative.[392] We hear that they are 'fools' (νήπιοι) and we are told about their 'reckless behaviour' (ἀτασθαλίαι); all this on a return journey (νόστος), which is quite separate from that of their leader,[393] and in the course of which they destroy themselves. Odysseus is not in any sense responsible for their death. So far from being expected to 'save the people', Odysseus does extra hours when trying to save his companions. What this opening would sound like if rephrased in terms of *laoi* we know from Eupeithes' version in book 24.[394] It would

---

[391] *Od.* 1.1–8.
[392] For the narrative perspective conveyed by the Odyssean proem see Rüter (1969) 45, Clay (1976) 313–17 and (1983) 34–8, Pucci (1982) 40, 59 n. 19, Nagler (1990); Cook (1995) 32 sees a 'transfer of *atasthaliai* from the protagonist onto his *laos* in the *Odyssey*', glossing over the crucial transformation into 'companions' (ἑταῖροι).
[393] The fact that only the return (νόστος) of the companions, but not that of Odysseus, is mentioned in the proem of the *Odyssey* deserves more careful consideration than it has received so far; contrast Hor. *Ep.* 1.2.21.
[394] See above p. 108.

not make a comfortable story. The people of the giant king Eurymedon may be described as perishing 'by their own reckless folly';[395] but even the *Odyssey* could not hope to sustain for long this skewed picture of Homer's people against the pull of the genre.

Losing the people is stigmatised throughout early Greek hexameter poetry, including the *Odyssey* itself. Hector in the *Iliad* chooses to die in response to his mistake. Agamemnon weeps bitter tears over the thought that he might come back home 'with bad repute' (δυσκλεής), for having lost 'many people' (πολὺν λαόν).[396] Not so Odysseus. He loses everybody, but because his group is called 'companions' – and not, as Eupeithes suggests, *laoi* – this becomes an altogether different matter.

The Odyssean narrator, then, uses the term 'companion' not just because it happens to come with the tale he wants to tell. Rather, by raising them to the status of a highly charged gloss *vis-à-vis* the *laoi*, he makes a larger point about the relationship between single agent and group which seems specifically directed against an Iliadic understanding of Homer's people. Right from the beginning the *Odyssey* promotes its own version of social violence against the powerful model; and the implications for Odyssean story-telling are far-reaching indeed.

A group of companions, however large, can perish without laying blame on their leader. What is more, they can perish and thereby *make* their leader's fame, if that fame is to consist in individual bereavement and suffering. I have already pointed to the focalising bias in favour of the single agent, which is built into the Greek word ἑταῖρος ('companion'):[397] as has often been remarked, this bias is all-pervasive in the *Odyssey*,[398] and it manifests itself at many different levels. Consider the case of the so-called *Apologoi*. When Odysseus embarks on his first-person narrative in book 9, he promises

---

[395] See above pp. 103 and 115. [396] *Il.* 9.13–22.
[397] See above p. 131. [398] See especially Clay (1983) 34–8.

to tell the story of 'his return' (νόστον ἐμόν), which Zeus sends him (μοι).[399] But although he insists that the story is his, there is reason to believe that books 9–12 are at least as interested in the fate of Odysseus' men.[400] In most of the episodes some of them die. Odysseus' narrative ends as soon as all his companions are gone.[401]

For Odysseus to say that he sings about *his* return, then, is not so much a matter of narrative content as it is one of narrative perspective. Odysseus presents the story of his group as his own, true to what I have termed the 'overall focalising bias' of the epic.[402] Another, closely related move, is to call the group 'companions'. Alcinous combines the two when he guesses the reason for Odysseus' grief towards the end of book 8.[403] As he suspects, Odysseus grieves because of what happened to his companions, and the focalising effect of the term is brought home even more forcefully by the glosses he employs (πηός, κασίγνητος, 'kinsman', 'brother'). Odysseus' travels are his *because* they are about his companions.

That Alcinous has indeed hit upon a crucial point is obvious not only from the *Apologoi* themselves, but also from the proem and the versions of the plot given elsewhere in the text. When Teiresias, for example, predicts that Odysseus will return 'badly' he explains this by adding: 'having lost all your companions'.[404] On this reading, the catastrophe of the companions becomes the defining part of Odysseus' return.[405] Their fate is seen not as one aspect of their leader's suffering but as its most salient feature. Without their death, there can be no return, no *Odyssey*. Thus the decision to tell a tale of companions, not *laoi*, becomes programmatic to the extent

---

[399] *Od.* 9.37f.; cf. 9.12f., 15, 11.376.
[400] Olson (1995) ch. 3 and esp. 61.
[401] The Charybdis-narrative makes up for the lack of adventure on Odysseus' part with what is left over from the companions' catastrophe: *Od.* 12.426–46.
[402] Cf. Pucci (1997) 153: 'Because of this tremendous bias in favor of the narrator [i.e. Odysseus] we are attached to that "narrating I" who makes us see him in a privileged light, different from the others, suffering because of the others.'
[403] *Od.* 8.577f., 581, 584–6.
[404] *Od.* 11.113f.; cf. 2.174–6, 9.534.
[405] *Od.* 11.114 νεῖσθαι ('to return home').

that things could not be otherwise.[406] The misfortunes of the collective come to stand for those of its leader; they make his fame, as reported by the Odyssean Muse and by himself.

The narrative of lost companions shapes and explains the tale of Odysseus' travels in the wilderness. To elaborate this a little further I now turn to two supporting narratives of divine revenge. The wrath of Helios and that of Poseidon have sometimes been thought to exclude one another, with the result that one of them was athetised.[407] No such operation is necessary.[408] Far from interfering with one another, Helios and Poseidon offer two complementary views of Odysseus' disastrous return. One sheds light on the fate of the group, the other explains that of the leader.[409] And as we would expect in a text which makes the catastrophe of a group the cause for its leader's fame, the former is subsumed under the latter.[410]

The story of Helios' wrath is embedded in Poseidon's just as the downfall of the group is seen as a function of their leader's fame throughout the *Odyssey*. Helios guarantees the important element of innocence on Odysseus' part; hence his role at the beginning of the text and when the catastrophe itself is reported. I quote from the episode on Thrinacie:

> Ζεῦ πάτερ ἠδ' ἄλλοι μάκαρες θεοὶ αἰὲν ἐόντες,
> τῖσαι δὴ ἑτάρους Λαερτιάδεω Ὀδυσῆος.[411]
>
> Father Zeus, and you other everlasting and blessed
> gods, punish the companions of Odysseus, son of Laertes.

It is quite clear from what Helios says that the point of his revenge is not Odysseus' fate but that of his companions. Indeed, anything else would have come as a surprise. Odysseus

---

[406] Cf. Pucci (1997) 153f.; although he seems to use *laoi* to refer to Hesiod's *demos*, his remarks are pertinent here.
[407] E.g. Schwartz (1924), Pfeiffer (1928), Schadewaldt (1970).
[408] See Fenik (1974), Friedrich (1987), (1991), Segal (1994) 195–227.
[409] Thus already Pfeiffer (1928) col. 2362f. in the framework of an analyst reading.
[410] Divine wrath ('Götterzorn') in Homer is analysed by Irmscher (1950). Jörgensen (1904) studies narrative perspective and its effect on the divine. Segal (1994) takes a first step towards looking at the Odyssean gods as focalising devices. The present argument is indebted to him.
[411] *Od.* 12.377f.

does not want to land on Thrinacie in the first place;[412] he issues warnings;[413] he then goes off at the right moment and falls asleep.[414] The companions' activity alone leads to the sacrilege and consequently their demise.[415] The opposite is the case with the Poseidon-narrative, which embraces and accommodates the more narrowly defined one associated with Helios. Poseidon explains the catastrophe of the group as a function of their leader's. He brings back together what Helios keeps apart and puts it into the larger framework of Odyssean homecoming.

Helios is offended only by the companions and asks Zeus to take revenge on them alone. The Poseidon-narrative, by contrast, starts and ends with Odysseus.[416] Odysseus decides to meet Polyphemus against his men's will.[417] He provokes the curse – once more against their recommendation[418] – by giving away his name, ultimate guarantee of his fame.[419] In reply Polyphemus offers two alternative versions of Odysseus' homecoming.[420] The first one is 'no *nostos*'. But since Odysseus in the *Odyssey* has to return and live, his group must die for him: hence Polyphemus' second alternative, which is also that of Teiresias and the narrative at large.

The Odyssean story of lost 'comrades', with its complicated divine apparatus and elaborate supporting narratives of revenge, gives structure and direction to Odysseus' travels through the wilderness. Their death secures his narrative sur-

---

[412] *Od.* 12.260ff.
[413] *Od.* 12.297ff., 320ff.
[414] *Od.* 12.333ff.
[415] Earlier readers of the Thrinacie episode sometimes exculpate the group; see Focke (1943), Heubeck (1954). Today it is generally agreed that Odysseus' companions bring about their own downfall; see Andersen (1973), Tsagarakis (1982–3), Friedrich (1987), Olson (1995) ch. 3 and esp. 59–61; cf. 211f.
[416] Readers have often disagreed on whether the adventure with the Cyclops entails an act of transgression on Odysseus' part. See e.g. Friedrich (1991), *contra* Brown (1996). However, there seems to be little doubt that the problem – and hence the story – is his.
[417] *Od.* 9.224–30.
[418] *Od.* 9.494–500.
[419] *Od.* 9.502–5; note that Odysseus asks Polyphemus to spread (φάσθαι) his fame; cf. Cook (1995) 94.
[420] *Od.* 9.530–6.

vival; his good fame depends on their downfall. But Odyssean companions do not simply allow for the story of homecoming to be told. Rather, they help perform the crucial transformation into the 'first-person bias', that focalising stratagem which becomes a hallmark of the Odyssean narrative project. While the 'shepherd of the people' ought to save his people, Odyssean groups die for their leader.

The leader kills his group

I have argued for a view of Odysseus' companions as a group that dies for its leader. Similar things can be said about the suitors. They too become a function of Odysseus' good fame, which they help to articulate through their own collective downfall.[421] In Teiresias' prophecy, revenge (ἀποτίσεαι) and return (ἐλθών) are closely linked.[422] The narrative of homecoming is once again told at the expense of a group and to the advantage of the single agent; and, as was the case with Odysseus' companions, a supporting narrative of justice restored results in a tale which is even more forcefully directed than it would otherwise be.

Both companions and suitors die for the narrative survival of their leader, and they do so in contrast with epic *laoi*. I have argued that this contrast is in many ways at the heart of the *Odyssey*, as it redefines social interaction over and against the powerful model of Homer's people. However, the fate of Penelope's suitors does not simply replay the perspectival shift from *laoi* to 'companions' but adds a further, characteristic twist. If 'companions' die for their leader, 'suitors' die at his hands. They are not lost but killed; and killed not only with

---

[421] Little has been written on epic courtship. Most of the existing studies concentrate on marriage and the economic and social exchanges it involves; see e.g. Lacey (1966), Vernant (1980), Redfield (1982) with further literature. Scholarship on the Odyssean suitors tends to concentrate on what is perceived to be the 'political' impact of their existence. See e.g. Rose (1975), Farron (1979–80), Nicolai (1984), Halverson (1985) and (1986); see also Westrup (1930), Whitman (1958) 307, Donlan (1973) 152f.; the seemingly 'objective' problem how many suitors there are belongs here; see e.g. Kirchhoff (1879) 510, Bassett (1918) 43, Merkelbach (1969) 100, Dawe (1993) 607.
[422] *Od.* 11.113–18.

HOMER'S PEOPLE

the full knowledge of those involved, but also with the approval of the *Odyssey* itself and the narrative tradition at large.

Once again I start by giving an overview of the epic usage in so far as it is relevant here. I first ask how suitors are treated in the texts and how this compares to the other groups we have been looking at. *Laoi* in early Greek epic push toward the open end of permanent well-being.[423] This is particularly true for *laoi* in the *Odyssey*.[424] A group of 'companions' is less protected, and we have seen in the last section how this can be exploited by a narrative of communal catastrophe such as the one told in the *Odyssey*. Epic suitors are always on their way to an end.[425] In so far as a 'wedding', γάμος, is their only *raison d'être*, they form the most teleologically dynamic collective of early Greek hexameter. There are no suitors after marriage.

Another point is closely related. The group on its way to marriage is not only teleologically dynamic but also – as a group – left without a clear social function. Suitors as a collective serve no purpose other than that of disappearing as suitors. No one is obliged or even interested in sustaining suitors in the longer run, and there is little solidarity built into the group itself. In the place of mutual obligation we find merciless competition.[426] 'Companions' (ἑταῖροι), we recall, divide among themselves rewards (τιμή) bestowed by their leader. 'Suitors' compete for the only possible way of avoiding defeat. They are not only more teleologically directed than companions, but also less cohesive as a group.

They are also more threatened. This last point is of particular importance to the present discussion and therefore needs

---

[423] See above ch. 1 and esp. 'Society and the stone'.
[424] See above ch. 2, '*Laoi* in the *Odyssey*', pp. 110–26.
[425] For the meaning and possible etymologies of Greek μνηστήρ ('suitor') see Frisk (1960–70) *s.v.* μιμνήσκω, Chantraine (1968–80) *s.v.* μιμνήσκω, Thieme (1980), *LfgrE s.v.* μνάομαι.
[426] E.g. *Od.* 18.275–7, where μνηστεύειν ('to woo') in Penelope's words is glossed by ἀλλήλοις ἐρίζειν ('to compete/fight with one another'). When Redfield (1982) 182 argues that Greek marriage is 'usually conceived of as a problem for women', he is obviously not speaking with epic courtship in mind.

to be documented carefully. Here is a first example from Hesiod:

> ... οὐ γὰρ ἶσ[ον ἀμφοτέροισιν
> ἆθλον ἔκειθ'· ἦ μέν ῥα π[οδώκης δῖ' Ἀταλάντη   5
> ἵετ' ἀναινομένη δῶρα [χρυσῆς Ἀφροδίτης,
> τῷ δὲ περὶ ψυχῆς πέλε[το δρόμος, ἠὲ ἁλῶναι
> ἠὲ φυγεῖν...[427]

> ... for the two were not competing for
> the same prize; swift-footed godlike Atalante
> ran refusing the gifts of golden Aphrodite.
> But for him the race was for his life, between being caught
> or escaping...

In Atalante's race from the Hesiodic *Catalogue of women*, Hippomenes not only runs for a wife, but also for his life. Γάμος, 'marriage', is of course the end of the chase that Hippomenes himself would wish to bring about. But he can do so only by escaping the alternative end, death:

> καὶ δὴ ἔχεν δύο μῆλα ποδώκης δῖ' Ἀτ[αλάντη,
> ἐγγὺς δ' ἦν τέλεος· ὃ δὲ τὸ τρίτον ἧκε χ[αμᾶζε·
> σὺν τῷ δ' ἐξέφυγεν θάνατον καὶ κῆ[ρα μέλαιναν,
> ἔστη δ' ἀμπνείων καί [[428]

> And swift-footed, godlike Atalante had already two apples
> and he/she was close to the end; but he threw the third to the ground
> and with it he escaped death and black doom
> and stood panting, and ...

Hippomenes' victory appears to be at least as much a matter of escaping death as it is of winning a partner.[429] In fact, there is little to suggest a clear distinction between the two.[430] Who is close to what 'end' (τέλος) in v. 21? More probably Hippomenes to that of his dreams (γάμος), but the alternative of Atalante finally catching up on him (θάνατος) seems also possible. The ensuing ambiguity is not, I would suggest, a

---

[427] Hes. fr. 76.4–8 (M–W).
[428] Hes. fr. 76.20–3 (M–W).
[429] Cf. Pi. *P.* 9.121–3.
[430] Cf. *Od.* 17.476 (πρὸ γάμοιο τέλος θανάτοιο, 'before marriage the end of death'); cf. also *Od.* 24.124 (τέλος θανάτοιο, 'the end of death') and *Od.* 20.74 (τέλος γάμοιο, 'the end of marriage'). The gods of epic, who do not die, also do not marry; γάμος ('marriage') and related words are not normally used of them.

mere accident of clumsy versification. Rather, the fact that we (together with the narrative voice) are having difficulties separating the possible outcomes of the race reflects their close interrelation.

In the case of collective courtship, Hippomenes' alternative re-emerges as a differentiation into the lucky *one* 'man' (ἀνήρ) who reaches the 'goal of marriage' (τέλος γάμοιο) and the group of 'suitors' (μνηστῆρες) who do not.[431] Epic 'suitors' (μνηστῆρες) never marry, which means that as a group they are inevitably doomed. Doomed to lose face (τιμή), lose a household (οἶκος), and finally, lose a life. The suitors of Helen as described in fragments 196–204 of the Hesiodic *Catalogue of women* may serve as a good example. At first sight they look reassuringly long-lived. The wooing itself takes place in a peaceful and orderly fashion, and there is no hint of a violent show-down at the end. However, on closer inspection we discover the pattern outlined above.

Tyndareos' famous oath highlights the basic problem: group solidarity up to and beyond 'the end of marriage' (τέλος γάμοιο) has to be *enforced* by an oath which 'everyone' (πάντες) only takes because they hope for a way out:

> ... τοὶ δ' ἀπτερέως ἐπίθον[το
> ἐλπόμενοι τελέειν πάντες γάμον· ἀλλ' ἄ[ρα πάντας
> Ἀτρε[ίδ]ης ν[ίκησε]ν ἀρηΐφιλος Μενέλαος
> πλεῖ[στ]α πορών...[432]
>
> ... and they obeyed quickly,
> hoping all to accomplish the marriage; but the
>   son of Atreus defeated them all [?],
> Menelaus who is dear to Ares,
> giving the most gifts ...

The very insistence with which the word 'everyone' (πάντες) recurs in this context (vv. 40, 45, 47a and possibly 47b) reminds us that only one of Helen's suitors will in the end be

---

[431] Hes. fr. 204.18 (M–W) is the only passage in early Greek hexameter poetry where the word 'suitor' occurs in the singular; interestingly, it describes a 'suitor' who does not actually exist. For the 'man' in marriage see e.g. *Il.* 6.350, 24.60, *Od.* 16.77, 20.335; cf. also *Il.* 3.49.
[432] Hes. fr. 204.46–9 (M–W).

successful. In fact, whatever the outcome of their competition, the group as a whole must lose it. This may have been implied in line 47 of fragment 204. But even if we discount the verse as doubtfully restored, the juxtaposition of the group and the lucky *one* in vv. 48f. of the same fragment is telling enough: 'suitors' as such have nothing to win.

In the catalogue of Helen's suitors, as elsewhere in early Greek hexameter poetry, the group of suitors cannot succeed as a whole. Judging from the Hippomenes–Atalante story and the logic of 'marriage or death' this means that all the Achaeans have to die, for they are all 'hoping to accomplish the marriage' (ἐλπόμενοι τελέειν ... γάμον ... v. 47). This is indeed how Hesiod motivates the end of the demigods in the *Catalogue of women*. His Achaeans are of course not killed on the spot for being unsuccessful courtiers. However, in the long run the somewhat artificial prolongation of their status as suitors has precisely this effect.[433] Unfortunately, fragment 204 is incomplete and may be corrupt in parts. But the *nexus* between death outside Troy and the courtship of Helen is clear: Helen's suitors must die.[434]

In Hesiod, the end of the suitors is also the end of an era. The *Odyssey* is less ambitious than that, although end-of-the-world imagery plays its role there too.[435] The emphasis, at any rate, is elsewhere, namely on the fact that the 'man' has been found before the wooing even started. This refocusing of our group is important for what suitors become in the *Odyssey*, but it does not fundamentally alter what has been argued so far. Homer's people as a group have all the sympathy of the epic tradition; μνηστῆρες, 'suitors', have none.

We have reached the moment at which the argument could be substantiated and modified by a close study of Penelope's

---

[433] Hes. fr. 204.58–62 (M–W); cf. Hes. *Op.* 161–73.
[434] It may be significant that Menelaus, who wins the hand of Helen and survives the war, does not himself appear as a suitor; similarly, we may note that Odysseus, another survivor, knows the outcome of the competition in advance and therefore woos from a distance. Such details would have posed a challenge to the narrative skills of the Hesiodic bard without necessarily affecting his overall model.
[435] As discussed in Auffarth (1991).

suitors in the *Odyssey*. I have suggested that the Odyssean picture is in some ways typical of suitors in epic, more typical perhaps than has been acknowledged so far. And yet, it is equally clear that the *Odyssey* develops what it finds in a very specific direction. Odyssean suitors are illegitimate from the start. They are cast as perverse guests who eat up a household without engaging in any of the activities associated with traditional courtship.[436] They have been suitors for too long, and more than once the suspicion arises that they are all too happy with their lives without a future. When the members of this group finally enter the contest which defines them as suitors, there can be no lucky *one* among them because the 'man' (ἀνήρ) has long been found.[437] All this deserves careful study, which cannot be undertaken here.[438] Rather than going into further detail, let us return to the question how 'suitors', the Odyssean group, complete the transformation of Homer's people into the Odyssean world as seen with the 'first-person bias'.

There are no 'suitors' in the *Iliad*. Even at the basic level of word usage they represent the Odyssean alternative to Homer's people in its most uncompromising form. I have tried to capture some of the implications this has for the present argument. If Homer's people must live, Odyssean suitors *must* die. Violence is always in the air in the context of epic courtship, but the *Odyssey* in particular encourages us to think of 'the man' slaughtering 'the suitors' as something necessary and proper. Iliadic leaders die for not having rescued their people. The Odyssean 'first-person bias' is most fully asserted at the point where the potential leader kills his (potential) group.

I have argued that this situation is created in stages. There is a narrative *crescendo* from the fate of Odysseus' companions to that of Penelope's suitors in the *Odyssey* which

---

[436] For the relationship between 'courtship' (μνηστύς) and 'guest friendship' (ξενίη) see e.g. Levy (1963), Reece (1993) ch. 8.
[437] As we are constantly reminded in bks. 21–2.
[438] For further study of the Odyssean suitors see above n. 421; see also Allen (1939), Saïd (1979), Matsumoto (1981), Byre (1988), Nagler (1990), Katz (1991), Scheid-Tissinier (1992), Olson (1995) ch. 10.

gradually transforms and eventually subverts the defining features of life among the *laoi*. As we have seen, this process directly involves Homer's people themselves. Indeed, it is integrated into a larger movement towards the well-being of the *laoi* outside the narrative. The model picture of Phaeacia, the perfect world of the 'blameless king', the end of the war and the narrative in book 24 can all be seen as stages on our journey toward the end of ends as prophesied by Teiresias: Odysseus dies among the prospering people. Paradoxically, then, the shift of narrative interest from Homer's people to 'suitors' in the *Odyssey*, which can be read as a sustained attack on the needs and privileges of the *laoi*, is at the same time presented as a salutary social operation on their behalf. The people are dead, long live the people.

Conclusion

I have argued for a reading of the *Odyssey* which acknowledges the importance of Homer's people as well as addressing the question why they are superseded by 'companions' and 'suitors'. *Laoi* are present throughout and serve to assert generic continuity as well as marking a narrative goal. At the same time, the *Odyssey* rejects any deeper thematic continuities. Against what I have called the *laos* ideology of early Greek epic, it refuses to assume that the leader has to save his group. Like Achilles, Odysseus turns around the well-known picture; but whereas Achilles has to pay dearly for his decision, Odysseus comes out on top.

If the *Iliad* is the *laos* epic of early Greek hexameter *par excellence*, the *Odyssey* is in many ways its counterpart. It would be misleading to say that it is uninterested in the plight of the *laoi*, but there is a striking difference in approach. The *Iliad* sees their situation as deeply problematic and fundamentally beyond reform. By contrast, the *Odyssey*, telling the story of Odysseus among 'companions' (ἑταῖροι) and the 'man' among 'suitors' (μνηστῆρες), promises progress by singling out two groups of 'non-people' which it destroys in the interest of the larger whole.

At one level, then, the *Odyssey* overturns the vision of responsible leadership which it inherits. The group dies for its leader. However, this act of rearrangement is presented in terms of a second, no less interesting one. The loss and killing of Odysseus' groups, who are so pointedly refused the status of *laoi*, points toward the welfare of the *laoi* themselves. Internal violence, if understood 'rightly', benefits the whole. Achilles was brought down because 'companions' and 'people' could not be neatly separated. In the *Odyssey* this separation is upheld against all odds. To be sure, Eupeithes, Eurymachus or Agelaos would have told a different story. To them the people killed by their own (potential) leader is a scandal as it would be a scandal by Iliadic standards. By Odyssean standards – and in Odyssean terminology – it is not only possible but also necessary.

When all is said and done, we return to the *laoi* and their leader; this time without a bloodbath. As was the case at the end of the *Iliad*, aetiological progress is in the air. And again, this progress is not itself narrated. The oaths are hardly taken and all is over. And yet, there is a clearer sense this time that a new and better world is in the making, a world which Teiresias at least can already foresee. What the *Iliad* only hints at as a possibility becomes a promise in the *Odyssey*; and what is a promise in the *Odyssey* becomes self-assured retrospective in other archaic and classical texts. The people in these texts have long been saved. Outside Homer, the *laoi* leave behind their suffering to become what we might call the 'founding people' of successful institutional structures. What this could mean for the performance of Homeric poetry will be discussed in the third and last chapter of this study.

3
LAOS EPIC IN PERFORMANCE

In chapter 1 I argued that the *laoi* of epic are a group of people situated at the most basic level of survival, a group, moreover, that is left without effective social structures and as a result is prone to communal catastrophe, as expressed in the traditional phrase 'he destroyed the people' (ὤλεσε λαόν). Early Greek hexameter poetry sometimes hints at the possibility of institutional progress but generally suppresses it. Unmitigated crisis is at the centre of its concerns.

In chapter 2 we saw that Homeric epic is song about the *laoi* in a thematically significant way. Achilles' story in the *Iliad* is based on their destruction. The epic does not tell of the fall of Troy – which Agamemnon hopes for and Hector fears – but instead the catastrophe of the people on both sides. The *Iliad* openly asserts the importance of the people for Homeric narrative, and in so doing deplores their institutional weakness. The *Odyssey* takes a different approach. Here 'companions' (ἑταῖροι) and 'suitors' (μνηστῆρες) take the place of *laoi*. The people themselves are removed from the narrative foreground and promised a future life in bliss.

In a third and last step I wish to reformulate the questions of language and text I have studied so far, in terms of performance and occasion. As I shall argue, the fact that the *Iliad* and to a lesser extent the *Odyssey* are song about the *laoi* is significant for their earliest performances, too.

Homer's people are the typical audience of public speech.[1] More specifically, they are an audience of epic.[2] The Odyssean narrator does not tell us explicitly that epic is sung to the

---
[1] For speech-making among Homer's people see ch. 1, pp. 34f., 38 with n. 107, and 41 with n. 120.
[2] *Od.* 8.471f., 13.27f.: cf. also Hes. *Op.* 768.

assembled people, but it is hard to see why he calls the bard 'honoured by the people' (λαοῖσι τετιμένον) if he does not assume this to be the case. Archaic Greek listeners at least must have assumed it for Homer himself, as is shown by the testimony of Simonides:

> οὕτω γὰρ Ὅμηρος ἠδὲ Στασίχορος ἄεισε λαοῖς.[3]
>
> For this is what Homer and Stesichorus sang to the people.

Simonides refers to a hypothetical 'original' performance in which Homer – and Stesichorus – sang (ἄεισε) to the people (λαοί). It is as yet unclear how this relates to a historical audience. But whatever the answer to that question, Simonides' words certainly invite us to study the relationship between the *laoi* within Homer's text and their counterpart, the *laos*, or *leos*, outside it.[4] In the following pages I propose to do just that. I wish to ask whether there were, in archaic and classical Greece, contexts of performance which correspond to Simonides' paradigmatic 'singing to the people', and if so, what they can contribute to our understanding of the texts.

This chapter, then, brings to completion a gradual shift. I started by discussing early Greek epic as a genre which embraces all texts and occasions. Chapter 2 looked at the ways in which the epic tradition is explored in Homer, allowing for a variety of performance contexts, but limiting the range of texts under consideration. In this third chapter I aim to come as close as possible to the historically unique *Gesamtkunstwerk* of Homeric epic sung to an early audience of *laoi*. The new task also poses a new challenge. So far we have been able to rely on a relatively well-preserved, relatively unified body of text. In many ways the material studied in this last section

---

[3] Simon. fr. 564.4 (*PMG*); for other audiences as *laoi* see Pi. *P.* 12.22–4, fr. 42.3f., B. 13.228–31, Sus. fr. 1 (West), Ar. *V.* 1015f., *Ra.* 676, *Th.* 39; discussion on pp. 174ff.
[4] *Leos* is the Attic form, which on the whole is synonymous with Homeric and Panhellenic *laos*; in order to avoid cumbersome repetitions I do not always cite both versions where one might expect them (for example the statement that 'the word *laos* is rare in archaic and classical Greek prose' is true for both forms). Where specific passages are discussed I follow their usage; for the special case of *leos* ritual see n. 98; for an attempt to interpret the difference between the two forms see n. 180.

of the argument is neither. There exist no detailed records of early performances of Homeric poetry, and as a consequence we shall have to draw on a wide range of more or less tangential, more or less disparate sources.

Two problems arise. First, it is difficult to treat all these sources with an equal amount of attention. Future study will inevitably bring to light details which the present study plays down or overlooks. Secondly, it is in the nature of the argument that it approaches a performance context on the basis of recorded text. Performances, however, cannot be reduced to written text alone.[5] Neither of these problems is easily overcome, and the primary aim of this chapter is not to demonstrate that they can be. In other words, I do not here wish to provide a full account of Homer's people in the texts of archaic and classical Greece; nor do I intend to capture in detail any actual occasion of epic performance. Rather, it is my hope that by the end of the chapter some performative parameters will have emerged; parameters which can be of use to our understanding of Homer's people and so of Homer's texts.

Some preliminary considerations

It has become a commonplace of classical scholarship to posit a close link between Athenian tragedy and fifth-century Athenian civic discourse. After the ground-breaking work carried out by Vernant and others,[6] few scholars today would not feel the need to locate tragedy in its historical and social context. In the words of Goldhill:

> If we wish to understand the force and direction of Greek tragedy, it is impossible not to bring into consideration the city of Athens, which gave rise to the institution of the tragic festivals and which ... can be regarded as offering specific conditioning to its dramas.[7]

---

[5] For the role of performance in the study of oral poetry see Lord (1960), Finnegan (1977); for Homer see Nagy (1979), (1996b).
[6] E.g. Vernant and Vidal-Naquet (1988).
[7] Goldhill (1986) 57; see also Goldhill (1990), (1997).

The lawcourt, the assembly, the hoplite warfare of the Athenian citizen-body, the various public rituals that were dispersed over the calendar year, together with less tangible aspects of world-view, form a web of implications and assumptions that come into play whenever the theatre of Dionysus fills for performance. As has often been pointed out, this is not a matter of mere 'reception'. The *theates* is not a passive witness to a spectacle put on for him by 'the authorities' or 'the poet'. Rather, as Longo argues,[8] his role as a participant is mirrored in the very structure of our plays.

Today such volumes as *Nothing to do with Dionysos?* and *The Cambridge companion to Greek tragedy* bear witness to thirty years of scholarship on the tragic performance, the tragic audience and the civic ideology behind them both.[9] As a result of this activity the project of exploring tragedy in its context, although far from complete and in itself inexhaustible,[10] has taken on revolutionary dimensions. This has no parallel in Homeric studies.

Ever since Parry and Lord[11] argued that Homeric poetry is deeply rooted in early Greek performance contexts, the problem of an appropriately context-oriented response has been on the agenda of classical scholars. On the one hand critics such as Muellner,[12] Foley,[13] and Kahane[14] developed sophisticated ways of reading the epic formula, thus paving the way for a study of Homeric culture as it is stored in the recurrent phrase and theme. Others were more concerned with the connection between text and language on a larger scale, arguing that what the Greeks came to subsume under the label 'Homer' does not so much reflect the activity of an 'actual' source, but rather provides the authorised stage where song is

---

[8] Longo (1990), first published in 1978.
[9] Winkler and Zeitlin (1990), Easterling (1997).
[10] How precisely tragedy would have been received in its historical setting is still subject to lively debate; see for example the recent challenge to 'democratic' readings led by Griffith (1995) and (1998).
[11] E.g. Parry (1971), Lord (1960), (1991), (1995).
[12] Muellner (1976) and (1996).
[13] Foley (1991).
[14] Kahane (1992), (1994).

SOME PRELIMINARY CONSIDERATIONS

to be 'found', claimed and displayed afresh from performance to performance. Different traditions of song compete for this stage, each offering different possibilities of what 'Homer' could be. Considerable critical sophistication was brought into play to explore how the shape and meaning of our epics reflect this ongoing process of agonistic recomposition.[15]

Formulaic studies on the one hand, and a more thematic approach to the epic tradition on the other, provided the methodological frame I have so far used in an attempt to describe the place of Homer's people in the story-telling of early Greek epic. Having thus far aimed at locating the concept within Greek hexameter poetry and Homer in particular, I now attempt to situate my findings within the context of archaic and classical Greek performances. Since there is no established way of doing this, my investigation will have to depend on a methodological experiment which is not altogether unproblematic.

There are good reasons why Homeric epic has not so far seen the close contextual scrutiny that has so successfully been applied to tragedy and the City Dionysia. Early evidence for performance is scanty, while later accounts abound with tendentious and anachronistic glosses.[16] One watershed has been particularly important. Mainly through Athenian influence, the performance and reception of Homeric poetry changed character dramatically in the sixth and fifth centuries. Since any earlier traces cannot be recovered beyond what is found in the texts themselves, there has seemed to be little hope for improvement. The ensuing *aporia* is stated succinctly by Redfield, who, as an honourable way out of the problem, recommends self-enlightened resignation: 'We should not speak of the "background" of the poems, as though we could reconstruct Homeric society and then apply this reconstruction to interpretation of the poems.'[17] Although Redfield acknowledges that a historically specific early context for our reading

---

[15] E.g. Nagy (1979), Sinos (1980), Clay (1983).
[16] For collections of the relevant material see n. 23.
[17] Redfield (1975) xi; cf. Silk (1987) 27f.

of Homer would be desirable, he is sceptical as to whether we will ever be able to find one. For him as for so many other readers, Greek epic is uttered into a space which lies *before* contexts. Homer in particular occupies that mythical position of absolute beginning about which no further questions can be fruitfully asked.

Redfield's is not the only possible response to our impasse, and in the wake of the 'tragic revolution' as we might call it there have been attempts at doing precisely what he says cannot be done. Three different approaches may be singled out. First, scholars have tried to place the Homeric poems in the historical context of dark age and archaic Greece. Others fuse text and occasion by studying the performative assumptions inherent in Homeric epic. Finally, some critics have argued that the Homeric poems can profitably be read in the context of archaic and classical ritual practice.

I have already mentioned the large group of scholars who try to locate the Homeric poems within the historical development of the *polis*.[18] Since I cannot here offer anything like an exhaustive evaluation of their various attempts, Seaford's book *Reciprocity and ritual* may serve as a recent example. Seaford argues that the *polis*, with its ideas and institutions, is largely absent from the Homeric poems. Instead we find public rituals of varied description, which shape the narrative and set it in a pre-political frame. The diachronic development of the Homeric tradition is reflected synchronically in the structure of the poems as they have come down to us. On Seaford's reading, both the *Iliad* and the *Odyssey* move towards a politically more developed mode of social interaction.[19]

I do not wish to comment here on the problems one might find with Seaford's analogy between historical and narrative teleology. For the purposes of the present project it is enough to say that his approach tells us little about how the Homeric epics would have been performed and received in a specific context. In this respect Seaford's problems are characteristic

---

[18] For literature and discussion see Introduction, 'Between the omnipresent hero and the absent *polis*'.
[19] Seaford (1994), esp. chs. 1 and 5.

SOME PRELIMINARY CONSIDERATIONS

of the two generations of Homerists who followed after Parry. The need to place the epics was felt, but a lack of external evidence rendered the results of any such attempt too general to be helpful.

One way of tackling this difficulty is to concentrate on the performative structures that the texts themselves offer us. This approach has mainly been associated with the *Iliad*. Starting from the assumption that the epic is too long to be performed *en bloc*, critics have tried to reconstruct possible performances by breaking it down into sections. Recent literature tends to postulate three such sections of more or less equal length, suggesting that each part was performed on a separate day. This approach is more specific than that adopted by Seaford. At the same time, however, its results must remain more speculative. Most important of all, they teach us little about how the poem and its audience conspired in the joint enterprise of creating meaning through performance.[20]

A third approach is more pertinent to the present project. In recent years classicists have begun to compare the Homeric texts with historical cult practice. Two such attempts should be mentioned here, both based on the *Odyssey*. Auffarth sees the epic as inspired by the Ionian festival of the Anthesteria, presenting Odysseus as a Dionysus-figure who comes to redress a reversal of social norm.[21] Cook emphasises ritual context rather than ritual structure.[22] The *Odyssey* was very probably performed at the Great Panathenaea from the sixth century onwards,[23] and this is taken as a starting-point for a

---

[20] Heiden (1996) discusses the earlier attempts of Wade-Gery (1952), Davison (1965), Schadewaldt (1975), Taplin (1992) and Stanley (1993). He also offers his own solution, according to which the *Iliad* was (first ?) performed in the following three blocks: bks. 1–8 (first day), bks. 9–15 (2nd day), bks. 16–24 (3rd day).
[21] Auffarth (1991); for detailed criticism see Baudy (1993).
[22] Cook (1995).
[23] It should be noted from the outset that we know little about what went under the name 'Homer' in the sixth and fifth century. *Pace* Nagy (1992) 39 the Panathenaea makes no exception. Since the sources never refer to any particular poems, we are left to guess the range of song available on this occasion. The evidence is collected in Allen (1924) 226–38 and Kotsidu (1991) 41–4. It seems safe to assume that the *Iliad* and the *Odyssey* were among the canonical Panathenaic texts from early on, and this is what I assume here. However, I do not wish to imply that they were the only ones.

sustained comparison between the epic and the festival. Both Auffarth and Cook have to press their evidence in order to make the results more coherent; but for all its shortcomings their approach points in the right direction.

Auffarth saw that the lack of context which plagued earlier Homeric scholarship can be overcome if we activate hitherto neglected intertexts. Ritual provided them. Cook added the Great Panathenaea as the decisive point of reference. The Panathenaea is not of course the only festival for which early performances of Homeric poetry are attested. But since we know more about it than we do about any comparable occasion, it represents an obvious test case for the present project.

The present study, then, makes a fresh attempt at reading Homeric epic within an archaic and classical Greek performance context. On the way to this goal, three questions need to be addressed. First, how was the term *laos* understood in archaic and classical times? This concerns the generic–temporal distance between early Greek hexameter poetry and other texts. How stable is the understanding of 'Homer's people'? Can we make out changes, and if so what are they? Second, we need to ask where and when potential archaic and classical Greek audiences of Homer would have encountered the concept *laos*. This question concerns the institutional and ritual dimensions of our term, which are little developed in epic. Third, we need to clarify how the understanding of the term *laos* was affected by specific performance contexts. How does the Great Panathenaea, for example, fit into the picture? What does it add? In answer to this last question I consider the performance of *laos* epic at the most important state festival of archaic and classical Athens.

Homer's people outside Homer

Let me start with the question of semantic continuity between early epic *laos* and the term as it was used in archaic and classical Greece. Earlier critics have argued that between the two there occurs a shift in social realities which brings about a fundamental change in the meaning of the word.[24] Starting from the assumption that the *laoi* of epic denote a social class, these critics describe the further development of the word in terms of the fortunes of that class in archaic and classical times. We have already seen one reason why this picture is flawed. Homer's people are not a class. But scholars have also been mistaken in their view of how the word *laos* developed in later times. I argue that there was in fact a strong continuity of usage between epic and other texts and that the discontinuities found may be explained with reference to performative context and generic outlook rather than historical development.[25] Epic as a genre concerns itself with an aspect of the people which is less prominent in other archaic and classical texts. Those texts in turn put their emphasis on points which epic on the whole plays down. The difference can be described in terms of the opposition myth vs ritual.[26] Elements of ritual are submerged in epic, but they are dominant outside it.

Similarities

Archaic and classical Greek *laoi* do not fundamentally differ from their counterpart in epic. In order to substantiate this claim, which is crucial to the overall argument, I first go in search of Homer's people as they appear in the texts of archaic and classical Greece. My survey aims to cover the surviving material down to the fourth century BC. While only a limited number of passages are discussed in detail, relevant parallels are listed in the footnotes.

As was the case in early epic, archaic and classical texts are favourably disposed towards the *laoi*. This is often expressed

---

[24] E.g. Harmatta (1981) 159; for further discussion and literature see Introduction, 'Between the omnipresent hero and the absent *polis*'.
[25] I cannot here attempt to solve the problem of why archaic and classical *laos* occurs less frequently in prose than it does in poetry; a partial answer will emerge in the course of the discussion.
[26] The terms are used as developed in Nagy (1979), (1990a); for more detailed discussion see ch. 3, 'The founding people' and '*Leos* ritual', especially pp. 173f.

LAOS EPIC IN PERFORMANCE

in the form of prayer. In Pindar, for example, we can easily recognise elements of the epic usage: the people need to be saved, and the lyric voice sympathises with this wish by asking a god to act as a good shepherd.[27]

Through the metaphor of the 'shepherd of the people' the *laoi* of epic are cast as dependent on single agents who save them. Outside epic issues of leadership are less important, but the pair of group and leader is still known both in its basic form[28] and in an institutionally more developed guise.[29] The relevant social contexts are also familiar: assembly, *agon*, battlefield and funeral.[30]

Just like their counterpart in epic, the *laoi* outside epic serve to define important social contexts, while remaining helpless when left to themselves. We have seen already that in their need for support they often receive the sympathetic attention of the texts. Another example of this can be found in Timotheus, where once again the context is one of prayer:

ἀλλ' ἑκαταβόλε Πύθι' ἀγνὰν
ἔλθοις τάνδε πόλιν σὺν ὄλβῳ,
πέμπων ἀπήμονι λαῷ
τῷδ' εἰρήναν θαλλούσαν εὐνομίᾳ.[31]

---

[27] E.g. Pi. *O.* 13.24–8; cf. *P.* 8.41–56, where ἀβλαβής ('unharmed') should be compared with *Il.* 6.223; cf. also Pi. *N.* 9.31f., *Pae.* 1.9f.; cf. also *CEG II* 852 with discussion and further literature.

[28] For the single agent and the *laos* in general see Callin. fr. 1.18f. (West), Alc. fr. 356 (*PLF*), Simon. *ep.* 36.4 (Page), Pi. *O.* 1.89, 8.25–30, 9.59–66, 13.24–8 (of a god), *P.* 3.85, 4.107, 152f., 5.94f. (of a hero in cult), 8.41–56, 10.31, *I.* 6.53f., B. 1.112–19, 9.30–5, 11.64–76, A. *Pers.* 787–9, *Supp.* 517f., *A.* 188f. (implied of Agamemnon), *Ch.* 363–6, S. *Aj.* 1100f., *Tr.* 194f., *OT* 144, *OC* 741f., 884–900, E. *Hec.* 8f., 510, *Supp.* 329, 387, 664, 744, *HF* 1389, *Ion* 1577f., 1592–4, *Ph.* 1227, 1239, 1467, Ar. *Eq.* 163f., *Av.* 1271–7, Hdt. 2.129.1.

[29] For gathering the *laos* see Pi. *P.* 9.54f., A. *Supp.* 517f., S. *OT* 144, *OC* 884–900, E. *Ion* 1140, *Or.* 873, Ar. *Pax* 296–8, 632; for dispersing them see Ar. *Pax* 551f., *Av.* 448–50; the role of the herald is discussed below in ch. 3, 'Ritual formulae'; for *laoi* and the mantic space see Pi. *O.* 6.58–61, A. *Supp.* 92–5 (in close contact with Homeric parallels).

[30] For the 'assembly' (ἀγορή) see Simon. *ep.* 16.10 (Page); for the *agon* see Xenoph. fr. 2.15 (West), Pi. *P.* 12.24, B. 9.35, 13.228–31; for the battlefield see e.g. A. *Pers.* 728f. and *passim*; for the funeral see Pi. *P.* 5.94f. (of a hero in cult), E. *Hec.* 508ff., *HF* 1389–93.

[31] Tim. fr. 791.237–40 (*PMG*).

but far-shooting Apollo,
come, I beseech you, with prosperity to this holy city
and bring to this unharmed people
a peace which blooms with good rule.

Pindar is not the only poet who displays sympathy for the *laoi*. Timotheus shows a similar concern, and in doing so alludes to the familiar scenario of communal catastrophe implied in the epithet ἀπήμων ('*un*harmed'). For reasons which will be discussed later, this theme is less common outside epic. But it is still prominent enough: a sympathetic general outlook is frequently counterbalanced by a reality in which the people perish.

Examples that support this last point can be found throughout the texts of our period. When Alcaeus for instance complains that 'Poverty subdues a great people', he echoes some of the formulae studied in chapter 1.[32] Even more pertinent are the following variations:

Βα.   ναυτικὸς στρατὸς κακωθεὶς πεζὸν ὤλεσε στρατόν.
Δα.   ὧδε παμπήδην δὲ λαὸς πᾶς κατέφθαρται δορί;[33]

Queen: The defeat of the naval army destroyed the army on foot.
Darius: So utterly has the whole people been destroyed by the spear?

Perhaps owing to a more general stylistic sensitivity Aeschylus avoids the epic phrase 'he destroyed the people' (ὤλεσε λαόν).[34] But with 'he destroyed the army' (ὤλεσε στρατόν) and 'the people have been destroyed' (λαός ... κατέφθαρται) he comes close enough.[35] Another example of variation may be found in Euripides:

... ὑβρίζων τ' αὖθις ἀνταπώλετο
Κάδμου κακόφρων λαός ...[36]

... but now their rioting brings them down in turn,
the malignant people of Cadmus ...

---

[32] Alc. fr. 364 (*PLF*); for the relevant formulae in epic see Appendix A.3.
[33] A. *Pers.* 728f.
[34] For the stylistic principle according to which tragedy aims to move 'away from Homer' see Björck (1950) 217.
[35] For 'army', στρατός, as a gloss on *laos* see n. 127.
[36] E. *Supp.* 743f.

The text evokes not only the epic formula 'he destroyed the people' (ὤλεσε λαόν), but also the mechanism of negative reciprocity attached to it. The variation, admittedly, is bold. It is the group, this time, who misbehave; but Euripides could not have played with the characteristics of Homer's people in the way he does, had he not been familiar with the epic usage.[37]

Archaic and classical texts often follow the precedent of epic, at the same time avoiding downright imitation. We have seen that this well-known tendency can also be found in the case of the *laoi*. Here is an example from Herodotus' Ionian prose:

ἐλπίζων γὰρ ὁ Ἀλυάττης σιτοδείην τε εἶναι ἰσχυρὴν ἐν τῇ Μιλήτῳ καὶ τὸν λεὼν τετρῦσθαι ἐς τὸ ἔσχατον κακοῦ, ἤκουε ...[38]

For Alyattes, expecting to find the Milesians reduced to the extremity of distress by famine, was told ...

The parallels with epic are not difficult to see.[39] The *laoi* of epic are never far from 'the extremity of distress', and whatever other reason Herodotus might have for his choice of phrase, he certainly alludes to an epic theme.[40] Now, we have seen that in epic the people's weakness is counterbalanced by what I called their 'conceptual strength'.[41] A similar phenomenon is found in other texts. Archaic and classical *laoi* are often seen to provide a criterion for the well-being of life in the world at large. For example, the picture drawn in Euripides' *Helen* is very much that of *Iliad* 1, *Odyssey* 19 and Hesiod's *Works and Days*:

Χο. βροτοῖσι δ' ἄχλοα πεδία γᾶς
     ⟨∪−∪−∪∪−⟩
     οὐ καρπίζουσ' ἀρότοις,
     λαῶν δὲ φθείρει γενεάν,

---

[37] Epic itself points the way; cf. *Od.* 7.58–60.
[38] Hdt. 1.22.3; cf. 2.129.1; for Herodotus' view of the *laos* as the 'founding people' see pp. 169f.
[39] Cf. *Il.* 17.225f. in particular.
[40] Other examples are found in Pi. *P.* 12.11f., *I.* 6.53, fr. 140a.55f. (?), B. 11.64–76, 13.117–20, A. *Pers.* 945, *Th.* 343f., *A.* 189, *Ch.* 363–6, E. *Supp.* 728–30, *Hel.* 1319–31, *Ph.* 1235, *Rh.* 410.
[41] See above ch. 1, 'Society and the stone'.

SIMILARITIES

> ποίμναις δ' οὐχ ἵει θαλερὰς   1330
> βοσκὰς εὐφύλλων ἑλίκων·[42]
>
> Chorus: Earth, green gone from her fields, would give
>   food no more in the sown lands, [?]
>   and she [Demeter] destroyed the generation of people.
>   For the flocks she shot out no longer
>   tender food from the curling leaves.

The goddess Demeter is upset about having lost her daughter, and her wrath precipitates a crisis of Euripides' *laoi* as well as of crops and flocks. They perish because of a serious problem of social interaction; in good epic fashion, the people serve as an indicator of the success of life in the most general terms.

Elsewhere in archaic and classical texts the normative force of the people is made even more explicit. They judge, they save or destroy, they name.[43] The rather diffuse notion of 'conceptual strength' thus comes into sharper focus. Why that is, and what the change could mean will be discussed presently. First we must note the full extent of semantic continuity between epic and other genres.

In the *Helen*, Euripides makes his chorus sing about the catastrophe of the people as caused by an angry god. We have already seen examples of prayer on behalf of the *laoi*, and there are many more passages in archaic and classical Greek texts where the people interact with the gods. Apollo, Athena and Zeus stand in a particularly close relationship with them.[44] Other deities, too, take an interest, or are asked to do

---

[42] E. *Hel.* 1327–31; the textual difficulties are discussed by Kannicht (1969) *ad loc.;* for the relevant parallels in epic see above ch. 1, 'Society and the stone'.

[43] This is particularly marked in Aeschylus' *Supplices* 366f., 399–401, 484f., 517f., 975–7; the role of the *laos* in this play deserves careful study; other examples for the power of the *laoi* are the group as judge: A. *Eu.* 638f., Tim. fr. 791.206–12 (*PMG*), going back to Hes. *Op.* 768; the *laos* names: E. *Heracl.* 86, *Andr.* 19f., *IT* 1452, *Ph.* 290, *IA* 281; cf. *CEG* II 890; the *laos* intervenes against transgressive behaviour: S. *Ph.* 1242f., *OC* 884–6, E. *Heracl.* 922–5, *Supp.* 467f.; the *laos* decides issues concerning the whole community: E. *Hec.* 508–10, *Supp.* 481, *Ph.* 1238f., 1460; for declarations of war and peace see also n. 127 below.

[44] Apollo: Thgn. 776, Pi. *P.* 9.54f., *Pae.* 1.8f., 2.1–5, A. *Eu.* 15f., E. *Andr.* 1089, *Ion* 1140, Tim. fr. 791.237–40 (*PMG*); the genre of the *Paean* seems particularly important in this context; see n. 103; Athena: A. *Eu.* 996–9, E. *Heracl.* 922f., *IT* 960, 1452, *Erechtheus* fr. 360.48f. (Nauck); Zeus: Pi. *O.* 13.24–8, *N.* 9.31f., Ar. *Pax* 62.

so, further underlining the closeness of the group to its epic counterpart.[45]

Laoi are the object of divine anger or grace. This is true both in epic and in other texts.[46] The term laos continues to denote the social world vis-à-vis the gods, and as such it is also used of a world that is situated at the most fundamental level of survival and procreation. Accordingly, we find once more the images of plant and animal growth which were used to express the well-being of the community in epic. They recur with some frequency and throughout the genres, for example:

> Παιά]ν δὲ λαῶν γενεὰν δαρὸν ἐρέπτοι
> σαό]φρονος ἄνθεσιν εὐνομίας.[47]
>
> Long may Paean wreathe the generation of the people
> with the flowers of wise order.

Note again the context of prayer. The people are seen as vulnerable, and their longing for help is sympathetically articulated by the speaker. In some ways the expression 'with the flowers of wise order' (σαόφρονος ἄνθεσιν εὐνομίας) goes beyond what is known from hexameter poetry, but we may also note that archaic and classical laoi show much the same tendency to 'flourish' or 'wither' as did their counterpart in epic. Another example of this can be found in Timotheus:

> ὁ γάρ μ' εὐγενέτας μακραί-
> ων Σπάρτας μέγας ἁγεμὼν
> βρύων ἄνθεσιν ἥβας
> δονεῖ λαὸς ἐπιφλέγων.[48]
>
> for the well-born, long-lived
> great leader of Sparta,
> the people flourishing with the blossoms of youth,
> attack me with burning anger.

The passage is interesting for more than one reason, but let us for now concentrate on the phrase 'blossoms of youth' (ἄνθεα ἥβας), which Timotheus uses in conjunction with the laoi. The

---

[45] Artemis: B. 11.115–17; Hera: Pi. N. 10.35; Persephone: Pi. N. 1.13–17.
[46] See above ch. 1, 'Society and the stone'.
[47] Pi. Pae. 1.9f.
[48] Tim. fr. 791.206–9 (PMG).

expression itself does not occur in epic, but the idea is familiar.[49] The term *laos* continues to represent the human community at its most basic level; and once again this is illustrated by images of plant and animal life.

They culminate in the myth of collective autochthony as we find it, for example, in Pindar.[50] While there are differences between Pindar's narrative of autochthonous birth and epic versions,[51] it is important that we first note the similarities; the *laoi* continue to be seen as an inclusive group which predates social differentiation, and this is most fully expressed in the image of autochthonous growth from stones. In each case the etymologising word play λαός–λᾶας (*laoi* = 'stone-people') helps to make the connection.

At the beginning of this section, I claimed that the meaning of *laos* in archaic and classical Greek texts is in important ways the same as that of its counterpart in epic. This has been substantiated by a number of points:

– Archaic and classical Greek *laoi* are a group in need of protection.
– Their need to be saved is generally regarded with sympathy.
– In order to survive they depend on the action of single agents.
– This is expressed in familiar terms, both at a basic level and in more institutionally developed contexts such as the *agore*, the *agon*, etc.
– Archaic and classical *laoi*, like their counterpart in epic, are closely linked to the gods, notably Apollo, Zeus, Athena.
– The group functions as a criterion for the well-being of a larger world.

---

[49] See above ch. 1, 'Society and the stone'.
[50] Pi. *O.* 9.41–6; other examples include schol. Pi. *O.* 9.68a, 70a–d (quoting Epicharmus, Philochorus and anonymous mythographers), *P.* 12.11f. (implying the word play 'people'–'stone'; cf. Eust. 1 p. 39.11–13 (van der Valk)), E. *Ion* 29, *Erechtheus* fr. 360.5–8 (Nauck), *CEG* II 824.2. Cadmus' sown men are perhaps the most famous autochthonous collective of archaic and classical Greece; see Vian (1963) ch. 7; they are regularly called *laos*: S. *OT* 144, *OC* 741, E. *Supp.* 329, 467, 664, 743f., *Ph.* 1227, 1239, 1467. On parallels with the Deucalion story see Vian (1963) 171. Also relevant are the passages which link the *laoi* to the land they live on: Phryn. Trag. fr. 5 (Kannicht/Snell), A. *Supp.* 517, 976, *Eu.* 290, E. *Heracl.* 316, *HF* 1389, *Ion* 1577f., *Rh.* 426, Adespota fr. 428 (Kannicht/Snell) = Pollux 9.13. The association of the *laos* with autochthony remains stable in later times.
[51] See ch. 3, 'Differences'.

– Its all-encompassing qualities are conceptualised in images of plant growth and animal life which culminate in the myth of collective autochthony; here, as in epic, we find the etymologising word play λαός–λᾶας (*laoi* = 'stone-people').

Having established the fundamental continuity between Homer's people and archaic and classical *laoi*, let us now turn to the differences between them.

Differences

The differences between the *laoi* of epic and their counterpart in other genres become apparent when we take a closer look at the issue of social structure. Epic concentrates on the interaction between groups and leaders as encapsulated in the formula 'shepherd of the people' (*ποιμὴν λαῶν). Outside epic, we do not find the same emphasis. The idea of the shepherd is known, but where it occurs it is applied to a god rather than a human being.[52] A certain lack of interest in the problems involved is also apparent. Theognis' account is characteristic. He invokes Apollo for help against an external enemy.[53] As for internal strife, Theognis remains unusually abstract. It is not the human leader who causes the catastrophe of the people, but an impersonal notion of strife (στάσις λαοφθόρος), which could almost be taken as a divine force. Editors do in fact capitalise a similar power in a related passage of Alcaeus, which I have already mentioned.[54] Although the general idea – destruction of the people – is so familiar that it was cited above to support the semantic and ideological continuity of the term *laos* across generic boundaries, Alcaeus departs from the epic usage in the same characteristic way as Theognis does. Both are concerned with a general state of affairs, not the rudimentary structure of group and leader.[55]

---

[52] *CEG II* 852 (ii).
[53] Thgn. 773–81.
[54] Alc. fr. 364 (*PLF*); cf. above p. 155.
[55] Cf. Alc. fr. 356 (*PLF*). Here as elsewhere the epic usage does not simply disappear.

Alcaeus blames 'poverty' (Πενία), Theognis can say that 'internal strife' (στάσις) destroys the people. For the purposes of the present argument this need not be seen as a matter of historical development. Archaic and classical texts are still concerned with the safety of the *laos*, and, as was the case in epic, a concern with communal survival is often rendered more urgent by 'actual' catastrophe. However, outside epic we do not on the whole focus on the shepherd as a guardian of the group's well-being, and do not tend to see the success and failure of communal life exclusively in terms of leadership. Once again, it should be stressed that there are many possible explanations for this change, from *Geistesgeschichte* to generic constraints. I do not wish to press any particular model here. Whatever the reasons for the discrepancy, its effects are quite clear. Archaic and classical life among the *laoi* is not the hopeless struggle we saw in epic. Theognis' and Alcaeus' abstractions open a path to permanent improvement, for 'strife' and 'poverty' can be overcome.

Non-epic texts are (relatively) uninterested in the pair of shepherd and group precisely because they allow for the possibility of social progress. The structure of leader and people is re-interpreted in terms of a more abstract and less permanent problem, a problem which can be solved by social change. For instance, in Bacchylides as in Homer, and in early Greek hexameter poetry at large, a crisis of social interaction may result in the catastrophe of the *laoi*:

    νεῖκος γὰρ ἀμαιμάκετον
βληχρᾶς ἀνέπαλτο κασιγνήτοις ἀπ' ἀρχᾶς   65
Προίτῳ τε καὶ Ἀκρισίῳ·
    λαούς τε διχοστασίαις
ἤρειπον ἀμετροδίκοις μάχαις τε λυγραῖς.[56]

    For a stubborn strife
had sprung up from a slight cause between the brothers
Proetus and Acrisius,
    and they had been ruining the people with feuds
that broke the bounds of law and with dire battles.

[56] B. 11.64–8.

Here as in epic, the people perish because of their leaders. But Bacchylides also highlights a fundamental difference between the epic usage of our term and the way other Greek texts understand it. While epic depicts the crisis of *laoi* without dwelling on institutional solutions, Bacchylides allows for a way out:

> λίσσοντο δὲ παῖδας Ἄβαντος
>   γᾶν πολύκριθον λαχόντας   70
> Τίρυνθα τὸν ὁπλότερον
> κτίζειν, πρὶν ἐς ἀργαλέαν πεσεῖν ἀνάγκαν,
> Ζεύς τ' ἔθελεν Κρονίδας
> τιμῶν Δαναοῦ γενεὰν
>   καὶ διωξίπποιο Λυγκέος   75
> παῦσαι στυγερῶν ἀχέων.[57]

But they [the people] besought the sons of Abas
    that they would share the fertile land between them,
and that the younger should make a new seat at Tiryns
before they all fell into grievous straits.
Then Zeus the son of Cronus,
honouring the race of Danaus
    and Lynceus, urger of steeds,
was willing to give them rest from their cruel woes.

The second half of Bacchylides' story is no longer typical of epic. One of his leaders goes and founds a city. Early Greek hexameter poetry does not on the whole offer a solution to the problems of the *laoi* beyond the abortive one of negative reciprocity,[58] despite occasional glimpses of a brighter future, especially in Homer. Bacchylides shifts the balance; his people successfully implore their leaders to change their situation, and this is achieved and sanctioned by the setting up of a new social structure.

Bacchylides neatly sums up the difference between *laoi* in early epic and *laoi* as other archaic and classical Greek texts understand them. The underlying concept of a mythically or historically 'early' society, a society in crisis and without permanent institutions, is the same for them as it was for Homer, Hesiod and the other epic poets. However, outside epic, the

---

[57] B. 11.69–76.   [58] See above ch. 1, 'Negative reciprocity'.

emphasis is no longer on the (insoluble) problem of survival. We concentrate instead on the progress made. *Laoi* become the 'founding people', a group that aetiologically predates social progress. They enter archaic and classical Greek discourse not to expose the incurable vulnerability of social life, but to celebrate its successful transformation.

The founding people

The rudimentary structures of Homer's people are transformed in archaic and classical texts to become the source of institutional progress. What is transient and at risk in the world of Homer becomes stable from the point of view of other genres. In Bacchylides it was a new *polis* which decisively changed the situation. In Pindar the solution to the people's problems lies in the perpetuation of successful leadership through hero cult:

> μάκαρ μὲν ἀνδρῶν μέτα
> ἔναιεν, ἥρως δ' ἔπειτα λαοσεβής.[59]
>
> He was blessed among men in life,
> then a hero revered by the people.

Between the fresh start suggested in Bacchylides and the adherence to a successful model in Pindar, archaic and classical Greek texts offer many ways in which social life is aetiologically transformed. Let us look in more detail at some of the examples which are important to the present argument. I start with a narrative of social beginning *par excellence*: collective autochthonous birth.

The autochthonous group is aetiological of society in that it makes possible every other form of social life.[60] As could be seen in chapter 1, early Greek hexameter epic knows of and sometimes invokes this idea in connection with the *laos*, but it does so relatively rarely, and not always in a positive way.

---

[59] Pi. *P.* 5.94f.
[60] For *laos* as the autochthonous group in archaic and classical Greece see above n. 50.

Achilles in the *Iliad* not uncharacteristically turns the pattern of autochthony on its head and has the *laoi* revert to being stones.[61] One may contrast his attitude with the myth of Deucalion, as told in Pindar's 9th Olympian Ode:

> ... φέροις δὲ Πρωτογενείας
> ἄστει γλῶσσαν, ἵν' αἰολοβρέντα Διὸς αἴσᾳ
> Πύρρα Δευκαλίων τε Παρνασσοῦ καταβάντε
> δόμον ἔθεντο πρῶτον, ἄτερ δ' εὐνᾶς ὁμόδαμον
> κτισσάσθαν λίθινον γόνον·   45
> λαοὶ δ' ὀνύμασθεν.[62]

> ... Sing instead of Protogeneia's town,
> where by decree of Zeus, with dazzling thunder,
> Pyrrha and Deucalion stepped down from Parnassus
> and set up the first home and without a bed founded
> a united stony offspring;
> and they were called 'people'.

In Pindar's words the autochthonous coming into being of the *laoi* looks ahead to social progress. Pyrrha and Deucalion establish the first house, where they 'found' (κτίσσαι in the Greek – the *polis* is not far away) the offspring which is first characterised in terms of its more political counterpart *demos* before being 'named' (ὀνυμάσαι) *laoi*.[63] Pindar's language resounds with institutional terminology. Far from lapsing back into their origins, his *laoi* push towards the institutional life which is to develop out of them: the functioning household, the *demos*, the city. As the word ὁμό-δαμος ('*united* in one people') implies, the world he describes is still relatively undifferentiated. But lack of differentiation, for Pindar, does not bode catastrophe. On the contrary, his stony people embody the promise of successful future structure, most notably the *polis*.

Pindar's description is typical. Throughout archaic and classical Greek texts, the autochthonous *laos* is linked with the city. In a passage from Euripides' *Ion* this is done in a partic-

---

[61] *Il.* 24.611; this movement from the people back to the stone is also attested in Pi. *P.* 12.11f.
[62] Pi. *O.* 9.41–6.
[63] For *demos* and *laos* see above ch. 2, n. 316; see also ch. 3, nn. 140 and 180.

ularly striking way.[64] Hector in the *Iliad* had hoped to integrate the people into his task of saving Troy, but in the end failed to reconcile the two. By merging the autochthonous *laos* of Athens with their *polis*, Athena in the *Ion* combines in harmonious coexistence what was prone to disruption in the more pessimistic vision of Homeric poetry.

To illustrate how close autochthonous birth can come to the establishment of social structures I next offer a passage from Philochorus. Because this takes us into the third century BC, the passage cannot count as evidence in the strict sense. It does, however, throw an interesting light on the issues in question. Here are the relevant lines as quoted in the Pindaric scholia:

Ἐπίχαρμος ἀπὸ τῶν λάων τῶν λίθων ὠνομάσθαι λαούς φησιν. ὁ δὲ Φιλόχορος ἀπὸ Κέκροπος· οὗτος γὰρ βουλόμενος τὸ τῶν Ἀθηναίων γένος πληθυνθῆναι ἐκέλευσεν αὐτοὺς λίθους λαβεῖν καὶ ἐνεγκεῖν εἰς τὸ μέσον· ἐξ ὧν ἔγνω δισμυρίους αὐτοὺς ὄντας. ἀπὸ Κέκροπος οὖν φησι τοὺς ὄχλους ⟨λαοὺς⟩ ὠνομάσθαι.[65]

Epicharmus says that the people (*laoi*) are so called from the *laes*, that is, stones; but Philochorus says from Cecrops. For Cecrops, wanting the race of the Athenians to become more numerous, asked them to pick up stones and bring them forward. From this he learnt that they were 20,000. So he says the crowds were called 'people' from Cecrops.

At first sight, the episode makes little sense. Why should Cecrops, wanting the race (γένος) of the Athenians to 'become more numerous' (πληθυνθῆναι), ask them to bring stones? That he goes on to count them has little to do with his initial plan. Another ancient commentator tellingly writes ἐπιγνῶναι ('to review') instead of πληθυνθῆναι ('to become more numerous').[66] For the very reason that this is easy to understand, it must be taken as a banal variant and was rightly rejected by Jacoby.[67] It was Jacoby, too, who first saw where the problem originates.[68]

Philochorus plays on an older story. Cecrops' attempt to enlarge the population points to the well-known crisis of life

[64] E. *Ion* 29f.; cf. also *Ion* 1572–8.   [65] Schol. Pi. *O.* 9.70b.
[66] Schol. Pi. *O.* 9.70c.   [67] *FGrHist* 328 fr. 95.
[68] *FGrHist ad* 328 fr. 95 (vol. IIIb pp. 399f.).

among Homer's people. But true to his rationalising tendencies, Philochorus transforms the pattern of autochthonous birth into a narrative of social reform – what had been an amorphous mass is now a group of 20,000.[69] In Homer the stone had implied a threat. In Pindar, it allowed for a number of acculturating acts, naming among them. Philochorus betrays the same optimistic tendency when he turns the stone into a token of communal countability. The beginning is placed at the centre of social life.[70]

There are more examples of the *laos* as an autochthonous community in archaic and classical Greece,[71] but enough has been said to illustrate the crucial point. Both early Greek hexameter poetry and other Greek archaic and classical texts associate life among the people with collective autochthonous birth. The underlying idea is the same in each case: autochthonous groups are marked as socially inclusive, historically early, etc. But, whereas Homer alludes to the idea only to describe the breakdown of social interaction, other archaic and classical writers adopt a different stance: their *laos*, too, represents a 'primitive' world, but one which is rife with new institutions, and in particular the *polis*.

Epic poetry is on the whole uninterested in setting up cities. While we do find a number of foundation narratives involving the *laoi*,[72] none of them is quite successful or important enough to dispel the impression that early Greek hexameter poetry, Homer included, plays down the salutary effect of

---

[69] Cf. Eust. 1 p. 38.30–3 (van der Valk). Cecrops in particular was an object of Philochorean rationalisation; cf. *FGrHist* 328 fr. 93 with Jacoby's note *ad loc.*

[70] For the link between Cecrops and the *laoi* see also *CEG II* 890. A negative doublet of Philochorus' version is reported by Pherecydes, *FGrHist* 3 fr. 22a–c. Pherecydes may not have used the word *laos*, but the story he tells is clearly relevant here. For the close connection between the term *laos* and the 'sown men of Thebes' (Σπαρτοί) see n. 50. Here as elsewhere Thebes can be seen as a negative counterpart of an Athenian success story; see Zeitlin (1990). Note, however, that in Pherecydes, too, the result of the crisis is the formation of a citizen body (πολῖται). Hecataeus' 'city of slaves' may be related; see *FGrHist* 1 fr. 345 and Vidal-Naquet (1986) p. 207 with n. 7.

[71] See above n. 50.

[72] E.g. the building of the Achaean wall (*Il.* 6.449–53); the settlement of Rhodes (*Il.* 2.653–70); the emigration of Odysseus and 'all his people' (*Od.* 4.174–6); cf. also *h.Ap.* 77f.

polis foundation.[73] As we have come to expect, this is different in other archaic and classical Greek literature. The Delphic oracle, for example, when referring to the settlers of a new city routinely calls them *laoi*.[74] As often, relatively late oracles preserve ideas that are also attested much earlier. In Pindar, for example, the familiar process of 'gathering the people' leads directly to the founding of a city.[75] The Homerising language in which this is expressed helps to highlight the differences with Homer, especially with the chaotic assembly of *Iliad* 2.

In Homer the gathering of the people does not usually lead to the establishment of a permanent social structure. By contrast, archaic and classical texts insist that definite progress can be made. In Pindar the lyric voice prays to Zeus that he may give the *laos* over to the 'lawful splendour of city life'.[76] In another context Pindar praises the life-giving qualities of Camarina:

τὰν σὰν πόλιν αὔξων, Καμάρινα, λαοτρόφον.[77]

augmenting your city which feeds the people, Camarina.

The new *polis* of Camarina, shortly after it has been founded, is seen as a means of ensuring the survival of the people. Λαοτρόφος ('which feeds the people') brings us back to the sphere of nutrition and growth. Everyone needs to be fed. But from now on social institutions stabilise the uncertainties of primeval nurture. The word λαοτρόφος, needless to say, is not found in epic.

---

[73] The Achaean camp in the *Iliad* is built without sacrifices (6.449f.); it is not spacious enough to accommodate the people (*Il.* 14.34) and will be destroyed as soon as the war is over (*Il.* 12.1–35). Odysseus' resettlement is never actually brought about. Neoptolemus' expedition to Rhodes forms a short excursus within the *Catalogue of ships*; *h.Ap.* 77f. represents the nightmare scenario of a settlement without *laoi*. Perhaps Hesiod in the *Works and days* goes furthest in allying city and *laoi*; but here, too, the city does not work a decisive transformation.

[74] 229 (P–W), 302 (P–W) and perhaps also 363 (P–W); the usage remains stable well into late antiquity.

[75] Pi. *P.* 9.54f.; note especially the word ἀρχέπολις ('ruling the city'), which may also convey associations of political beginning; for the process of 'gathering the people' see above ch. 1, 'Social structures', and Appendix A.4.

[76] Pi. *N.* 9.31f.

[77] Pi. *O.* 5.4; see also *O.* 6.60.

Pindar in our last passage looked at the *laoi* from the point of view of the newly established *polis*. His words can be taken to refer back to the historically unique event of city foundation, but the fact that the founding act is perpetuated in the epithet λαοτρόφος ('which feeds the people') also suggests that the transformation is never complete. Just as the *laoi* outside epic look ahead to future progress, the archaic and classical *polis* retains for ever the memory of the decisive step. Plato's Athenian stranger points out that the model city of the *Laws* could not exist without them.[78] The existence of a *laos* (here *leos* in the Attic form) is the necessary precondition for everything that follows. Not only do the people need and therefore move toward the structure of the *polis*, but the existence of the *polis* in turn depends on them being there.

In the *Iliad*, this situation of mutual dependence led to a conflict of priorities.[79] In other archaic and classical literature we find city and people in harmonious symbiosis. In Sophocles' *Antigone*, for example, Haimon mentions the city's founding people not so much in remembrance of the founding act itself, but as the consensual basis of all existing institutions.[80] Haimon is careful to avoid any opposition between the city and the *leos*. In his words, the people are committed to the city (ὁμό-πτολις, 'united in the *city*') as well as taking us back to a state of primeval unity (ὁμό-πτολις, '*united* in the city'). This must be the meaning of the much debated word ὁμόπτολις. It harks back to Pindar's ὁμόδαμος ('united in one people'), and like its Pindaric precursor it promises an all-inclusive, yet institutionally committed, social world.[81]

Another version of the same phenomenon is found in Euripides,[82] who has the chorus of his play *Heraclidae* introduce

---

[78] Pl. *Lg.* 707e1f.; for earlier parallels see Pi. *O.* 9.59–66, *P.* 9.54f., *N.* 1.13–17, B. 1.119.
[79] See above ch. 2, '*Laoi* in the *Iliad*', pp. 83–95.
[80] S. *Ant.* 731–4; also Pi. *Pae.* 2.48, A. *Supp.* 366f., *Eu.* 775 and 997, E. *Heracl.* 922f., Ar. *Ach.* 162f.; Thgn. 53–6 deplores a perverse state of disjunction.
[81] Jebb (1888) *ad loc.* already offers the right translation but does not adduce the decisive parallel; Kamerbeek (1978) *ad loc.* returns to Campbell's mistaken rendering 'her fellow-citizens in this town of Thebes'; see Campbell (1871) *ad loc.*
[82] E. *Heracl.* 8of.

THE FOUNDING PEOPLE

their *laos* as being 'of the four cities' (τετράπτολις) and 'settled together' (ξύνοικος). Just as in Pindar and Sophocles all social structure was entailed in the 'primitive' notion of the *laos*, the founding people, Euripides, too, reminds us that existing institutions can always be re-merged in remembrance of the founding act.[83]

I have studied in some detail the tendency of archaic and classical *laos* to imply and predate the structures of the *polis*. This was done in two ways. First, in terms of mythical and historical chronology, the *laoi* are the founding people in that they predate institutional life. Second, from the point of view of the already existing *polis*, the founding people embrace and underpin modern institutional differentiation. These perspectives can be traced consistently in the Greek texts of the archaic and classical eras. On the one hand, the *laoi* are seen as the social world which aetiologically predates all political institutions. On the other hand, the basis on which any given political structure is built – the *laoi* – can always be evoked in the 'present day'.

When Herodotus talks about the founding of a colony, he does so in a way which has by now become familiar:

ἐπειδὴ ὅ τε Ἀναξανδρίδης ἀπέθανε καὶ οἱ Λακεδαιμόνιοι χρεώμενοι τῷ νόμῳ ἐστήσαντο βασιλέα τὸν πρεσβύτατον Κλεομένεα, ὁ Δωριεὺς δεινόν τε ποιεύμενος καὶ οὐκ ἀξιῶν ὑπὸ Κλεομένεος βασιλεύεσθαι, αἰτήσας λεὼν Σπαρτιήτας ἦγε ἐς ἀποικίην ...[84]

As a result of this Dorieus was indignant when, on the death of Anaxandrides, the Spartans followed their usual custom and put the eldest son, Cleomenes, on the throne. Unable to bear the prospect of being ruled by Cleomenes, he asked the Spartans for a body of people (*leos*) and took them off to found a settlement elsewhere.

The word *leos* is rare in Herodotus, and its usage in the context of colonisation (ἀποικίη) must be significant. Note that Herodotus' settlement does not predate political structures as such. Sparta is already there before the crisis and will continue

---

[83] Words of the root **oik-* ('household' etc.) and of the root **p(t)ol-* ('city' etc.) are often combined in conjunction with the *laos*. It is characteristic of our term that it blurs the fundamental structural opposition between city and household.
[84] Hdt. 5.42.2; cf. also 4.148.1.

to exist afterwards. However, the rejection of custom (νόμος) on the part of the younger brother leads to a temporary breakdown of existing institutions.[85] Having undergone a phase of political uncertainty, Sparta is split and refounded.

Archaic and classical *laoi* do not necessarily refer back to a time where no stable institutions exist. More important than an absolute historical or mythical date is the dynamic nature of the process. The phenomenon of colonisation is in principle contemporary to the texts studied here; and yet it entails the same mechanisms as 'original' settlement in myth, of which it can be seen as a variant. In both cases the word for the group involved is *laos*. We might say that while in myth the *laoi* are remembered as being historically early, in present times they either evoke (and reaffirm) the founding consensus or serve to mark a crisis which leads to political (re-)formation.

The myth of the 'settling together' (*synoikismos*) of Athens under Theseus illustrates well this last point. The version of it that interests me here goes back to Aristotle and is preserved for us in Plutarch.[86] On the one hand, the story is of course set in the early days of Athens. However, just as the process of colonisation reported by Herodotus does not actually predate the city of Sparta, so Theseus in Aristotle's account only enlarges an already existing *polis* (τὴν πόλιν αὐξῆσαι βουλόμενος). In order to do so he assembles the founding people, *leoi*. In Herodotus, this process was mapped onto a modern crisis of social institutions. By rejecting the custom (νόμος) of Sparta Dorieus plunges his city into a state of pre-political turmoil. In Aristotle, too, chronologies begin to shift, but this time in the opposite direction. His assembly of the *leoi* is of course set in the early pre-history of Athens. However, it also functions as an *aition* of Athenian political life, an *aition* which is replayed every time the Athenian herald repeats Theseus' announcement: 'come hither, all ye people' (δεῦρ' ἴτε πάντες λεῴ).[87] In other ways too Aristotle projects the lan-

---

[85] The story is closely reminiscent of B. 11.64–76.
[86] Plu. *Thes.* 25.1 = Arist. fr. 384 (Rose).
[87] For further discussion see pp. 180, 182f.

THE FOUNDING PEOPLE

guage of his own time back into the mythical–historical situation he describes. When Theseus calls everyone on equal conditions (ἐπὶ τοῖς ἴσοις) he uses an element of the historical process of colonisation.[88]

The spontaneous breakdown of political structure described in Herodotus and the organised re-enactment implied in Aristotle's account are closely related. They both represent ways in which the founding activities of the *laoi* may be replayed in the present. Such an alliance between past and present is alien to epic, but can be found throughout the rest of our archaic and classical sources. A passage from Euripides' *Iphigenia in Tauris* provides another good example.[89] The *leos* is there presented both as the primeval group which is as yet lacking the institutional structure it is about to attain and the group of people who feast in remembrance of the decisive change.[90] The past is replayed in the present; the festival instituted by Athena preserves a memory of the moment at which (a) custom (νόμος) was established.[91]

Another, more famous example of the same phenomenon is found in Aeschylus' *Eumenides*:

Αθ.   κλύοιτ' ἂν ἤδη θεσμόν, Ἀττικὸς λεώς,
        πρώτας δίκας κρίνοντες αἵματος χυτοῦ.
        ἔσται δὲ καὶ τὸ λοιπὸν Αἰγέως στρατῷ
        αἰεὶ δικαστῶν τοῦτο βουλευτήριον.[92]

Athena: If it please you, people of Attica, hear now my decree,
        who are judging the first case of bloodletting.
        In future times there will always be this council of judges
        for the army of Aegeus.

When Athena institutes the Areopagus it is once again the people who experience the decisive change.[93] As indicated by the contrast between 'now' / 'the first case' (ἤδη / πρώτας δίκας) and 'in the future' / 'always' (αἰεί / τὸ λοιπόν), the unique

---

[88] Th. 1.27 with Gomme (1945) *ad loc.*; much later Nicolaus of Damascus uses the phrase in conjunction with the term *laos*; see *FGrHist* 90 fr. 28.
[89] E. *IT* 1450–61; cf. *IT* 958–60.
[90] Cf. *IT* 1452 and 1458.
[91] *IT* 1458.
[92] A. *Eu.* 681–4.
[93] Cf. A. *Eu.* 638f.

point at which institutional progress was achieved in the past is endlessly re-enacted. What the gloss 'army' (στρατός) adds in line 683 will be discussed later.[94] For now we note the role of the *leos* in the making and remaking of a social structure. Euripides, too, has some interesting things to say about this:

Αγ. ὁρῶ δ' ὄχλον στείχοντα καὶ θάσσοντ' ἄκραν,
οὗ φασι πρῶτον Δαναὸν Αἰγύπτῳ δίκας
διδόντ' ἀθροῖσαι λαὸν ἐς κοινὰς ἕδρας.[95]

Messenger: I see a crowd go streaming up to take their seats on the hill –
the same place where they say that Danaus first stood trial with Aegyptus
and gathered the people into shared seats.

Once again I leave the process of glossing for later discussion (λαός, 'people', alternates with ὄχλος, 'crowd') and concentrate on the aetiological character of the scene.[96] When Danaus first gathers the Argives into the 'shared seats' (κοιναὶ ἕδραι) of the lawcourt, they are a *laos*. And once again what they are and do 'then' is replayed 'today'. An example of what this process might have been thought to look like when transposed into the present can be found in Aristophanes' *Birds*.[97] Something like Pisthetairos' foundation feast must have been celebrated at regular intervals throughout the political world of archaic and classical Greece.

I have argued that the idea of institutional progress is relatively marginal to *laoi* in early Greek hexameter poetry. In Homer such progress is sometimes promised or alluded to but never fully realised. As we have seen, it is crucial to other archaic and classical Greek descriptions of *laoi*. Two things are important to note. First, the *laoi* outside epic, like their counterpart within, belong to an early stage of social life. Second, unlike Homer's people, the *laoi* of archaic and classical Greek texts are cast as 'the founding people' – that is to say, they are thought to embody and aetiologically predate social institutions. Past and present are closely intertwined. On the one hand, modern institutional differentiation is ex-

---

[94] See n. 127.   [95] E. *Or.* 871–3.   [96] See n. 127.   [97] Ar. *Av.* 1271–7.

plained with reference to the *laos* in the past; on the other, the primeval situation can be replayed in the present. Where this is done we enter the realm of ritual.

Leos ritual[98]

The difference between the *laoi* of epic and *laoi* in other texts can now be rephrased in terms of the presence or absence of ritual elements. A short clarification of my use of the term 'ritual' may be in place. As will be obvious to any reader of recent work in the field, there are various definitions of ritual which range from the vague to the nuanced.[99] My aim is to be both specific and brief. I call 'ritual' social practices that are carried out (relatively) regularly and within a (relatively) stable institutional framework. It is characteristic of such practices that they are encouraged by and in turn articulate 'custom' (νόμος), but not everything that is customary in archaic and classical Greece need therefore have been played out in elaborate ritual proceedings.

Here, as in chapter 1, I wish to emphasise the flexible nature of the concepts used. Like the formula of epic, archaic and classical Greek ritual may be said to articulate 'the doctrine, ideology and culture' of a given society without thereby imposing absolute boundaries.[100] Both formula and ritual manifest themselves in recurrent patterns of speech and action, but they crystallise processes which go far beyond the surface phenomenon of 'mere repetition'. Their close relationship finds expression in the fact that quasi-ritual action makes up

---

[98] I write '*leos* ritual' because the form *laos* was not used at Athens in ritual addresses. For the linguistic opposition between (Attic) *leos* and *laos* (of the Achaeans) see n. 180.

[99] For a general overview see Bell (1992) and (1997). Recent developments in the study of ancient Greek ritual are documented by Morris (1993); Osborne in the introduction to Hornblower and Osborne (1994) provides an outline of ritual activity in democratic Athens. For useful working definitions of ritual see Burkert (1985) 8, Bruit Zaidman and Schmitt Pantel (1992) 27. The present argument is indebted to Turner (1969), (1974), (1982), who sees ritual as complementary to social structure. Turner's ideas are clarified and further developed in Grimes (1982), Ashley (1990), Alexander (1991).

[100] Cf. pp. 15f.

much of the formulaic apparatus of epic while formulaic speech is typically part of archaic and classical Greek ritual. The latter observation will be of particular interest here.[101]

In the following pages I argue that for an archaic and classical Greek audience of Homer, the word *laos* (or, in its Attic form, *leos*) was specifically associated with successful ritual action. Since most of our evidence comes from Athens, and since the argument is moving towards the performance of Homer at an Athenian state festival,[102] I shall concentrate on *leos* ritual as a characteristically Athenian version of what is likely to have been a much more widespread phenomenon.

The traditional pronouncements 'hear, ye people' (ἀκούετε λεῴ) and 'come hither, all ye people' ((δεῦρ') ἴτε, πάντες λεῴ) are of central importance here. These formulae represent an important 'crystallising point' of social life in that they persist relatively unchanged over the times and occasions. In this respect they closely compare with the generically stable formulaic core of *laos* epic as established in chapter 1. In other ways, however, they strikingly differ. While the formulae of epic point to collective disaster, the formulae of Athenian communal ritual offer a controlled way of transforming the structured world of political life into the primeval world of the *laos*, which calls for institutional (re-)formation and enables the community to (re-)affirm its basic consensus as well as its present structures.

Ritual formulae

Leos ritual has a long tradition in Greek culture. From the relatively unstable procedures of epic to the well-defined context of a Pindaric *Paean*, we see the *laoi* playing their part in the more or less formalised, more or less regular assertion of

---

[101] 'Custom', νόμος, in its archaic and classical meaning is not a Homeric term, and it is therefore doubtful whether we should speak of 'ritual' in Homer in the same way in which that term has proved useful for other times and genres. For the relationship between νόμος ('custom') and νομός ('allotment', 'pasture' etc.) in epic see *LfgrE s.v.*

[102] See above ch. 3, 'Some preliminary considerations'.

social order and institutional life.[103] In this study I concentrate on how such ritual was carried out in archaic and classical Athens. However, I do not wish to suggest that Athenian procedures were necessarily unique. Rather, it is the nature of our task that points us towards Athens.

Like other ritual action, *leos* ritual is articulated by (more or less) standardised gestures. As in most other cases of early Greek ritual, almost all these gestures are lost to us, and we must be grateful for the two noteworthy exceptions that survive.[104] The pronouncements 'hear, ye people' (ἀκούετε λεῴ) and 'come hither, all ye people' ((δεῦρ') ἴτε πάντες λεῴ) made by the herald to the *leoi* can be reconstructed for archaic and classical Athens from the literary sources. Rather than singling out particular occasions, I study the phenomenon in general terms.[105]

In chapter 1 I noted that the herald of epic carries in himself the seed of institutional progress. I further noted that Homer's people are not often addressed directly.[106] Both these observations conform to an overall picture of *laoi* in unresolved crisis. In archaic and classical texts, the situation changes dramatically. Here the herald assumes a role of central importance. At Athens in particular his direct address to the *leoi* becomes the all-pervading token of institutional stability in the *polis*. Of the original announcements only imitations and parodies survive. Nevertheless, some inferences can be made on the basis of our sources.

---

[103] For epic see above ch. 1; for the *Paean* see the material collected in Käppel (1992) and especially Thgn. 773–9, Pi. *Pae.* 1.8–10, 2.1–5, 48, 6.177–81, Ar. *Pax* 551–5 (?), Tim. fr. 791, 237–40 (*PMG*). The association between the *laos* and the *Paean* remains stable in later times.

[104] Strictly speaking they are three: ἀκούετε λεῴ ('hear, ye people'); ἴτε πάντες λεῴ ('go, all ye people'); and δεῦρ' ἴτε πάντες λεῴ ('come hither, all ye people'), each with variants; see appendix B. For convenience the latter two phrases are treated together.

[105] There are two Attic festivals for which the relevant formulae are attested: the Choes (Ar. *Ach.* 1000f. with E. *IT* 958–60) and the Chalceia (S. fr. 844.1–3 (Radt)); for three others they can be reconstructed with some probability; the Brauronia or Tauropolia (E. *IT* 1450–61), the Chytroi (Ar. *Ra.* 219) and perhaps the Lenaea (Ar. *V.* 1015f., *Ra.* 676; cf. *Prolegomena de comoedia* XVIIIb 1 and 2 (Koster)). For the Panathenaea see n. 142.

[106] See above pp. 34 (the herald) and 55 with n. 47 (no direct address to the *laoi*).

LAOS EPIC IN PERFORMANCE

By way of an introduction I start with two non-Attic texts. Pindar and Bacchylides sometimes use the term *laos* with reference to their audience.[107] For instance, in Pindar fr. 42 'all the people' (πᾶς λαός) is used to refer to the audience of Pindaric poetry.[108] This observation must immediately be modified, for Pindar's audience is not simply a mass of bystanders who find themselves listening to a good song. Rather, they become a *laos* at a specific performative moment, the moment where something is 'shown' (δεκνύναι). As far as the *laos* is concerned, Pindar's activity mirrors that of the herald. It *shows* (note the visual metaphor), and *showing* through language is strictly speaking a matter of the herald. What Pindar leaves implicit is spelled out by his younger colleague Bacchylides:

> τὰν εἰκ ἐτύμως ἄρα Κλειώ
> πανθαλὴς ἐμαῖς ἐνέσταξ[εν φρασίν,
> τερψιεπεῖς νιν ἀ[ο]ιδαὶ
> παντὶ καρύξοντι λα[ῶ]ι.[109]

If indeed all-blooming Clio
  dripped it into my heart,
sweetspeaking songs
  will announce him to all the people.

Once again the addressee of choral song is 'all the people' (πᾶς λαός), this time identical with the spectators at the athletic *agon*.[110] Bacchylides is more explicit than Pindar. His songs will expressly 'act as a herald' (καρῦξαι); but the underlying idea is similar for both. Like the herald, the poets Pindar and Bacchylides change the structure of their social world by the announcements they make to the *laos*.

What we have seen so far is not entirely new. The assemblies (ἀγών, ἀγορή) of epic already functioned as a stage on which the structure of the people was determined. But Pindar and Bacchylides add a strong institutional emphasis. It is the

---

[107] Pi. fr. 42.3–5, B. 13.228–31; for the *Paean* see above n. 103.
[108] Pi. fr. 42.3–5.
[109] B. 13.228–31.
[110] For *laoi* at the epic *agon* see above ch. 1, 'Social structures'; for archaic and classical examples see ch. 3, 'Similarities'.

herald's job *always* to act as a herald. As we move into the sphere of Attic language and literature, this tendency towards repetition and institutionalisation becomes ever more prominent. Here is another poet in the pose of the herald:

> ἀκούετε λεῴ· Σουσαρίων λέγει τάδε
> υἱὸς Φιλίνου Μεγαρόθεν Τριποδίσκιος.
> κακὸν γυναῖκες· ἀλλ' ὅμως ὦ δημόται
> οὐκ ἔστιν οἰκεῖν οἰκίαν ἄνευ κακοῦ.
> καὶ γὰρ τὸ γῆμαι καὶ τὸ μὴ γῆμαι κακόν.[111]

> Hear, ye people: this is what Susarion says,
> Philinus' son, Megarian from Tripodisc.
> Women are a pest. But all the same, oh demesmen,
> no household can exist without aforesaid pest:
> for marry or stay single, either's damnable.

First we note the aetiological character of the address. What Susarion as a herald proclaims is not, of course, an innovation in the strict sense. By his time men and women have long shared a household (οἶκος), and the problems that arise from this have been discussed by Hesiod, Semonides and others.[112] Susarion's address to the founding people (λεῴ) does not in any trivial sense change their world. However, the speaker clearly employs an aetiological gesture (the invention of woman, marriage etc.), which appeals to archaic and classical Greeks precisely because it reflects a contemporary problem with the organisation of public and family life. Addressing this concern, Susarion adopts and replays the primeval gesture of an announcement (κήρυγμα) to the people (λεῴ).

We have left the context of choral song without finding a radical change in tone. The announcement to the founding people creates a (pseudo-)ritual context in which the structure of a social world changes. Note that Susarion uses the term *leoi* only once, in his opening address, while he says δημόται ('demesmen') later in his speech. *Leos* remains strictly a

---

[111] Sus. fr. 1.1–5 (West); the date and generic status of the fragment is debated; the evidence is assembled most recently in *PCG VII* 664f.; for the purposes of the present discussion the fragment is treated as an example of archaic or classical verse as in West (1976) 183f.

[112] E.g. Hes. *Works and days*, *Catalogue of women*, Semon. fr. 7 (West).

matter of scene-setting. More importantly, however, Susarion does not simply imitate the pose of a herald as Pindar and Bacchylides had done. Rather, his first two words are themselves an example of 'herald speak', direct quotes, that is, of the formula 'hear, ye people' (ἀκούετε λεῴ), which was current in archaic and classical Athens and which is frequently attested in drama.[113] For example:

> Κη.   ἀκούετε λεῴ· κατὰ τὰ πάτρια τοὺς Χοᾶς
>   πίνειν ὑπὸ τῆς σάλπιγγος.[114]
>
> Herald: Hear, ye people: everyone drink the jugs
>   to the trumpet, according to ancient custom.

Like Susarion, Aristophanes quotes the formula 'hear, ye people' (ἀκούετε λεῴ), this time putting it into the mouth of a 'real' herald (κῆρυξ). As a result we find ourselves thrown into a historically specific ritual context – Aristophanes in fact closely parodies one of the better-known Attic festivals, the Choes.[115] More could be said about the place of the announcement within that festival, but for now we note that Aristophanes takes to its institutional extremes the same stance that we have found to varying degrees in Pindar, Bacchylides and Susarion. The herald has taken centre stage. Again, an aetiological innovation in the strict sense is not implied. However, behind his invitation to act 'according to the customs of the fathers' (κατὰ τὰ πάτρια) we can still sense the prototypical first time at which those customs were instituted.[116]

Like Pindar and Bacchylides, Susarion and Aristophanes draw on patterns of ritual action and aetiological change, when they use the word *laos*. However, only the latter two quote historically 'real' practice (ἀκούετε λεῴ). This is typical

---

[113] Cf. Dunbar (1995) *ad* Ar. *Av.* 448–50: 'Clearly a traditional Athenian proclamation-opening'. The relevant passages are collected in Appendix B.1. Susarion as the 'inventor of comedy' employs a formula which is highly relevant to later definitions of comedy as a genre; see *Prolegomena de comoedia* XVIIIb 1 and 2 (Koster).
[114] Ar. *Ach.* 1000f.
[115] See above n. 105.
[116] This is borne out by the aetiology of the event as given in other sources; cf. van Leeuwen (1901) *ad* Ar. *Ach.* 961.

of fifth-century Athens, where the ritual model of life among the *laoi*, as formalised in stock phrases, becomes overwhelmingly prominent. Let me adduce two related passages from tragedy. The first comes from Aeschylus' *Eumenides* and has been discussed already. It is the famous scene in which Athena sets up the Areopagus.[117] Athena in the pose of the herald is known from epic, but she never directly addresses the people there.[118] In Aeschylus she uses a modified version of 'hear, ye people' (ἀκούετε λεῴ) only in her direct address, glossing with 'army' (στρατός) where she explains further developments.[119] 'May you now listen' (κλύοιτ' ἂν ἤδη) will hardly have been a standard form. But although Athena blunts the formulaic impact of the phrase by changing the wording, she also brings to the fore its performative aspect by reserving it for her address. Homer's people are rarely addressed *qua laos*. In an Attic context the word tends to be used above all in direct address, a point which further attests to its close association with ritual practice. Here is another, perhaps even more striking, example of the same phenomenon:

Τα.   ... σημαίνει δέ μοι
          σιγὴν Ἀχαιῶν παντὶ κηρῦξαι στρατῷ.   530
          κἀγὼ καταστὰς εἶπον ἐν μέσοις τάδε·
          "Σιγᾶτ', Ἀχαιοί, σῖγα πᾶς ἔστω λεώς,
          σῖγα σιώπα." νήνεμον δ' ἔστησ' ὄχλον.[120]

Talthybius: ... and he ordered me
          to proclaim silence from the entire army of the Achaeans.
          And I stood up in the middle and said:
          'Be quiet, Achaeans, all the people quiet,
          be silent! Silence!' And I made the crowd calm down.

Again we see the pattern which points to ritual practice: Talthybius uses the term *leos* in direct speech only. Before and after his address, when he comments on his actions, he uses the glosses 'army' (στρατός) and 'crowd' (ὄχλος).

---
[117] A. *Eu.* 681–4; note the other two aetiological addresses later in the play: v. 775 (Orestes to the *leos*) and vv. 996f. (the Furies to the *leos*).
[118] See above ch. 1.
[119] For similar glosses see A. *Eu.* 566 and 569.
[120] E. *Hec.* 529–33.

LAOS EPIC IN PERFORMANCE

I have laid out in some detail the usage of the Athenian formula 'hear, ye people' (ἀκούετε λεώ). It has a close relative, which can also be located in cult: 'come hither, all ye people' ((δεῦρ') ἴτε πάντες λεώ).[121] I have already discussed the passage from Aristotle which traces the origins of this phrase back to Theseus,[122] and which brings together many relevant elements of the archaic and classical word *laos*: its use in public announcements, the aetiological character of the occasion (if *leoi* are the founding people, Theseus is the founding king), its ritual overtones. Typical for the Athenian context is the Attic form *leos*. There can be little doubt that Theseus' words were uttered by historically 'real' heralds. Once again they are faithfully recalled in drama:

Τρ.   ἀλλ' ὦ γεωργοὶ κἄμποροι καὶ τέκτονες
       καὶ δημιουργοὶ καὶ μέτοικοι καὶ ξένοι
       καὶ νησιῶται, δεῦρ' ἴτ' ὦ πάντες λεώ.[123]

Trygaeus: You peasants and merchants and carpenters
           and craftsmen and immigrants and foreigners
           and islanders, come hither, O all ye people.

Leaving aside the question to what occasion Aristophanes alludes, we can confidently conjecture that he is inspired by historical practice. Another scene from drama, this time from Euripides' *Phaethon*, combines the phrases 'go, ye people' (ὦ ἴτε λαοί) and 'silence among the people' (σῖγ' ἔστω λεώς) in an elaborate description of ritual procedures.[124] We note again the role of the herald. The scene is of course adapted to the needs of the play. But even in such remote settings as the edge of the world, the well-known ritual gestures are clearly recognisable.[125]

We can conclude that the formula 'come hither, all ye people' ((δεῦρ') ἴτε πάντες λεώ), like its relative 'hear, ye people' (ἀκούετε λεώ), was current in Athenian ritual of the archaic

---

[121] The relevant passages are collected in Appendix B.2.
[122] Plu. *Thes.* 25.1 = Arist. fr. 384 (Rose); see above pp. 170f.
[123] Ar. *Pax* 296–8.
[124] E. *Phaeth.* 109–18 (Diggle).
[125] In passing I note that Panhellenic *laos* alternates with Attic *leos*. For discussion see n. 180.

and classical period. We may further specify that the variant ἴτε λεώ ('go, ye people') was used to see off processions, while the fuller 'come hither, all ye people' (δεῦρ' ἴτε πάντες λεώ) (re-)enacts the implications of the phrase 'to gather the people' (λαὸν ἀθροῖσαι). It is this latter phrase which most obviously constitutes the founding act itself and was appropriately associated with Theseus.

A passage from Euripides' *Orestes*, which I have quoted already, is illuminating in this context.[126] Half-way through the play a messenger describes the process by which the people of Argos gather for the court case against Orestes. In the course of his description he recalls the aetiological 'first time' when a court was convened under Danaus. First the participants in the legal case are simply called a 'crowd' (ὄχλος).[127] But when the speaker wants to express the aetiological significance of their action, he switches to *laos*. The change is telling. The force of the formulae discussed in this section rests precisely on transforming a situation without meaning and historical depth into that significant moment between past and present at which institutional progress takes place. This is the moment of *leos* ritual.[128]

As a corollary to the argument presented so far, let us consider two more points. The first concerns the formula ἀκούετε

---

[126] E. *Or.* 871–3; cf. above p. 172.

[127] The two main glosses on the term *laos* in Attic Greek and beyond are ὄχλος ('crowd') and στρατός ('army'); for the former see e.g. E. *Hec.* 529–33, *Or.* 871–3, Ar. *Ra.* 211–19 and the Atticistic lexica; for στρατός ('army') see e.g. Pi. *P.* 8.52–5, A. *Pers.* 126–30, 728f., *Eu.* 681–4; E. *Hec.* 530–2; the last passage together with E. *Supp.* 467, 669, Ar. *Pax* 296–300, 551, 1316f. and especially Ar. *Av.* 448–50 suggests that the *leos* was involved in declarations of war and peace; cf. Dunbar (1995) *ad* Ar. *Av.* 448–50. Λαός = ὄχλος seems to be younger than λαός = στρατός and is above all attested for Athens. The two glosses στρατός ('army') and ὄχλος ('crowd') are complementary and can be seen as reflecting the hopes and fears associated with the *laoi* in the *polis*: while ὄχλος ('crowd') expresses a threatening lack of diversification, στρατός ('army') implies the absence of differences which would impede effective group activity in times of crisis. The phenomenon deserves closer study than can be undertaken here.

[128] The word *leos* has already been used in *Or.* 846. When Electra asks whether Orestes has left the house in a fit of madness the chorus reply that he has gone to the Argive people (πρὸς δ' Ἀργεῖον λεών) to stand trial. If the allusion to the trial in Aeschylus' *Eumenides* raises expectations of an aetiological solution to Orestes' suffering, this is made more poignant by Euripides' use of the word *leos*.

λεῴ ('hear, ye people') and the injunction of collective restraint (εὐφημεῖν) which it entails. Time and again we encounter variants of the phrase which draw attention to this aspect, both in comedy and in tragedy.[129] The fact that Homer's people do not speak can be seen as an indication of their hopeless dependence.[130] For their counterpart in archaic and classical Athens silence becomes a sign of ritual order and a promise of the progress that ensues.

A second point is more relevant to the formula 'come hither, all ye people' ((δεῦρ') ἴτε, πάντες λεῴ). Again it concerns the character of the founding people of Attica as a group that is closely linked to ritual. Expressions such as 'all the people' (πᾶς λεώς) are frequent in archaic and classical times,[131] but they are particularly noteworthy in (pseudo-)-ritual contexts.[132] As we have seen already, comedy in particular can playfully elaborate on the phrase by providing endless lists of those involved.[133] There is more than just a joke here. As Aristophanes in particular reminds us, not all the Attic people who gather as *leoi* need to be Athenian citizens.[134] Indeed, the term can include metics and foreigners and even women and slaves.[135] *Leos* ritual creates a world of overarching communal life. Even on occasions where non-

---

[129] For comedy see Ar. *Th.* 39 with schol. *ad loc.* The question whether we should read *laos* with the scholia or *leos* with MS *R* is significant. See n. 180. For tragedy see E. *Supp.* 669f.; cf. *Hec.* 532f.; compare the passages where the assembled *laoi* break their silence in situations of extreme tension: B. 3.5–9 (restored), 9.30–5, S. *Tr.* 783 with an interesting combination of disruption and restraint; E. *Hec.* 553 with *Or.* 901 (variant reading), perhaps also *Tr.* 522; cf. *Il.* 18.502 for precedent; A. *Pers.* 592 describes the breakdown of discipline.
[130] Cf. ch. 1, n. 111.
[131] As they are in epic; see above ch. 1, 'Society and the stone'.
[132] Cf. Appendix B.2.
[133] Ar. *Pax* 296–8, quoted above p. 180.
[134] The standard combination is Ἀττικὸς λεώς ('Attic people') not *Ἀθηναῖος λεώς ('Athenian people') or *λεώς Ἀθηνῶν ('people of Athens'). This has important implications for our term. Synchronically, not everyone who may be said to be 'Attic' is also 'Athenian'; see e.g. Loraux (1993) ch. 3 and especially pp. 116f. (women may be 'Attic', but not 'Athenian'). From a diachronic perspective, the adjective 'Attic' harks back to a time where the city of Athens – and hence 'Athenians' – do not yet exist. Both points are characteristic of the term *leos*. For an exception to the rule see *CEG* II 890 (λαὸς Ἀθηναίων, 'people of the Athenians').
[135] For foreigners and metics see Ar. *Pax* 296–8; for women and slaves see Arist. *Pr.* 922b with E. *Phaeth.* 102–18 (Diggle) and Ar. *Ach.* 1000–4.

citizens were not 'actually' involved (as they clearly were not in the historical activity of the Areopagus), the founding assembly is envisaged as temporarily abolishing social strata. *Leos* ritual was the prime occasion on which the community reminded itself of who it was made of. Everyone had to be there when society started.

Public announcements (κηρύττειν) to the *laos* in archaic and classical Greece signal a process of primeval crisis and institutional progress. By collapsing and thereby temporarily abolishing social differentiation, they create a context in which institutional progress can and must take place. At Athens this process is formalised in the two standard addresses we have looked at. One is used to gather and dismiss the assembly of *leoi* and to set processions on their way. The other urges restraint and makes room for the transforming act itself. None of this differs in principle from what the herald does in epic.[136] But in archaic and classical times, especially at Athens, a strong ritual–aetiological slant is added. We know what we have achieved, because we know that we once were – and still are – the *leos* of Attica.

A festival of institutional progress

Communal ritual in fifth-century Athens was often regarded as *leos* ritual, and it is possible that the address to the *leos* was in fact one of its defining features.[137] The formula 'come here, all ye people' became the Athenian κήρυγμα *par excellence*. Its relative, 'hear, ye people' (ἀκούετε λεῴ), was so common that even at a much later stage it could be exploited in jokes.[138] Demes that did not use it prove the rule by giving rise to negative aetiologies.[139] Possible alternatives such as 'hear ye citizens' (*ἀκούετε πολῖται), or 'hear, ye people' – with *demos* for 'people' – are unattested and would at any rate

---

[136] See above ch. 1, 'Social structures'.
[137] For historical examples see above n. 105.
[138] Ath. 8.41.
[139] Plu. *Thes.* 13.4; cf. Philoch. *FGrHist* 328 fr. 108 with Jacoby's note *ad loc.*

be uncomfortably partial.[140] The scarcely gendered, inclusive, pre-political *leos* is the obvious concept for the large-scale ritual group in archaic and classical Attica. It is more probable than not that our formulae would have been uttered at every such occasion, the (Great) Panathenaea among them;[141] but whether or not we accept this to be likely, such occasions could certainly – and very often were – *looked at* as gatherings of the Attic *leos*, the founding people.

We are now ready to return to our initial question. I started this chapter by asking how Homer's people would have been received by an archaic and classical Greek audience. The argument so far has been that the Athenians, an example of such an audience, would have associated the term *laos* with institutional progress in myth and ritual. Earlier on I argued that Homeric epic – while allowing for the possibility of a better world – on the whole exposes the vulnerability of Homer's people. This must have made a striking contrast to the experience of any Greek audience, but it must have struck the Athenians in particular because they knew their 'founding people' primarily from *leos* ritual.

The effect would have been all the more remarkable on occasions where the Athenian audience was specifically encouraged to see itself as the Attic *leos* (Ἀττικὸς λεώς) on their way from uninstitutional early life to the political structures of the city. The Great Panathenaea was such an occasion. This festival, I claim, did not simply provide a space in which the inhabitants of Attica collectively staged the performance of Homeric poems and with them the fate of Homer's people. Rather, the (Great) Panathenaea can in itself be seen as a

---

[140] For an etymology of Greek δῆμος as 'that which is divided' see Frisk (1960–70) s.v. δῆμος, Palmer (1963) 188f., Chantraine (1968–80) s.v. δαίομαι, LfgrE s.v. δῆμος, Wyatt (1994–5) 169, who also suggests that the word *laos* is etymologically rooted in the sense 'that which is gathered together'; cf. ch. 2, n. 316.

[141] For this part of the argument I concentrate on the Great Panathenaea, assuming the festival to remain relatively stable as regards the issues and time-span that are relevant here; for Homeric performances at the Great Panathenaea see Lycurg. *Against Leocrates* 102 with Kotsidu (1991) 41–4; for a dynamic model of ritual see Geertz (1973), Grimes (1982), Morris (1993); an attempt to write the early history of the Panathenaea is made e.g. in Davison (1958), Mikalson (1976), Robertson (1985) and (1992).

A FESTIVAL OF INSTITUTIONAL PROGRESS

prime dramatisation of early life and institutional progress at Athens. As such it is in stark contrast with the story told in Homer.

There are two ways of supporting the claims I have just made. First, there is the direct evidence for *leoi* at the Great Panathenaea. It is varied and tantalising, and, as so often in matters of cult practice raises more questions than it solves.[142] The present study cannot hope to tackle any of these questions in depth; and since my point here does not depend on details of ritual procedure, I have adopted a second, more general approach.

The direct evidence aside, it can be argued that the proceedings of the Great Panathenaea betray a number of characteristics which encourage identification of its celebrants with the founding people of Attica (Ἀττικὸς λεώς). This suggestion is independent of whether or not such identification was ever made explicit, for example, in the form of the ritual pronouncements we have studied so far, though there are good reasons to believe that they were. What I wish to argue here is that the Great Panathenaea provided a performative framework in which the complementary narratives of Homer's people (ὤλεσε λαόν) and the founding people (ἀκούετε λεῴ) were encouraged to intersect and resonate.

Laoi in archaic and classical Greek myth and ritual function as 'the founding people', a group on its way to institutional progress. In myth they predate the founding of a city, of a cult, or a lawcourt, and their aetiological character is re-played at Athens in the form of *leos* ritual. The Panathenaea is perhaps the one Attic festival which most ostensibly plays out processes of social formation. About its privileged position in the Athenian calendar year N. Loraux writes: 'At each

---

[142] The *leokoreion* as the starting-point of the Panathenaic procession is of prime importance here; see Th. 6.75.3, Arist. *Ath.* 18.3. Robertson attractively explains the name as referring to the 'place where the *leos* is ordered' (λεώς + κορεῖν/ κοσμεῖν); see Robertson (1992) 103–5, restated in (1996) 58. The idea goes back to Curtius (1894), who in turn takes up a suggestion made by Müller (1873) 146; cf. also Frazer (1898) *ad* Paus. 1.5.2; though the etymology is not attested for archaic and classical Athens. Another important clue is given much later, in *IG* 2(2) 5006.1–4 = 466 (P–W). The problem starts when we try to fill the gap between the reign of Hadrian and the earliest history of the festival.

celebration of the Panathenaea, the history of Athens begins, or begins anew.'[143] The origins of the festival were traced back to the arch-Athenian Erichthonius[144] and sometimes to Theseus.[145] As Deubner comments: 'The symbol of the political unification of Attica is the name of Theseus, and so the name Panathenaea was linked to him.'[146] The aetiological character of our festival is mirrored in its structure. As has often been pointed out, the Panathenaea was socially comprehensive, featuring citizens of all age groups as well as women, metics and slaves.[147] Everyone has to be there when Athens is founded. The different groups were on display in a procession which led from the city gates to the religious and political heart of Athens, the Acropolis. On the way we hear of such ancient customs as the so-called 'contest of the sideman' (*apobates*), a combination of chariot race and foot race.[148] The culminating sacrifice involved a contribution by all Attic towns as well as the colonies and allies,[149] allowing the city to replay the founding acts of settlement (*synoikismos*) and colonisation in cult.[150] Among the festivals of Athens the Panathenaea most obviously bridges the gap between pre-political 'early times' and political life as it is 'now'. This is the occasion at which the city founds other cities and is itself, in Loraux's words, founded and refounded every year afresh.

The (Great) Panathenaea, then, was in important ways the founding occasion of Athenian political life. But it was also crucial at a more fundamental level. The archaic and, as yet, little understood contest of *euandria*[151] that formed part of

---

[143] Loraux (1993) 42.
[144] Hellanicus in *FGrHist* 323a fr. 2, Androtion in *FGrHist* 324 fr. 2; cf. Istros in *FGrHist* 334 fr. 4; for discussion see Jacoby *ad loc.*, Loraux (1993) ch. 1.
[145] Paus. 8.2.1; see also schol. Pl. *Prm.* 127a and Phot., Suda *s.v.*
[146] Deubner (1932) 22f.
[147] For the comprehensive character of the occasion see e.g. Parker (1996) 91.
[148] For further details and discussion see pp. 189f. below.
[149] Deubner (1932) 34, quoting schol. Ar. *Nu.* 386; cf. Castriota (1992) 200, Sourvinou-Inwood (1994) 271f. with n. 10, Jameson (1994) 307.
[150] Deubner (1932) 34; cf. Levi (1968) 1 189, Parke (1977) 33.
[151] For a possible link between the *laos* and the *euandria* see Pi. *N.* 10.36 and Ezek. *Exag.* 203 in a context which imitates fifth-century Athenian tragedy; for the nature of the *euandria* see Boegehold (1996) 97–103, Goldhill (1994) 355f., Crowther (1985).

the festivities suggests that at the Panathenaea the Athenians also celebrated their manpower.[152] Another point is closely related. It has recently been argued that the Athenian *ephebeia* of later times ended on 28 Hecatombaion, the day of the Panathenaic procession.[153] While the evidence does not allow us to reach certainty on this point, the prominence of young men on the Parthenon frieze clearly testifies to the importance of ephebic participants.[154] Political progress is accompanied by the coming into being of a new generation of citizen soldiers. The well-being of a society's (a city's) youth and the well-being of the *laos* are closely linked in the term νεολαία, 'young folk', a word which appears in Attic literature from Aeschylus onwards.[155] Timotheus praises the 'blossoms of youth' (ἄνθεα ἥβης) as a hallmark of the Spartan *laos*,[156] suggesting that the phenomenon was seen to be more than just Attic; and the testimony of early epic further suggests that, throughout archaic and classical Greece, the well-being of the *laos* was linked to that of the (male) youth of a given society.[157] The term νεολαία ('young folk') indicates that at Athens this connection was particularly close.[158]

---

[152] Compare the myths of enlargement in Plu. *Thes.* 25.1 = Arist. fr. 384 (Rose) and Philochorus in schol. Pi. *O.* 9.70b–c = *FGrHist ad* 328 fr. 95; see also A. *Pers.* 116–27, where it is feared that the city will be 'void of men' (κένανδρος) after the *leos* has left; cf. *Pers.* 729f.; for a positive version see Hdt. 8.136.2.

[153] Robertson (1992) 108–14, who also suggests a Peisistratean origin; it is unlikely that the *ephebeia* as described in Arist. *Ath.* 42 predates the fourth century; cf. Wilamowitz (1893) I 191–4; however, institutional reform does not preclude strong continuity in terminology and social practice. On the question of a pre-Lycurgan *ephebeia* see Pélékidis (1962) *passim*, esp. 9 and 52, Vidal-Naquet (1986) 97–9, Winkler (1990) 26–31.

[154] It is discussed, from a political perspective, by Osborne (1987) 103–5.

[155] A. *Pers.* 669, *Supp.* 686–8, Ar. fr. 73 (*PCG*); E. *Alc.* 103 may be corrupt – see Dale (1954) *ad loc.*

[156] Tim. fr. 791.206–9 (*PMG*).

[157] Epic 'people' (λαός) and 'young men' (κοῦροι) stand in a close thematic and formulaic relationship with one another; cf. especially the phrases λαὸς Ἀχαιῶν and κοῦροι Ἀχαιῶν at the end of the hexameter line.

[158] According to Kassel/Austin *ad* Ar. fr. 73, νεολαία ('young folk') in Aristophanes reflects the language of tragic choruses. Phot. *s.v.* νεολέως [*sic*] may preserve the Attic form, in which case it should be accentuated on the second syllable (*Thesaurus Linguae Graecae s.v.*) and perhaps the explanatory ἔφηβος ('young man') changed to ἔφηβοι in the plural ('young men'); see Favis (1950) 81 and Georgacas (1958) 172f. In a late Attic inscription the ephebes are themselves called a *leos*: *IG* 2(2) 3744.1–4; cf. *IG* 2(2) 3765.

Timotheus uses imagery of plant growth to describe the beauty of youth (ἥβη), and he sees both as a characteristic feature of the Spartan *laos*. The Panathenaic procession shows analogous features. Because of such elements as the θαλλοφόροι ('twig-bearers') and the sacred olive branch (εἰρεσιώνη), the Great Panathenaea has been called an agrarian festival.[159] We can now understand how these disparate elements come together in the overall aetiological character of the occasion. The Panathenaic procession is envisaged as a social world at the moment of growth and reproduction. It dramatises precisely that test-case of social life where collective crisis leads on to the rise of a renewed social world whose survival is in turn secured by new institutions, above all a new 'contract' with the patron goddess.[160] Institutional progress becomes a function of communal well-being and *vice versa*. This is the world of the founding people, and it was formalised at Athens as *leos* ritual.

Laos epic in performance

I have argued for a number of aspects which would have encouraged sixth or fifth-century celebrants of the Great Panathenaea to see themselves as a gathered *leos*. This suggestion does not end our search for early Homeric audiences, nor does it exhaust possible explanations of what the Athenians were celebrating at their most important state festival;[161] but it can tell us something about what Homer's people might have meant to a Panathenaic audience as opposed to that of any other performance context; such as, say, the symposium, the school, or other festivals. Let us, finally, draw together the different strands of the argument.

---

[159] Mommsen (1898) 8–10, 57f.; Farnell (1896) 296f. is more cautious; cf. Burkert (1966) 25.

[160] For Athena's connection with the *laos* in epic see above ch. 1, 'Society and the stone'. For her relationship with 'her' *leos* in tragedy see A. *Eu.* 996–9, E. *Heracl.* 923, *IT* 960, 1452, *Erechtheus* fr. 360.48f. (Nauck).

[161] For further study of the Panathenaea see e.g. Kotsidu (1991), Robertson (1992), Neils (1992), (1994), (1996).

Simonides tells us that Homer sang to the *laoi*.[162] But quite apart from his testimony and from what epic itself can tell us about the audience of epic song,[163] it is hard to believe that the celebrants at the Great Panathenaea would not have reacted with a mixture of recognition and rejection to what they heard. The people of Attica, too, were a *laos*, or could see themselves as such – and what they saw when they chose to look was likely to provoke a strong reaction to the story told in Homer. If Simonides is to be trusted, archaic and classical Greeks could always conceptualise Homeric poetry as being sung to the people. But the Panathenaic context adds a more specific framework. For the Athenians the *laos* that counted most was, and had to be, their own founding people, and this was never more true than at their founding festival, the (Great) Panathenaea. Under such circumstances, the vivid display of a *laos* so similar to and yet so radically different from their own must have been fully resonant. It is this resonance which I wish to explore in the remaining part of my discussion.[164]

In the following section I argue that at the Great Panathenaea the *laos* of Homer's epic and the *leos* of Athenian ritual intersect with and thus illuminate each other. I do not suggest that the Homeric texts as we have them were composed for the occasion or could only be understood as part of it.[165] Nor do I wish to reduce the Panathenaea to a mere setting for Homeric song. Rather, I suggest that in the context of its Panathenaic performance Homeric epic was likely to be perceived in the light of contemporary *laos* ideology as described throughout this chapter. In order to understand better how this may have worked, let me first introduce two analogous ways in which the ritual of the Great Panthenaea resonates with Homeric epic and *vice versa*.

I start with the *Iliad* as the core text of Homeric poetry and the so-called 'contest of the sidemen' (*apobatai*) as a crucial

---

[162] See above p. 146.
[163] Cf. p. 146, n. 3.
[164] The concept of resonance between myth and ritual is developed in Cook (1995) 8.
[165] Further discussed above pp. 147–52.

element of the Panathenaic procession. Dionysius of Halicarnassus spells out for us what is only ever implicit in cult.[166] The sideman (*apobates*) was typical of the Panathenaic procession in the fifth century, so much so that he forms a prominent part of the Parthenon frieze. As Simon writes: 'The chariots and apobatai are deliberately chosen here because they symbolize a time-honored contest and [are] typical of Athens.'[167] Simon takes up two points in Dionysius' description, the ancient descent of the *apobates* and his typically Athenian character. But she neglects a third: in the guise of *parabatai* the Athenian sidemen also feature in poetry. Dionysius says that 'the poets call them *parabatai*, the Athenians *apobatai*'. In drawing this distinction he seems to be referring to Homer in particular:

ἂν δ' ἔβαν ἐν δίφροισι παραιβάται ἡνίοχοί τε.[168]

and the charioteers and sidemen (*parabatai*) mounted the chariots.

Parallels between chariot-riding in Homer and at the Panathenaea have long been noted, and Thompson in particular has used them to argue for historical continuity between early hero-worship and the festival.[169] According to Thompson, the Panathenaic sideman (*apobates*) provides the kernel of ritual activity around which the other competitions of the festival developed. In fact, pseudo-Eratosthenes already links the invention of the chariot in general and that of the sideman in particular to the Panathenaea; and attributes them both to the arch-Athenian Erichthonius.[170] Again the Panhellenic gloss *parabates* is made to resonate with its local counterpart. One concept explains the other, and we can assume that just as the Hellenistic text can play on their similarity, fifth-

---

[166] D.H. *Roman antiquities* 7.73; cf. *AB* 426.
[167] Simon (1983) 62; cf. Connor (1987) 45 n. 31, quoting Harpocration *s.v.* ἀποβάτης and comparing D.S. 12.70.
[168] *Il.* 23.132; taken up by E. *Supp.* 677–9 in an epicising context.
[169] Thompson (1961), followed by Simon (1983) 62, Castriota (1992) 219, Robertson (1996) 57f.
[170] [Eratosth.] *Katast.* 13; cf. Hygin. *Astron.* 2.13.; cf. *Marmor Parium* 10 and the evidence assembled by Jacoby (1904) *ad loc.*; on Erichthonius see Loraux (1993) ch 1. and *passim*.

century Athenians at their festival would have compared the Homeric sidemen with their own Erichthonian version of the phenomenon.[171]

Parabatic chariot-riding is all-pervasive in the *Iliad*, but the passage I have quoted above is the only one where we find the noun.[172] Its context in the funeral of Patroclus seems significant. Like the Athenian sideman (*apobates*), Homer's *parabates* most prominently occurs as part of a ritual procession. However, in Homer we do not see the proud display of aetiological progress found in the Athenian version. Whether on the battlefield or at the funeral, the Iliadic sidemen hint at suffering and loss, while their Athenian counterparts celebrate the cunning of Erichthonius, who overcomes the crisis of early social life.

The relationship between crisis and aetiological progress that we have seen in the pair *parabates–apobates* is more obvious still in the offering of the garment to Athena in the *Iliad* and at the Great Panathenaea. Everything goes wrong in Homer. The procession fails; the city will be conquered.[173] An audience of Athenian celebrants cannot but have compared the *ad hoc*, uninstitutionalised, action in Troy with its own carefully prescribed and highly stylised doings.[174] Their *peplos* is a very special piece of cloth, and it is decidedly *not* offered *ad hoc*.[175] Quite the contrary: its acceptance is guaranteed through a long tradition of successful ritual.[176]

We have seen two examples of how the Great Panathenaea resonates with the *Iliad* and *vice versa*. Common gestures mark out an Athenian success story of institutional problem-solving. This is not to reduce Homeric poetry to a mere foil for Athenian self-appraisal. The *Iliad* is full of positive social

---

[171] The military chariot, also on the Parthenon frieze, was said to have been invented by Theseus; see Mommsen (1898) 140, quoting schol. Ar. *Nu.* 28.
[172] As noted in schol. *Il.* 23.132b, c.
[173] *Il.* 6.305–11.
[174] Solon fr. 4.1–4 (West) shows that such comparisons go back a long way.
[175] The garment offered by the Trojans is special in a different sense, in that it is characteristically ill-omened; cf. *Il.* 6.289–95.
[176] Davison (1958) 26 draws attention to this when he argues against the athetesis of *Il.* 6.271–311 advocated by Lorimer (1950) 442–8.

paradigms, and Athenian audiences in particular never tired of drawing on them. But side by side with the glorious exploits of heroic times and enwrapped in the beautiful diction of Panhellenic verse, there are also darker aspects to the world of Homer. One of them has been seen throughout this study: if the Homeric hero is better than we are now, the situation of Homer's people is worse. There may be pathos in their suffering, but there is little to commend it for emulation. Certainly the Athenians *qua leos*, the 'founding people' of Attica, would have known where they stood when they heard that Achilles or Agamemnon or Hector 'destroyed the people'; on the side of their own institutions, not of the Homeric 'shepherd of the people'; the side of progress, not of stagnation; of life, not death. To be sure, the members of the audience would have sympathised with what they heard – after all, the temptation of imagining oneself being led by Achilles must have been strong. But such sympathy could never go beyond a certain point. At the Great Panathenaea, if anywhere, we (Athenians) must realise the differences between founding people and Homer's people, 'us' and 'them' – if only so as to find our way back into 'our' world and refound the city.

So much for Troy and the prime example both of Homeric story-telling and of story-telling about Homer's people. Things are slightly different on Ithaca, the rocky island. Despite the overwhelming generic pull of phrases such as 'he destroyed the people' the *Odyssey* ostensibly presents a narrative of social progress through social cleansing. The leader comes home, bringing death to some but prosperity to all. No matter that companions and suitors are lost on the way. They could be but are not 'in fact' seen as the *laoi*. The seemingly endless line of leaders destroying their *laoi* is curtailed with a dramatic gesture in book 24 and at the end of ends, as the 'true' account has it, the people will prosper.

As we have seen, there are traditional elements to the *Odyssey*'s revisionary zeal. *Laoi* turn into 'companions' as soon as we enter the world of *nostos*, thus inaugurating the transformation into what I have called the epic's overall 'first person bias'. In other ways, too, the switch from Troy to *nostos* proves important. If we take a closer look at the ever-flourishing tradition of return narratives which attached itself to the Homeric enterprise and of which the *Odyssey* itself is only the most prominent example, it appears that Homeric homecomings have a potential of converting the Panhellenic challenge posed by Homer's people into countless aetiological solutions.

Once again, a Hellenistic text spells out for us what is meant. In Strabo, Homer's people overcome the crisis of war and displacement by founding a *polis*. For Strabo, Homer's people have themselves become the founding people.[177] The *Odyssey* does not go as far as that. But for all their problems, Odyssean *laoi* are on the whole more lucky than their counterpart in the *Iliad*. The end of narrative and violence in book 24 may come abruptly; and the repeated promise of a better future may strike us as lame. But these gestures do go some way toward building a bridge between the fate of Homer's people and what we have seen in chapter 3. Placing itself in the transitional world of the returns the *Odyssey* approaches – without fully realising – the sort of institutional transformation which the Athenians themselves know they have long achieved.[178]

The ritual of the Panathenaea does for the Athenians of the archaic and classical period what the *Odyssey* in the last consequence fails to deliver: the challenge of social life is met with a permanent institutional solution. For the Hellenistic author Strabo the *laos* on tour is both Homeric and local, part of the problem and part of the solution. In fact, the possibility of having it both ways was eagerly exploited by political communities throughout the Hellenistic world. At Athens the difference between 'our' *leos*, the founding people, and the *laos* of Homer remains more marked. I have argued that these two

---

[177] Strabo 13.1.53, 14.1.20, 14.4.3; for the purposes of the present argument, it does not matter that the *laos* of Strabo's first passage is Trojan.
[178] Athenian readers in particular may not have had difficulties comparing the 'rocky' island with their own notoriously 'rocky' piece of land; cf. *Il*. 3.201, *Od*. 1.247, 15.510, 16.124, 21.346, *RE s.vv.* Kranaoi, Κραναός; for further resonances between Attic myth and the *Odyssey* see Cook (1995).

realisations of one term form a pair of opposites which are mutually explanatory precisely because they are in important ways mutually exclusive. 'We' are Attic because we are *not* Homeric; we are – and must be – the founding people, because we are *not* doomed like the people of the Achaeans.[179]

Reflection on Homer's people at the Great Panathenaea addresses a concern which was important to the Athenians as it would have been to any other political community in archaic and classical Greece. There had to be, in the calendar of the *polis*, occasions on which to remember the founding acts of society. The Panathenaea was such an occasion. And yet, this most optimistic of festivals, that moment when the community reconstituted itself under the protection of its patron goddess, featured the performance of poetry which sang to the founding people the sorrows of Homer's *laoi*. The *Iliad* in particular as the most lengthy and most canonical of Homeric texts focuses on the negative aspects of their existence. The *Odyssey* leads us through relentless violence to the threshold of a better world only to break off and retreat into silence. For an Athenian audience this is only half the story, and not the half they would have emphasised for themselves. The problems described in Homer are 'Achaean'; their solution is left to the Athenians.[180]

There remains much we do not know or understand about the performances of Homer at the Great Panathenaea. At what point of the festival precisely was epic produced? How was it done? What texts were chosen at what time? More important still; how did the political changes of the fifth century affect performance practice and audience response? The present discussion does not claim to answer any of these important questions. What I do hope to have shown is one aspect of life in the *polis* which would very likely have shaped the

---

[179] Conveniently, Homeric epic says next to nothing about Attic *laoi* in particular; see n. 182.
[180] The difference between Attic *leos* (Ἀττικὸς λεώς) and epic/Panhellenic *laos* (λαὸς Ἀχαιῶν) articulates this divide. Although the form *leos* is known to epic, it is used only in a few personal names; and although the Athenians knew and understood the word *laos*, they never used it for their own ritual practice. Drama stands between epic and ritual and therefore uses both forms; see Björck (1950).

expectations and preoccupations of an early Panathenaic audience.

For Homeric audiences of the sixth and fifth century the central issue concerning Homer's people would always have been the possibility of institutional progress. At Athens this is not only made more poignant by the presence of a strong ritual model; the Athenians are also invited to reflect on Homer's people and with them their status as the founding people of Attica by the very nature of the Panathenaea as a performance context. When the people of Attica met at the beginning of their political year to (re)found Athens once again, they celebrated their capacity of stepping out and being 'the founding people', the one *leos* among the *laoi*.[181] Somewhere on the way Homer's people made possible a crucial reflection on what that meant. History had begun; the people of Attica had once again gathered to live.[182]

Conclusion

As we have seen in chapter 1, early Greek epic sings about the incurably vulnerable nature of the *laoi*. Their defining structure, encapsulated in the metaphor of the 'shepherd of the people' (*ποιμὴν λαῶν), fails; as a result, the leaders are said to have 'destroyed the people' (ὤλεσε λαόν). Homer elaborates on this narrative in a highly significant fashion. The *Iliad* goes out of its way not to tell the fall of Troy which both Agamemnon and Hector expect. Instead, it sings about Achilles and the fall of the people on both sides. In a different way, the *Odyssey*, too, pays tribute to the genre's fascination with the

---

[181] For an example of a select *laos* outside Athens see Tim. fr. 791.236 (*PMG*) with Wilamowitz (1903) 63; note that the *laoi* of the Achaeans serve as a foil for local pride.

[182] Plutarch tells us that the Iliadic *Catalogue of ships* was read with proud awareness that only the Athenians appear in it as a *demos*: Plu. *Thes.* 25.3. If this is an old reading, it further develops the opposition between *laos* and *leos*, suggesting that Homer's people include everyone except the Athenians, who are this time associated with the more 'modern' and patriotically charged concept *demos*. For democratic tendencies to suppress the term *laos* see also ch. 1, n. 35; for the difference between *laos* and *demos* see ch. 2, n. 316 and ch. 3, n. 140.

laoi. Here the group is relegated to the narrative sidelines, its place taken by 'companions' and 'suitors'. I have argued that this entails a striking act of perspectival rearrangement. Odyssean groups die for their leader. At the same time, the *Odyssey* presents itself as leading Homer's people to the threshold of a better era. When Odysseus dies, the people prosper.

Early Greek epic as a whole tends to depict the crisis of the *laoi* as absolute, and although it gives glimpses of a better world, it does so in passing. By contrast, archaic and classical literature emphasises the possibility of aetiological progress. This process is narrated in myth but, more importantly, it is enacted in ritual. *Leos* ritual becomes the dominant model of life among the *laoi* in archaic and classical Athens. Formulae such as 'hear, ye people' (ἀκούετε λεῴ) and 'come hither, all ye people ((δεῦρ') ἴτε πάντες λεῴ) serve to gather what I called 'the founding people' of Attica and create a world in which institutional progress becomes necessary and possible.

The (Great) Panathenaea displays many of the characteristics associated with the Attic *leos*. As well as marking the beginning of the political year at Athens, the festival also served more generally as a celebration of the city's regenerative capacities. As 'a festival of institutional progress' the Panathenaea reflects on the preconditions of successful social life in subtle and varied ways. The performance of Homeric poetry is one of them.

From the point of view of life in the *polis*, the Greeks shared a pre-history, as long as it remained at a stage of unmitigated crisis. Institutional solutions could only speak to one particular audience. At the Panathenaea the city of Athens gave its own very specific answer to the challenge of communal life. It did so diachronically by remembering *autochthony* and *synoikismos* and by displaying the inventions of Erichthonius and Theseus on a symbolic march from the city gates to the *polis*. Synchronically, it celebrated the renewal of communal life through successful cult, and a successful transferral of power. Every four years, this proud display of institutional problem-solving was set against the backdrop of Homer's people, a social world without effective social structures.

Appendix A
EPIC FORMULAE

A.1 'Shepherd of the people' etc.

[−∪∪−∪∪−∪∪−∪∪] ποιμένα λαῶν *Il.* 1.263, 2.243, 4.296, 5.144, 6.214, 9.81, 10.3, 73, 406, 11.92, 187, 202, 506, 578, 598, 651, 842, 13.411, 14.22, 423, 516, 17.348, 19.386, 22.277, 23.389, *Od.* 3.469, 4.532, 17.109, Hes. fr. 23(a).34 (M–W)[?], fr. 193.1 (M–W), fr. 280.8 (M–W)
[28 Hom., 25 *Il.*, 3 [?] Hes.]

[−∪∪−∪∪−∪∪−∪∪] ποιμένι λαῶν *Il.* 2.85, 105, 254, 772, 4.413, 5.513, 566, 570, 7.230, 469, 11.370, 13.600, 15.262, 16.2, 19.35, 251, 20.110, 23.411, 24.654, *Od.* 3.156, 4.24, 528, 14.497, 15.151, 18.70, 20.106, 24.368, 456, Hes. fr. 141.19 (M–W), *Iliupersis* fr. 4.2 (Davies), Asius Samius fr. 1.3 (Davies)
[28 Hom., 19 *Il.*, 1 Hes., 1 *Iliupersis*, 1 Asius Samius]

[−∪∪−∪∪−∪∪−∪∪] ὄρχαμε λαῶν *Il.* 14.102 (*var. lect.* ἀνδρῶν), 17.12, 19.289, 21.221, *Od.* 4.156, 291, 316, 10.538, 15.64, 87, 167, Hes. fr. 301 (M–W)
[11 Hom., 7 *Od.*, 1 Hes.]

[−∪∪−∪∪−∪∪−∪∪] κοίρανε λαῶν *Il.* 7.234, 8.281, 9.644, 11.465
[−∪∪−∪∪−∪∪−] κοσμήτορε λαῶν *Il.* 1.16, 375, 3.236
[−∪∪−∪∪−∪∪−] κοσμήτορι λαῶν *Od.* 18.152
[−∪∪−∪∪−∪∪−] ἡγήτορα λαῶν *Il.* 20.383, Hes. fr. 43(a).58 (M–W), fr. 136.18 (M–W)
[−∪∪−∪∪−] λαῶν ἀγόν [−∪∪−−] Hes. fr. 25.34 (M–W)
λαῶν ... ἄναξ *Il.* 9.98; cf. *Od.* 2.234, 5.12 λαῶν οἷσιν ἄνασσε σημάντορες (sc. λαῶν) *Il.* 4.430f.

A.2 'Saving the people'

ἤ κέ σφιν νῆάς τε σαῷ καὶ λαὸν Ἀχαιῶν *Il.* 9.424
ὅππως κεν νῆάς τε σαῷς καὶ λαὸν Ἀχαιῶν *Il.* 9.681

APPENDIX A

αὐτὰρ ὅτ' ἐς νῆάς τε ἴδοι καὶ λαὸν Ἀχαιῶν *Il.* 10.14
Αἴαντε, σφὼ μέν τε σαώσετε λαὸν Ἀχαιῶν *Il.* 13.47
παυρότεροι θνήσκουσι, σαοῦσι δὲ λαὸν ὀπίσσω Tyrt. fr. 11.13 (West)

A.3 'Destroying the people'

(i) δυσκλέα Ἄργος ἱκέσθαι, ἐπεὶ πολὺν ὤλεσα λαόν *Il.* 2.115, 9.22
    [–∪∪–∪∪–∪∪–∪∪]   ὤλεσε λαόν *Il.* 22.107
    [–∪∪–∪∪–∪∪–]   ἀπὸ δ' ὤλεσε λαούς *Od.* 24.428
    [–∪∪–∪∪–∪∪–]   καὶ ἀπώλεσε λαούς *Od.* 9.265
    [–∪∪–∪∪–∪∪–]   ὀλέκοντο δὲ λαοί *Il.* 1.10
    [–∪∪–∪∪–∪∪–]   ὤλλυντο δὲ λαοί Hes. fr. 33(a).24
                             (M–W)
    [–∪∪–∪∪–∪]   ἀποφθινύθουσι δὲ λαοί *Il.* 5.643, Hes. *Op.* 243[1]

(ii) [–∪∪] ὤλεσε λαὸν ἀτάσθαλον [–∪∪– –] *Od.* 7.60
     [–∪∪] ὤλεσα λαὸν ἀτασθαλι- [–∪∪– –] *Il.* 22.104
(iii) [–∪∪–∪∪–∪] ἀπώλεσε λαὸν Ἀχαιῶν *Il.* 5.758
     [–∪∪–∪∪–∪] ἀπώλετο λαὸς Ἀχαιῶν *Il.* 6.223[2]
(iv) βούλομ' ἐγὼ λαὸν σῶν ἔμμεναι ἢ ἀπολέσθαι *Il.* 1.117
     νεῦσε δέ οἱ λαὸν σόον ἔμμεναι οὐδ' ἀπολέσθαι *Il.* 8.246[3]
(v) [–∪∪–∪∪–∪] δάμασσε δὲ λαὸν Ἀχαιῶν *Il.* 9.118
    [–∪∪–∪∪–] δέδμητο δὲ λαὸς ὑπ' αὐτῷ *Od.* 3.305
(vi) λαοὶ μὲν φθινύθουσι [∪–∪∪–∪∪– –] *Il.* 6.327, 9.593 var. lect. ant.
(vii) τιμήσας μὲν ἐμέ, μέγα δ' ἴψαο λαὸν Ἀχαιῶν *Il.* 1.454, 16.237
(viii) πέφνον λαὸν ἄριστον ἀμύνων Ἀργείοισιν *Od.* 11.500
      ὅσσον λαὸν ἔπεφνεν ἀμύνων Ἀργείοισιν *Od.* 11.518[4]
(ix) ἔσσεται ἦμαρ ὅτ' ἄν ποτ' ὀλώλῃ Ἴλιος ἱρή
     καὶ Πρίαμος καὶ λαὸς ἐϋμμελίω Πριάμοιο *Il.* 4.164f., 6.448f.
(x) τόφρα μάλ' ἀμφοτέρων βέλε' ἥπτετο, πῖπτε δὲ λαός *Il.* 8.67, 11.85, 15.319, 16.778

A.4 'Gathering the people'

(i) [–∪∪–∪∪–∪∪–∪∪] λαὸν ἀγείρας *Il.* 2.664
    [–∪∪–∪∪–∪∪–∪∪] λαὸν ἀγείρων *Il.* 4.377
    [–∪∪–∪∪–∪∪–∪∪] λαὸν ἄγειρεν *Il.* 11.716

---

[1] A variant leads on to number (ii): ἀλλ' ὁ μὲν ὤλεσε λαὸν ἀτάσθαλον ὤλετο δ' αὐτός *Od.* 7.60.
[2] Related: [–∪∪] λαὸν ὀλέσθαι Ἀχαιϊκόν [–∪∪– –] *Il.* 13.349. Number (iv) can be seen as a variant.
[3] Related: [–∪∪–∪∪–] ἐπεί κ' ἀπὸ λαὸν ὀλήται *Il.* 11.764.
[4] *Il.* 13.349 is related; see n. 2.

EPIC FORMULAE

[–⏑⏑–⏑⏑–⏑⏑–⏑⏑] λαὸν ἀγείρω *Il.* 16.129
[–⏑⏑–⏑⏑–⏑⏑–⏑⏑] λαὸν ἄγειραν *Od.* 3.140, Hes. *Op.* 652[5]
(ii) [–⏑⏑–⏑⏑–⏑⏑–] ἐσαγείρετο λαός *Od.* 14.248
[–⏑⏑–⏑⏑–⏑⏑–] ἠγείρετο λαός Hes. *Sc.* 475
[–⏑⏑–⏑⏑–⏑⏑–] ἐπεγείρετο [ἐπαγείρετο Vitelli] λαός Hes. fr. 75.11 (M–W)[6]
(iii) λαὸν ἀγείροντες [⏑⏑–⏑⏑–⏑⏑– –] *Il.* 11.770
λαὸν ἀγειρούσῃ [⏑⏑–⏑⏑–⏑⏑– –] *Il.* 4.28[7]

A.5 'Dispersing the people'

[–⏑⏑] λαὸν μὲν σκέδασον [⏑⏑–⏑⏑– –] *Il.* 19.171
[–⏑⏑] λαὸν μὲν σκέδασεν [⏑⏑–⏑⏑– –] *Il.* 23.162
[–⏑⏑] λαοὶ μὲν σκίδνασθ' [⏑⏑–⏑⏑– –] *Od.* 2.252[8]

A.6 Interaction between group and leader

(i) λαοὶ ἕποντ' [⏑⏑–⏑⏑–⏑⏑–⏑⏑– –] *Il.* 2.578, 16.551
λαοὶ ἕπονθ' [⏑⏑–⏑⏑–⏑⏑–⏑⏑– –] *Il.* 13.492, 710[9]
(ii) [–⏑⏑–⏑⏑–] παῦρος δέ οἱ εἵπετο λαός *Il.* 2.675
[–⏑⏑–⏑⏑–⏑] πολὺς δέ μοι ἕσπετο λαός *Od.* 6.164[10]
(iii) [–⏑⏑–⏑⏑–⏑⏑–⏑⏑] ὄρνυθι λαούς *Il.* 15.475, 19.139
(iv) [–⏑⏑–⏑⏑–] ὄτρυνε δὲ λαὸν ἅπαντα *Il.* 16.501, 17.559
[–⏑⏑–⏑⏑–] ὤτρυνε δὲ λαὸν ἅμ' αὐτῷ *Il.* 15.695[11]
(v) [–⏑⏑–⏑⏑–] τὸν δ' ἄλλον λαὸν ἀνώχθω *Il.* 11.189
[–⏑⏑–⏑⏑–] τὸν δ' ἄλλον λαὸν ἀνώχθι *Il.* 11.204
[–⏑⏑–⏑⏑–] ἄμα τ' ἄλλον λαὸν ἀνώγῃ Panyas. fr. 12.8 (Davies)
[–⏑⏑–⏑⏑–] σιωπᾶν λαὸν ἀνώγει *Il.* 2.280
metrical variant: λαοὺς [–⏑⏑–⏑⏑–⏑⏑–⏑] ἄνωγεν *Il.* 1.313
negative variant: [–⏑⏑–⏑⏑–⏑⏑–⏑⏑] λαὸν ἐρύκω *Il.* 24.658
cognate: [–⏑⏑–⏑⏑–] ἅμα δ' ἄλλον λαὸν ὄπασσον *Il.* 16.38; cf. also *Il.* 18.452
(vi) [–⏑⏑–] καὶ λαὸν ἐρυκάκετε [⏑⏑– –] *Il.* 6.80
[–⏑⏑–] καὶ λαὸν ἐρυκάκοι [–⏑⏑– –] *Il.* 7.342
positive variant: [–⏑⏑–] τί δὲ λαὸν ἀνήγαγεν [–⏑⏑– –] *Il.* 9.338

---

[5] Variant: λαὸς ἀπείρων Hes. *Sc.* 472; cf. λαὸν ἐρύκω *Il.* 24.658 and λαὸν ἐέργων *Il.* 12.201, 219; there seems to be a close link with formulae of the type λαός/λαὸν Ἀχαιῶν.
[6] Variant: [–⏑⏑–⏑⏑–⏑⏑–⏑⏑] ἔγρετο λαός *Il.* 24.789.
[7] Variant: λαὸν κηρύσσοντες ἀγειρόντων [⏑⏑– –] *Il.* 2.438.
[8] Variant: νῦν δ' ἀπὸ πυρκαϊῆς σκέδασον [⏑⏑–⏑⏑– –] *Il.* 23.158.
[9] Active variant: λαὸν ἄγων [⏑⏑–⏑⏑–⏑⏑–⏑⏑– –] *Il.* 10.79.
[10] Active variant: [–⏑⏑–⏑⏑–] πολὺ δὲ πλείστους ἄγε λαούς *Il.* 2.580.
[11] Metrical variant: ἢ οὐκ ὀτρύνοντος ἀκούετε λαὸν ἅπαντα *Il.* 15.506; negative variant: [–⏑⏑–⏑⏑–] κατὰ δ' ἔσχεθε λαὸν ἅπαντα *Od.* 24.530.

APPENDIX A

A.7 The activity of the herald

[–∪∪–] δ' ἄρα λαὸν ἐρήτυον [–∪∪– –] *Il.* 18.503
[–∪∪–] δ' ἄρα λαοὶ ἐρητύοντο [∪– –] *Od.* 3.155
[–∪∪–∪∪] λαός, ἐρήτυθεν δέ [∪– –] *Il.* 2.99

A.8 The inclusive nature of Homer's people

(i) [–∪∪–∪∪–∪∪–∪∪] λαὸν ἅπαντα *Il.* 15.506, 16.501, 17.559, *Od.* 2.81, 24.530[12]
(ii) Ἀλκίνοε κρεῖον, πάντων ἀριδείκετε λαῶν *Od.* 8.382, 401, 9.2, 11.355, 378, 13.38
(iii) τόνδ' ἄρα πάντες λαοὶ ἐπερχόμενοι θηεῦντο *Od.* 2.13, 17.64
(iv) [–∪∪–∪∪–∪] καὶ ἄλλους ἵδρυε λαούς *Il.* 2.191
    [–∪∪–∪∪–∪] καὶ ἄλλους ὄρνυθι λαούς *Il.* 15.475[13]
(v) [–∪∪–∪∪–] τὸν δ' ἄλλον λαὸν ἀνώχθω *Il.* 11.189
    [–∪∪–∪∪–] τὸν δ' ἄλλον λαὸν ἄνωχθι *Il.* 11.204
    [–∪∪–∪∪–] ἅμα τ' ἄλλον λαὸν ἀνώγῃ Panyas. fr. 12.8 (Davies)
    [–∪∪–∪∪–] ἅμα δ' ἄλλον λαὸν ὄπασσον *Il.* 16.38
    [–∪∪–∪∪–] ἅμα δ' ἄλλος λαὸς ἐπέσθω *Il.* 11.796[14]

A.9 'Many people'

(i) [–∪∪–∪∪–∪] πολὺν δ' ὅ γε λαὸν ἀγείρας *Il.* 2.664
    [–∪∪–∪∪–∪] πολὺν δέ μοι ὤπασε λαόν *Il.* 9.483[15]
(ii) δυσκλέα Ἄργος ἱκέσθαι, ἐπεὶ πολὺν ὤλεσα λαόν *Il.* 2.115, 9.22
(iii) [–∪∪–∪∪–∪] πολὺ πλεῖστοι καὶ ἄριστοι | λαοί (ἕποντ') *Il.* 2.577f., 817f.
    [–∪∪–∪∪–∪∪–] πολέες γὰρ ἅμ' αὐτῷ | λαοὶ ἕποντ' *Il.* 16.550f.
(iv) [–∪∪–∪∪–] πολὺ δὲ πλείστους ἄγε λαούς *Il.* 2.580
    [–∪∪–∪∪–] παυρὸς δέ οἱ εἵπετο λαός *Il.* 2.675[16]
(v) [–∪∪–] τοιόνδε τοσόνδε τε λαὸν Ἀχαιῶν *Il.* 2.120
    [–∪∪–] τοιόνδε τοσόνδε τε λαὸν ὄπωπα *Il.* 2.799
(vi) τόσσον λαὸν ἕπεσθαι [∪–∪∪–∪∪– –] *Il.* 4.430
    ὅσσον λαὸν ἔπεφνεν [∪–∪∪–∪∪– –] *Od.* 11.518

---

[12] Cf. *Od.* 4.176, 13.155f., Hes. *Th.* 84f., Tyrt. f.11.13 (West); related:
    [–∪∪–∪∪–∪∪–] καὶ λαὸς ἀπείρων Hes. *Sc.* 472
    [–∪∪–∪∪–∪∪–∪∪] λαὸν ἅμ' αὐτῷ *Il.* 15.695
    [–∪∪–∪∪–∪∪–∪∪] λαὸς ὑπ' αὐτῷ *Od.* 3.305.
[13] Cf. *Il.* 22.54.
[14] Cf. [–∪∪–∪∪–∪] πολὺν δ' ἅμα λαὸν ὄπασσε *Il.* 18.452.
[15] Cf. *Il.* 10.170, Hes. *Op.* 763f. with variant reading, fr. 33(a).2 (M–W).
[16] Cf. *Il.* 4.407.

EPIC FORMULAE

A.10 'The people of the Achaeans'

(i) [−∪∪−∪∪−∪∪−∪∪] λαὸς Ἀχαιῶν *Il.* 6.223, 7.434, 13.822, 23.156
(ii) [−∪∪−∪∪−∪∪−∪∪] λαὸν Ἀχαιῶν *Il.* 1.454, 2.450, 4.184, 5.573, 758, 7.306, 9.118, 424, 681, 10.14, 13.47, 196, 16.237, 822
(iii) [−∪∪−∪∪] λαὸν Ἀχαιῶν χαλκοχιτώνων *Il.* 2.163, 179 var. lect. ant., 4.199, 8.76 (variant of the standard form), 15.56.
(iv) [−∪∪−] κατὰ λαὸν Ἀχαιϊκόν [−∪∪−−] *Il.* 9.521
    [−∪∪−] λίπε λαὸν Ἀχαιϊκόν [−∪∪−−] *Il.* 15.218
    [−∪∪] λαὸν ὀλέσθαι Ἀχαιϊκόν [−∪∪−−] *Il.* 13.349
(v) [−∪∪−∪∪−∪] ἀπώλεσε λαὸν Ἀχαιῶν *Il.* 5.758
    [−∪∪−∪∪−∪] ἀπώλετο λαὸς Ἀχαιῶν *Il.* 6.223
    [−∪∪−∪∪−∪] δάμασσε δὲ λαὸν Ἀχαιῶν *Il.* 9.118
    [−∪∪−∪∪−] δέδμητο δὲ λαὸς ὑπ' αὐτῷ *Od.* 3.305
(vi) τιμήσας μὲν ἐμέ, μέγα δ' ἴψαο λαὸν Ἀχαιῶν *Il.* 1.454, 16.237

Appendix B
RITUAL FORMULAE

B.1 'Hear, ye people' etc.

(i) ἀκούετε λεῴ Sus. fr. 1.1 (West),[1] Ar. *Ach.* 1000, *Pax* 551, *Av.* 448, Plu. *Thes.* 13.4
(ii) κλύοιτ' ἂν ἤδη ... Ἀττικὸς λεώς A. *Eu.* 681
(iii) νῦν αὖτε λεῴ προσέχετε τὸν νοῦν Ar. *V.* 1015
(iv) σῖγα πᾶς ἔστω λεώς E. *Hec.* 532
   σῖγ' ἔστω λεώς E. *Phaet.* 118 (Diggle)
   σιγᾶτε λαοί E. *Supp.* 669
(v) εὔφημος πᾶς ἔστω λεώς Ar. *Th.* 39
(vi) ἀκούετε ναοί [νεῴ Meineke] Ath. 8.41

Related: S. *Aj.* 565, *OT* 144, E. *Ph.* 1227, Ar. *Pax* 1316f.

B.2 'Come hither, all ye people' etc.

(i) δεῦρ' ἴτε πάντες λεῴ Plu. *Thes.* 25.1
   δεῦρ' ἴτ' ὦ πάντες λεῴ Ar. *Pax* 296
   ἰὼ πᾶς λεώς ... μόλετε σὺν τάχει S. *OC* 884
(ii) ὦ ἴτε λαοί E. *Phaeth.* 112 (Diggle)
   βᾶτ' εἰς ὁδὸν δὴ πᾶς ὁ χειρῶναξ λεώς S. fr. 844.1 Radt
(iii) ὦ γαῖα Κάδμου, πᾶς τε Θηβαῖος λεώς
   κείρασθε, συμπενθήσατ', ἔλθετ' ἐς τάφον E. *HF* 1389f.

S. *OT* 144 and E. *Or.* 873 are related; see also E. *Supp.* 467.

---

[1] Cf. *Prolegomena de comoedia* XVIIIb 1 and 2 (Koster).

BIBLIOGRAPHY

Adkins, A. (1960a) *Merit and responsibility: a study in Greek values*, Oxford
  (1960b) ' "Honour" and "punishment" in the Homeric poems', *BICS* 7: 23–32
  (1970) *From the many to the one: a study in personality and human nature in the context of ancient Greek society, values and beliefs*, London
  (1972) *Moral values and political behaviour in ancient Greece*, London
  (1982) 'Values, goals and emotions in the *Iliad*', *CP* 77: 292–326
  (1987) 'Gagarin and the "morality" of Homer', *CP* 82: 311–22
Ahl, F. and Roisman, H. (1996) *The Odyssey re-formed*, Ithaca, NY
Alexander, B. (1991) *Victor Turner revisited: ritual as social change*, Atlanta, GA
Allen, T. (1924) *Homer: the origins and the transmission*, Oxford
Allen, W. (1939) 'The theme of the suitors in the *Odyssey*', *TAPA* 70: 104–24
Alvis, J. (1995) *Divine purpose and heroic response in Homer and Virgil: the political plan of Zeus*, Lanham, MD
Ameis, C., Hentze, C., Cauer, P. (1913) *Homers Ilias*, 7th edn, Leipzig
Andersen, Ø. (1973) 'Der Untergang der Gefährten in der *Odyssee*', *SO* 49: 7–27
  (1976) 'Some thoughts on the shield of Achilles', *SO* 51: 5–18
Andreev, J. (1988) 'Die homerische Gesellschaft', *Klio* 70: 5–85
Andrewes, A. (1961) 'Phratries in Homer', *Hermes* 89: 129–40
Arieti, J. (1983) 'Achilles' inquiry about Machaon: the critical moment in the *Iliad*', *CJ* 79: 125–30
Ashley, K. ed. (1990) *Victor Turner and the construction of cultural criticism*, Bloomington, IN
Athanassakis, A. (1992) 'Cattle and honour in Homer and Hesiod', *Ramus* 21: 156–86
Auffarth, C. (1991) *Der drohende Untergang: 'Schöpfung' in Mythos und Ritual im alten Orient und in Griechenland am Beispiel der Odyssee und des Ezechielbuches*, Berlin
Bakker, E. (1990) 'Homeric discourse and enjambement: a cognitive approach', *TAPhA* 120: 1–21
  (1993) 'Activation and preservation: the interdependence of text and performance in an oral tradition', *Oral Tradition* 8: 5–20
Bakker, E. and Kahane, A. eds. (1997) *Written voices, spoken signs*, Cambridge, MA

Bannert, H. (1987) 'Versammlungsszenen bei Homer', in *Homer: beyond oral poetry*, eds. J. Bremer, I. de Jong, J. Kalf: 15–29
Barrett, D. (1981) 'The friendship of Achilles and Patroclus', *CB* 57: 87–93
Bassett, S. (1918) 'The suitors of Penelope', *TAPhA* 49: 41–52
Baudy, G. (1993) Review of Auffarth (1991) in *Gnomon* 65: 577–85
Becker, A. (1995) *The shield of Achilles and the poetics of ekphrasis*, London
Bell, C. (1992) *Ritual theory, ritual practice*, Oxford
 (1997) *Ritual: perspectives and dimensions*, Oxford
Benjamin, A. ed. (1988) *Post-structuralist classics*, London
Bennett, M. (1997) *Belted heroes and bound women: the myth of the Homeric warrior-king*, Lanham, MD
Benveniste, E. (1973) *Indo-European language and society*, trans. E. Palmer, London
Björck, G. (1950) *Das Alpha impurum und die tragische Kunstsprache*, Uppsala
Blickman, D. (1987) 'The role of the plague in the *Iliad*', *ClAnt* 6: 1–10
Boegehold, A. (1996) 'Group and single competitions at the Panathenaia', in *Worshipping Athena*, ed. J. Neils: 95–105
Bölte, F. (1934) 'Ein pylisches Epos', *RhM* 83: 319–47
Bowersock, G., Burkert, W., Putnam, M. eds. (1979) *Arktouros: Hellenic studies presented to Bernard M. W. Knox on the occasion of his 65th birthday*, Berlin
Bowra, C. (1930) *Tradition and design in the Iliad*, Oxford
 (1952) *Heroic poetry*, London
 (1972) *Homer*, London
Brelich, A. (1958) *Gli eroi greci: un problema storico-religioso*, Rome
Brown, C. (1996) 'In the Cyclops' cave: revenge and justice in *Odyssey* 9', *Mnemosyne* 49: 1–29
Bruit Zaidman, L. and Schmitt Pantel, P. (1992) *Religion in the ancient Greek city*, trans. P. Cartledge, Cambridge
Burkert, W. (1966) 'Kekropidensage und Arrephoria: vom Initiationsritus zum Panathenäenfest', *Hermes* 94: 1–25
 (1985) *Greek Religion: archaic and classical*, trans. J. Raffan, Oxford
 (1987) 'The making of Homer in the sixth century B.C.: rhapsodes versus Stesichoros', in *Papers on the Amasis Painter and his world*, eds. D. von Bothmer et al.: 43–62
Byre, C. (1988) 'Penelope and the suitors before Odysseus, *Odyssey* 18.158–303', *AJPh* 109: 159–73
Cairns, D. (1993) *Aidôs: the psychology and ethics of honour and shame in ancient Greek literature*, Oxford
Calhoun, G. (1934) 'Classes and masses in Homer', *CPh* 29: 192–208, 301–16
 (1962) 'Polity and society: the Homeric picture', in *A companion to Homer*, eds. A. Wace and F. Stubbings: 431–52

Campbell, L. (1871) *Sophocles: the plays and fragments*, vol. 1, Oxford
Casewitz, M. (1992) 'Sur le concept de "peuple"', in *La langue et les textes en grec ancien: actes du colloque Pierre Chantraine*, ed. F. Létoublon: 193–200
Castriota, D. (1992) *Myth, ethos and actuality: official art in fifth-century B.C. Athens*, Wisconsin
Chadwick, H. (1912) *The heroic age*, Cambridge
Chantraine, P. (1968–80) *Dictionnaire étymologique de la langue grecque*, Paris
Clay, J. Strauss (1976) 'The beginning of the *Odyssey*', *AJPh* 97, 313–26
 (1983) *The wrath of Athena: gods and men in the Odyssey*, Princeton
Collins, C. (1996) *Authority figures: metaphors of mastery from the Iliad to the Apocalypse*, Lanham, MD
Collins, L. (1988) *Studies in characterization in the Iliad*, Frankfurt
Connor, W. (1987) 'Tribes, festivals, and processions; civic ceremonial and political manipulation in archaic Greece', *JHS* 107: 40–50
Cook, E. (1995) *The Odyssey in Athens: myths of cultural origins*, Ithaca, NY
Coulson, W. et al. eds. (1994) *The archaeology of Athens and Attica under the democracy*, Oxford
Crowther, N. (1985) 'Male beauty contests in Greece: the *euandria* and the *euexia*', *Antiquité Classique* 54: 285–91
Curtius, E. (1894) 'Das Leokorion', in *Gesammelte Abhandlungen*, vol. 1: 465–74, Berlin. First published in *Monatsberichte der k. preuss. Akademie 1878*: 77–87
Dale, A. (1954) *Euripides: Alcestis*, Oxford
Danek, G. (1988) *Studien zur Dolonie*, Vienna
Davison, J. (1958) 'Notes on the Panathenaea', *JHS* 78: 23–42
 (1965) 'Thucydides, Homer, and the "Achaean wall"', *GRBS* 6: 5–28
Dawe, R. (1993) *The Odyssey: translation and analysis*, Lewes, Sussex
Descat, R. (1979) 'L'idéologie homérique du pouvoir', *REA* 81: 229–40
Deubner, L. (1932) *Attische Feste*, Berlin
Dieterich, A. (1891) *De hymnis Orphicis*, diss. Marburg
Diggle, J. (1970) *Euripides: Phaethon*, Cambridge
Donlan, W. (1973) 'The tradition of anti-aristocratic thought in early Greek poetry', *Historia* 22: 145–54
 (1979) 'The structure of authority in the *Iliad*', *Arethusa* 12: 51–70
 (1989) 'The pre-state community in Greece', *SO* 64: 5–29
Dornseiff, F. (1937) 'Odysseus' letzte Fahrt', *Hermes* 72: 351–5
Dougherty, C. and Kurke, L. eds. (1993) *Cultural poetics in archaic Greece: cult, performance, politics*, Cambridge
Drews, R. (1979) 'Argos and Argives in the *Iliad*', *CPh* 74: 111–35
Dunbar, N. (1995) *Aristophanes: Birds*, Oxford
Dunkle, J. (1981) 'Some notes on the funeral games: *Iliad* 23', *Prometheus* 7: 11–18

Easterling, P. ed. (1997) *The Cambridge companion to Greek tragedy*, Cambridge
Edwards, M. (1966) 'Some features of Homeric craftsmanship', *TAPhA* 97: 115–79
  (1987) *Homer: poet of the Iliad*, Baltimore, MD
van Effenterre, H. (1977) 'Laos, laoi et lawagetas', *Kadmos* 16: 36–55
Erbse, H. (1972) *Beiträge zum Verständnis der Odyssee*, Berlin
  (1986) *Untersuchungen zur Funktion der Götter im homerischen Epos*, Berlin
Fagles, R. (1961) *Bacchylides*, New Haven, CT
Fanta, A. (1882) *Der Staat in der Ilias und Odyssee: ein Beitrag zur Beurteilung der homerischen Verfassung*, Innsbruck
Farnell, L. (1896) *The cults of the Greek states*, vol. 1, Oxford
  (1921) *Greek hero cults and ideas of immortality*, Oxford
Farron, G. (1979–80) 'The *Odyssey* as an anti-aristocratic statement', *StudAnt* 1: 50–101
Fatheuer, T. (1988) *Ehre und Gerechtigkeit: Studien zur gesellschaftlichen Ordnung im frühen Griechenland*, Münster
Favis, B. (1950) 'Κριτικὰ καὶ παλαιογραφικὰ εἰς τὸν 'Ησύχιον', *Lexikographikon Deltion* 5: 53–122
Fenik, B. (1974) *Studies in the Odyssey*, Wiesbaden
  ed. (1978) *Homer: tradition and invention*, Leiden
Fick, A. and Bechtel, F. (1894) *Die griechischen Personennamen*, 2nd edn, Göttingen
Finley, M. (1977) *The world of Odysseus*, 2nd edn, London
Finnegan, R. (1977) *Oral poetry: its nature, significance and social context*, Cambridge
Focke, F. (1943) *Die Odyssee*, Stuttgart
Foley, H. (1981) *Reflection on women in antiquity*, New York
Foley, J. (1991) *Immanent art: from structure to meaning in traditional oral epic*, Bloomington, IN
  (1999) 'What's in a sign?', in *Signs of orality*, ed. E. Mackay: 1–27
Fränkel, H. (1921) *Die homerischen Gleichnisse*, Göttingen
Frazer, J. (1898) *Pausanias' description of Greece*, vol. 2, London
Frazer, R. (1985) 'The crisis of leadership among the Greeks and Poseidon's intervention in *Iliad* 14', *Hermes* 113: 1–9
Friedrich, R. (1987) 'Thrinakia and Zeus' ways to men in the *Odyssey*', *GRBS* 28: 375–400
  (1991) 'The hybris of Odysseus', *JHS* 111: 16–28
Frisk, H. (1960–70) *Griechisches etymologisches Wörterbuch*, Heidelberg
von Fritz, K. (1966) 'Pandora, Prometheus und der Mythos von den Weltaltern', in *Hesiod*, ed. E. Heitsch: 367–410. First published in *The Review of Religion* 11 (1947): 227–60
Gagarin, M. (1987) 'Morality in Homer', *CPh* 82: 285–306

Geddes, A. (1984) 'Who's who in Homeric society', *CQ* 34: 17–36
Geertz, C. (1973) *The interpretation of cultures: selected essays*, New York
Georgacas, D. (1958) 'A contribution to Greek word history, derivation and etymology (Schluß)', *Glotta* 36: 161–93
Gnoli, G. and Vernant, J.-P. eds. (1982) *La mort, les morts dans les sociétés anciennes*, Cambridge
Godman, P. and Murray, O. eds. (1990) *Latin poetry and the classical tradition: essays in medieval and renaissance literature*, Oxford
Goldhill, S. (1986) *Reading Greek tragedy*, Cambridge
  (1990) 'The Great Dionysia and civic ideology', in *Nothing to do with Dionysos?*, eds. J. Winkler and F. Zeitlin: 97–129. First published in *JHS* 107 (1987) 58–76
  (1991) *The poet's voice: essays on poetics and Greek literature*, Cambridge
  (1994) 'Representing democracy: women at the Great Dionysia', in *Ritual, finance, politics*, eds. S. Hornblower and R. Osborne: 347–67
  (1997) 'The audience of Athenian tragedy', in *The Cambridge companion to Greek tragedy*, ed. P. Easterling: 54–68
Gomme, A. (1945) *A historical commentary on Thucydides*, vol. 1, Oxford
Gomme, A., Andrewes, A., Dover, K. (1970) *A historical commentary on Thucydides*, vol. 4, Oxford
Görgemanns, H. and Schmidt, E. eds. (1976) *Studien zum antiken Epos*, Meisenheim a. Glan
Greenblatt, S. and Gunn, G., eds. (1992) *Redrawing the boundaries: the transformation of English and American literary studies*, New York
Greenhalgh, P. (1972) 'Patriotism in the Homeric world', *Historia* 21: 528–37
Grene, D. and Lattimore, R. eds. (1953–72) *The complete Greek tragedies*, Chicago
Griffin, J. (1980) *Homer on life and death*, Oxford
Griffith, M. (1995) 'Brilliant dynasts: power and politics in the *Oresteia*', *ClAnt* 14: 62–129
  (1998) 'The king and the eye: the rule of the father in Greek tragedy', *PCPS* 44: 20–80
Grimes, R. (1982) *Beginnings in ritual studies*, Lanham, MD
Gschnitzer, F. (1971) 'Stadt und Stamm bei Homer', *Chiron* 1: 1–17
  (1976) 'Politische Leidenschaft im Homerischen Epos', in *Studien zum antiken Epos*, eds. H. Görgemanns and E. Schmidt: 1–21
  (1981) *Griechische Sozialgeschichte von der mykenischen bis zum Ausgang der klassischen Zeit*, Wiesbaden
  (1983) 'Der Rat in der Volksversammlung: ein Beitrag des Homerischen Epos zur griechischen Verfassungsgeschichte', *IBK* 22: 151–63 (= *Festschrift R. Muth*)
  (1991) 'Zur homerischen Staats- und Gesellschaftsordnung: Grund-

charakter und geschichtliche Stellung', in *Zweihundert Jahre Homer-Forschung*, ed. J. Latacz: 182–204

Güntert, H. (1932) 'Labyrinth: eine sprachwissenschaftliche Untersuchung', in *Sitzungsberichte der Heidelberger Akademie der Wissenschaften, phil.-hist. Klasse*, Heidelberg

Hadzisteliou-Price, T. (1973) 'Hero-cult and Homer', *Historia* 22: 129–45

(1979) 'Hero cult in the "age of Homer" and earlier', in *Arktouros: Hellenic studies presented to Bernard M. W. Knox*, eds. G. Bowersock, W. Burkert, M. Putnam: 219–28

Hainsworth, J. (1968) *The flexibility of the Homeric formula*, Oxford

(1991) *The idea of epic*, Berkeley, CA

(1993) *The Iliad: a commentary*, vol. 3, Cambridge

Halverson, J. (1985) 'Social order in the *Odyssey*', *Hermes* 113: 129–44

(1986) 'The succession issue in the *Odyssey*', *G&R* 33: 119–28

Hansen, W. (1977) 'Odysseus' last journey', *QU* 24: 27–48

Harmatta, J. (1981) 'Wort und Begriff λαός von der mykenischen Zeit bis ins 5. Jahrhundert v. u. Z.', in *Soziale Typenbegriffe*, vol. 3, ed. E. Welskopf: 156–62

Heiden, B. (1996) 'The three movements of the *Iliad*', *GRBS* 37: 5–22

Heitsch, E. ed. (1966) *Hesiod*, Darmstadt

Heubeck, A. (1954) *Der Odyssee-Dichter und die Ilias*, Erlangen

(1984a) 'DA-MO-KO-RO', in *Kleine Schriften*: 449–52, Erlangen. First published in *Atti e memorie del I congresso internazionale di micenologia*, vol. 2: 611–15, Rome 1968

(1984b) 'Gedanken zu griechisch λαός', in *Kleine Schriften*: 453–62, Erlangen. First published in *Studi linguistici in onore di V. Pisani*: 535–44, Brescia 1969

Heubeck, A., West, S., Hainsworth, J. (1988) *A commentary on Homer's Odyssey*, vol. 1, Oxford

Hoffmann, W. (1969) 'Die Polis bei Homer', in *Zur griechischen Staatskunde*, ed. F. Gschnitzer: 123–38, Darmstadt. First published in *Festschrift B. Snell*: 153–65, Munich 1956

Hölscher, U. (1978) 'The transformation from folk-tale to epic', in *Homer: tradition and innovation*, ed. B. Fenik: 51–67

(1989) *Die Odyssee: Epos zwischen Märchen und Roman*, 2nd edn, Munich

Hommel, H. (1955) 'Aigisthus und die Freier: zum poetischen Plan und zum geschichtlichen Ort der *Odyssee*', *Studium Generale* 8: 237–45

Hooker, J. (1989) 'Homer, Patroclus, Achilles', *SO* 64: 30–5

Hornblower, S. and Osborne, R. eds. (1994) *Ritual, finance, politics: Athenian democratic accounts presented to David Lewis*, Oxford

Irmscher, J. (1950) *Götterzorn bei Homer*, Leipzig

Jacoby, F. (1904) *Das Marmor Parium*, Berlin

BIBLIOGRAPHY

Jameson, M. (1994) 'The ritual of the Athena Nike parapet', in *Ritual, finance, politics*, eds. S. Hornblower and R. Osborne: 307–19
Janko, R. (1992) *The Iliad: a commentary*, vol. 4, Cambridge
Jeanmaire, H. (1939) *Couroi et courètes: essai sur l' éducation spartiate et sur les rites d' adolescence dans l' antiquité hellénique*, Lille
Jebb, R. (1888) *Sophocles: the plays and fragments; with critical notes, commentary and translation in English prose; part 3: Antigone*, Cambridge
  (1905) *Bacchylides: the poems and fragments*, Cambridge
de Jong, I. (1987a) 'The voice of anonymity: tis-speeches in the *Iliad*', *Eranos* 85: 69–84
  (1987b) *Narrators and focalizers: the presentation of the story in the Iliad*, Amsterdam
Jörgensen, O. (1904) 'Das Auftreten der Götter in den Büchern ι–μ der Odyssee', *Hermes* 39: 357–82
Kahane, A. (1992) 'The first word of the *Odyssey*', *TAPhA* 122: 115–31
  (1994) *The interpretation of order: a study in the poetics of Homeric repetition*, Oxford
  (1997) 'Hexameter progression and the Homeric hero's solitary state', in *Written voices, spoken signs*, eds. E. Bakker and A. Kahane: 110–37
Kamerbeek, J. (1978) *The plays of Sophocles: commentaries, part 3: The Antigone*, Leiden
von Kamptz, H. (1982) *Homerische Personennamen: sprachwissenschaftliche und historische Klassifikation*, Göttingen
Kannicht, R. (1969) *Euripides: Helena*, Heidelberg
Käppel, L. (1992) *Paian: Studien zur Geschichte einer Gattung*, Berlin
Katz, M. (1991) *Penelope's renown: meaning and indeterminacy in the Odyssey*, Princeton
Kern, O. (1933) 'Λαοί – die Laien', *ARW* 30: 205–7
King, K. (1987) *Achilles: paradigms of the war hero from Homer to the middle ages*, Berkeley
Kirchhoff, A. (1879) *Die homerische Odyssee*. 2nd edn, Berlin
Kirk, G. (1962) *The songs of Homer*, Cambridge
  (1968) 'War and the warrior in the Homeric poems', in *Problèmes de la guerre en Grèce ancienne*, ed. J.-P. Vernant: 93–117
  (1985) *The Iliad: a commentary*, vol. 1, Cambridge
  ed. (1985–93) *The Iliad: a commentary*, Cambridge
Kotsidu, H. (1991) *Die musischen Agone der Panathenäen in archaischer und klassischer Zeit: eine historisch-archäologische Untersuchung*, Munich
Kretschmer, E. (1930) 'Beiträge zur Wortgeographie der altgriechischen Dialekte', *Glotta* 18: 67–100
Kurz, G., Müller, D., Nicolai, W. eds. (1981) *Gnomosyne: menschliches Denken und Handeln in der frühgriechischen Literatur* (= *Festschrift W. Marg*), Munich

Lacey, W. (1966) 'Homeric ἕδνα and Penelope's κύριος', *JHS* 86: 55–68
Latacz, J. (1977) *Kampfparänese, Kampfdarstellung und Kampfwirklichkeit in der Ilias, bei Kallinos und Tyrtaios*, Munich
  ed. (1991) *Zweihundert Jahre Homer-Forschung: Rückblick und Ausblick*, Stuttgart
  (1996) *Homer: his art and his world*, trans. J. Holoka, Ann Arbor
Lattimore, R. (1951) *The Iliad of Homer*, Chicago
  (1965) *The Odyssey of Homer*, New York
Leaf, W. (1900–2) *The Iliad*, 2nd edn, London
Lebedev, A. (1996) 'A new epigram for Harmodios and Aristogeiton', *ZPE* 112: 263–8
van Leeuwen, J. (1901) *Aristophanis Acharnenses*, Leiden
Lejeune, M. (1965) 'Le δᾶμος dans la société mycénienne', *REG* 78: 1–22
Létoublon, F. ed. (1992) *La langue et les textes en grec ancien: actes du colloque Pierre Chantraine*, Amsterdam
  ed. (1997) *Hommage à Milman Parry: le style formulaire de l'épopée homérique et la théorie de l'oralité poétique*, Amsterdam
Levi, M. (1968) *Commento storico alla Respublica Atheniensium di Aristotele*, Milan
Levy, H. (1963) 'The Odyssean suitors and the host–guest relationship', *TAPhA* 94: 145–53
Lloyd-Jones, H. (1987) 'A note on Homeric morality', *CPh* 82: 307–10
Lohmann, D. (1970) *Die Komposition der Reden in der Ilias*, Berlin
  (1988) *Die Andromache-Szenen der Ilias: Ansätze und Methoden der Homer-Interpretation*, Hildesheim
Long, A. (1970) 'Morals and values in Homer', *JHS* 90: 121–39
Longo, O. (1990) 'The theater of the *polis*', in *Nothing to do with Dionysos?*, eds. J. Winkler and F. Zeitlin: 12–19. First published in *Dioniso* 49 (1978): 5–13
Lonsdale, S. (1990) *Creatures of speech: lion, herding, and hunting similes in the Iliad*, Stuttgart
Loraux, N. (1982) 'Mourir devant Troie, tomber pour Athènes: de la gloire du héros à l' idée de la cité', in *La mort, les morts dans les sociétés anciennes*, eds. G. Gnoli and J.-P. Vernant: 27–43
  (1993) *The children of Athena: Athenian ideas about citizenship and the division between the sexes*, trans. C. Levine, Princeton
Lord, A. (1960) *The singer of tales*, Cambridge, MA
  (1991) *Epic singers and oral tradition*, Ithaca, NY
  (1995) *The singer resumes the tale*, ed. M. Lord, Ithaca, NY
Lorimer, H. (1950) *Homer and the monuments*, London
Lynn-George, M. (1988) *Epos: word, narrative and the Iliad*, Basingstoke
  (1996) 'Structures of care in the *Iliad*', *CQ* 46: 1–26
Mackay, E. ed. (1999) *Signs of orality: the oral tradition and its influence in the Greek and Roman world*, Leiden

BIBLIOGRAPHY

Macleod, C. (1982) *Homer: Iliad book XXIV*, Cambridge
Maddoli, G. (1970) 'Δᾶμος e βασιλῆες: contributo allo studio delle origini della *polis*', *SMEA* 12: 7–57
Martin, R. (1989) *The language of heroes: speech and performance in the Iliad*, Ithaca, NY
  (1997) 'Formulas and speeches: the usefulness of Parry's method', in *Hommage à Milman Parry*, ed. F. Létoublon: 263–73
Matsumoto, N. (1981) 'Die Freier in der *Odyssee*', in *Gnomosyne: menschliches Denken und Handeln in der frühgriechischen Literatur* (= *Festschrift W. Marg*), eds. G. Kurz, D. Mueller, W. Nicolai: 35–41
McGlew, J. (1989) 'Royal power and the Achaean assembly at *Iliad* 2.84–393', *ClAnt* 8: 283–95
Merkelbach, R. (1969) *Untersuchungen zur Odyssee*, 2nd edn, Munich
Mikalson, J. (1976) 'Erechtheus and the Panathenaia', *AJPh* 97: 141–53
Mommsen, A. (1898) *Feste der Stadt Athen im Altertum*, Leipzig
Mondi, R. (1983) 'The Homeric Cyclopes: folktale, tradition and theme', *TAPhA* 113: 17–38
Moreau, A. ed. (1992) *L'initiation: actes du colloque international de Montpellier*, vol. 1, Montpellier
Morris, I. (1986) 'The use and abuse of Homer', *ClAnt* 5: 81–138
  (1993) 'The poetics of power', in *Cultural poetics*, eds. C. Dougherty and L. Kurke: 15–45
Morris, I. and Powell, B. eds. (1996) *A new companion to Homer*, Leiden
Morrison, J. (1992) *Homeric misdirection: false predictions in the Iliad*, Ann Arbor, MI
Most, G. (1997) 'Hesiod's myth of the five (or three or four) races', *PCPS* 43: 104–27
Moulton, C. (1974) 'The end of the *Odyssey*', *GRBS* 15: 153–69
Muellner, L. (1976) *The meaning of Homeric* εὔχομαι *through its formulas*, Innsbruck
  (1996) *The anger of Achilles*, Ithaca, NY
Müller, K. (1873) *De foro Athenarum* (= *Kunstarchaeologische Werke*, vol. 5), Berlin
Murnaghan, L. (1987) *Disguise and recognition in the Odyssey*, Princeton
Murray, O. (1990) 'The idea of the shepherd king', in *Latin poetry and the classical tradition*, eds. P. Godman and O. Murray: 1–14
Nagler, M. (1967) 'Towards a generative view of the Homeric formula', *TAPhA* 98: 269–311
  (1974) *Spontaneity and tradition: a study in the oral art of Homer*, Berkeley
  (1990) 'Odysseus: the proem and the problem', *ClAnt* 9: 335–56
Nagy, G. (1979) *The best of the Achaeans: concepts of the hero in archaic Greek poetry*, Baltimore, MD
  (1990a) *Greek mythology and poetics*, Ithaca, NY

(1990b) *Pindar's Homer: the lyric possession of an epic past*, Baltimore, MD
(1992) 'Homeric questions', *TAPhA* 122: 17–60
(1996a) *Homeric questions*, Austin, TX
(1996b) *Poetry as performance: Homer and beyond*, New York
Neils, J. (1992) *Goddess and polis: the Panathenaic festival in ancient Athens*, Princeton
(1994) 'The Panathenaia and Kleisthenic ideology', in *The archaeology of Athens and Attica under the democracy*, eds. W. Coulson et al.: 151–60
(1996) *Worshipping Athena*, Madison, WI
Nicolai, W. (1984) 'Zu den politischen Wirkungsabsichten des Odyssee-Dichters', *GB* 11: 1–20
Nisetich, F. (1980) *Pindar's victory songs*, Baltimore, MD
Olson, S. (1995) *Blood and iron: stories and storytelling in Homer's Odyssey*, Leiden
Osborne, R. (1987) 'The viewing and obscuring of the Parthenon frieze', *JHS* 107: 98–105
(1994) 'Democracy and imperialism in the Panathenaic procession: the Parthenon frieze in its context', in *The archeology of Athens and Attica under the democracy*, eds. W. Coulson et al.: 143–50
(1996) *Greece in the making*, London
Page, D. (1955) *The Homeric Odyssey*, Oxford
Palmer, L. (1963) *The interpretation of Mycenean Greek texts*, Oxford
Parke, H. (1977) *Festivals of the Athenians*, London
Parker, R. (1996) *Athenian religion: a history*, Oxford
Parry, M. (1971) *The making of Homeric verse: the collected papers of Milman Parry*, ed. A. Parry, New York
Pazdernik, C. (1995) 'Odysseus and his audience: *Odyssey* 9.39–40 and its formulaic resonances', *AJPh* 116: 347–69
Pedrick, V. (1983) 'The paradigmatic nature of Nestor's speech in *Iliad* 11', *TAPhA* 113: 55–68
Pélékidis, C. (1962) *Histoire de l' éphébie attique des origines à 31 avant Jésus Christ*, Paris
Pelling, C. ed. (1990) *Characterization and individuality in Greek literature*, Oxford
Peradotto, J. (1990) *Man in the middle voice: name and narration in the Odyssey*, Princeton
Petersmann, H. (1981) 'Homer und das Märchen', *Wiener Studien* n.s. 15: 43–68
Pfeiffer, R. (1928) Review of Schwartz (1924) and Wilamowitz (1927) in *Deutsche Literaturzeitung* 49: cols. 2355–72
Pinsent, J. (1983) "Ἑταῖρος/ἕταρον in the *Iliad*', in *Mélanges E. Delebecque*: 311–18, Aix-en-Provence

Postlethwaite, N. (1981) 'The continuation of the *Odyssey*: some formulaic evidence', *CPh* 76: 177–87
Pritchard, J. (1969) *Ancient Near Eastern texts relating to the Old Testament*, 3rd edn, Princeton
Pucci, P. (1982) 'The proem of the *Odyssey*', *Arethusa* 15: 139–62
  (1987) *Odysseus polytropos: intertextual readings in the Odyssey and in the Iliad*, Ithaca, NY
  (1997) *The song of the Sirens: essays on Homer*, Lanham
Quiller, Q. (1981) 'The dynamics of the Homeric society', *SO* 56: 109–55
Raaflaub, K. (1989) 'Die Anfänge des politischen Denkens bei den Griechen', *HZ* 248: 1–32
  (1991) 'Homer und die Geschichte des 8. Jh.s v. Chr', in *Zweihundert Jahre Homer-Forschung*, ed. J. Latacz: 205–56
  (1997a) 'Homeric society', in *A new companion to Homer*, eds. I. Morris and B. Powell: 624–48
  (1997b) 'Politics and interstate relations in the world of early Greek *poleis*: Homer and beyond', *Antichthon* 31: 1–27
Rabel, R. (1990) 'Apollo as a model for Achilles in the *Iliad*', *AJPh* 111: 429–40
Race, W. (1997) *Pindar II: Nemean odes, Isthmian odes, fragments*, Cambridge, MA
Redfield, J. (1975) *Nature and culture in the Iliad: the tragedy of Hector*, Chicago
  (1982) 'Notes on the Greek wedding', *Arethusa* 15: 181–201
Reece, S. (1993) *The stranger's welcome: oral theory and the aesthetics of the Homeric hospitality scene*, Ann Arbor, MI
Reinhardt, K. (1961) *Die Ilias und ihr Dichter*, Göttingen
Rihll, T. (1986) '"Kings" and "commoners" in Homeric society', *LCM* 11: 86–91
Risch, E. (1987) 'Die ältesten Zeugnisse für κλέος ἄφθιτον', *ZVS* 100: 3–11
Robertson, N. (1985) 'The origin of the Panathenaea', *RhM* 128: 231–95
  (1992) *Festivals and legends*, Toronto
  (1996) 'Athena's shrines and festivals', in *Worshipping Athena*, ed. J. Neils: 27–77
Rohde, E. (1966) *Psyche: the cult of souls and belief in immortality among the Greeks*, trans. W. Hillis, New York
Rose, P. (1975) 'Class ambivalence in the *Odyssey*', *Historia* 24: 129–49
  (1988) 'Thersites and the plural voices of Homer', *Arethusa* 21: 5–25
Rowe, C. (1983) 'The nature of Homeric morality', in *Approaches to Homer*, eds. C. Rubino and C. Shelmerdine: 248–75
Rubino, C. and Shelmerdine, C. eds. (1983), *Approaches to Homer*, Austin, TX
Russo, J. (1963) 'A closer look at Homeric formulas', *TAPhA* 94: 235–47
  (1966) 'The structural formula in Homeric verse', *YCS* 20: 210–40

(1997) 'The formula', in *A new companion to Homer*, eds. I. Morris and B. Powell: 238–60
Russo, J. and Fernandez-Galiano, M. (1992) *A commentary on Homer's Odyssey*, vol. 3, Oxford
Rüter, K. (1969) *Odysseeinterpretationen*, Göttingen
Saïd, S. (1979) 'Les crimes des prétendants, la maison d'Ulisse et les festins de l'Odyssée', in *Etudes de littérature ancienne*, 9–49, Paris
Sandys, J. (1919) *The odes of Pindar*, 2nd edn, London
Schachermeyr, F. (1950) *Poseidon und die Entstehung des griechischen Götterglaubens*, Berne
Schadewaldt, W. (1965a) *Iliasstudien*, Tübingen
  (1965b) *Von Homers Welt und Werk*, 4th edn, Stuttgart
  (1970) 'Der Helios-Zorn in der *Odyssée*', in *Hellas und Hesperien: gesammelte Schriften zur Antike und zur neueren Literatur*, vol. 1: 93–105, 2nd edn, Zurich. First published in *Studi in onore di Luigi Castiglioni*: 861–76, Florence
  (1975) *Der Aufbau der Ilias*, Frankfurt
Scheid-Tissinier, E. (1992) 'Les prétendants de l'Odyssée: une génération perdue', in *L'initiation: actes du colloque international de Montpellier*, vol. 1, ed. A. Moreau: 105–18, Montpellier
Schein, S. (1984) *The mortal hero: an introduction to Homer's Iliad*, Baltimore, MD
Schmidt, J. (1886) *Synonymik der griechischen Sprache*, vol. 4, Leipzig
Schofield, M. (1999) *Saving the city: philosopher-kings and other classical paradigms*, London
Schwartz, E. (1924) *Die Odyssee*, Munich
Scott, M. (1980) 'Aidos and nemesis in the works of Homer, and their relevance to social or co-operative values', *AClass* 23: 13–35
  (1981) 'Some Greek terms in Homer suggesting non-competitive attitudes', *AClass* 24: 1–15
Scully, S. (1990) *Homer and the sacred city*, Ithaca, NY
Seaford, R. (1994) *Reciprocity and ritual: Homer and tragedy in the developing city-state*, Oxford
Segal, C. (1971) *The theme of the mutilation of the corpse in the Iliad*, Leiden
  (1994) *Singers, heroes, and gods in the Odyssey*, Ithaca, NY
de Sélincourt, A. (1972) *Herodotus: The histories*, ed. A. Burn, Harmondsworth
Sheppard, J. (1922) *The pattern of the Iliad*, London
Silk, M. (1987) *Homer: the Iliad*, Cambridge
Simon, E. (1983) *Festivals of Attica*, Madison, WI
  (1985) *Die Götter der Griechen*, 3rd edn, Munich
Sinos, D. (1980) *Achilles, Patroclus and the meaning of philos*, Innsbruck
Skiadas, A. (1980) 'Das Aigisthos-Beispiel und die Schuld der Sterblichen (*Od.* 1.35–42)', *Archaiognosia* 1.1: 11–26

BIBLIOGRAPHY

Slater, W. (1969) *Lexicon to Pindar*, Berlin
Snodgrass, A. (1971) *The dark age of Greece: an archaeological survey of the eleventh to the eighth centuries*, Edinburgh
  (1982) 'Les origines du culte des héros dans la Grèce antique, in *La mort, les morts dans les sociétés anciennes*, eds. G. Gnoli and J.-P. Vernant: 107-19
Sommerstein, A. (1980) *Aristophanes: Acharnians*, Warminster
  (1985) *Aristophanes: Peace*, Warminster
Sourvinou-Inwood, C. (1994) 'Something to do with Athens: tragedy and ritual', in *Ritual, finance, politics. Athenian democratic accounts presented to David Lewis*, eds. S. Hornblower and R. Osborne: 269-90
Specht, F. (1944) 'Zur idg. Sprache und Kultur II: got. *fairhwus*', *ZVS* 68: 191-200
Stagakis, G. (1966) 'Therapontes and hetairoi in the *Iliad* as symbols of the political structure of the Homeric state', *Historia* 15: 408-19
  (1971) '*Ἑτα(ι)ρίζω* in Homer as a testimony for the establishment of an hetairos relation', *Historia* 20: 524-33
  (1975) *Studies in the Homeric society*, Wiesbaden
Stanley, K. (1993) *The shield of Homer: narrative structure in the Iliad*, Princeton
Steiner, G. (1996) *No passion spent: essays 1978-1996*, London
Stössel, H. (1975) *Der letzte Gesang der Odyssee: eine unitarische Gesamtinterpretation*, diss. Erlangen-Nuremberg
Strasburger, H. (1953) 'Der soziologische Aspekt der homerischen Epen', *Gymnasium* 60: 97-114
  (1954) 'Der Einzelne und die Gemeinschaft im Denken der Griechen', *HZ* 177: 227-48
Tannen, D. ed. (1982) *Spoken and written language: exploring orality and literacy*, Norwood
Taplin, O. (1980) 'The shield of Achilles within the *Iliad*', *G&R* 27: 1-21
  (1990) 'Agamemnon's role in the *Iliad*', in *Characterization and individuality in Greek literature*, ed. C. Pelling: 60-82
  (1992) *Homeric soundings: the shaping of the Iliad*, Oxford
Thalmann, W. (1984) *Conventions of form and thought in early Greek epic poetry*, Baltimore, MD
  (1988) 'Thersites: comedy, scapegoats and heroic ideology in the *Iliad*', *TAPhA* 118: 1-28
Thieme, P. (1980) 'Homerisch μνάομαι', *ZVS* 94: 124-40
Thomas, C. (1966) 'Homer and the polis', *PP* 21: 5-14
Thompson, A. (1961) 'The Panathenaic festival', *Archäologischer Anzeiger* 76: cols. 224-31
Tredennick, H. (1970) *Memories of Socrates and Symposium*, Harmondsworth

Tsagarakis, O. (1982–3) 'Odysseus und die Hybris seiner Gefährten', *Platon* 34–5: 77–88
Turner, V. (1969) *The ritual process: structure and anti-structure*, London
  (1974) *Dramas, fields, metaphors: symbolic action in human society*, Ithaca, NY
  (1982) *From ritual to theatre: the seriousness of human play*, New York
Ulf, C. (1990) *Die homerische Gesellschaft*, Munich
Vernant, J.-P. ed. (1968) *Problèmes de la guerre en Grèce ancienne*, Paris
  (1980) 'Marriage', in *Myth and society in ancient Greece*, trans. J. Lloyd: 45–70, Brighton, Sussex
Vernant, J.-P. and Vidal-Naquet, P. (1988) *Myth and tragedy in ancient Greece*, trans. J. Lloyd, New York
Vian, F. (1963) *Les origines de Thèbes, Cadmos et les Spartes*, Paris
Vidal-Naquet, P. (1986) *The black hunter: forms of thought and forms of society in the Greek world*, trans. A. Szegedy-Maszak, Baltimore, MD
Vilatte, S. (1988) 'Art et polis: le bouclier d' Achille', *DHA* 14: 89–107
Wace, A. and Stubbings, F. eds. (1962) *A companion to Homer*, London
Wade-Gery, H. (1952) *The poet of the Iliad*, Cambridge
Watkins, C. (1995) *How to kill a dragon: aspects of Indo-European poetics*, Oxford
van Wees, H. (1988) 'Kings in combat: battles and heroes in the *Iliad*', *CQ* 38: 1–24
  (1992) *Status warriors: war, violence and society in Homer and history*, Amsterdam
Welskopf, E. (1981a) 'Die Bezeichnungen λαός, δῆμος, πληθύς, ἔθνος in den homerischen Epen', in *Soziale Typenbegriffe*, ed. E. Welskopf, vol. 3: 163–92
  (1981b) *Soziale Typenbegriffe im alten Griechenland und ihr Fortleben in den Sprachen der Welt*, vol. 3, Berlin
Welwei, K.-W. (1983) *Die griechische Polis: Verfassung und Gesellschaft in archaischer und klassischer Zeit*, Stuttgart
Wender, D. (1978) *The last scenes of the Odyssey*, Leiden
West, M. (1976) *Studies in Greek elegy*, Berlin
  (1988) *Hesiod: Theogony and Works and days*, Oxford
  (1993) *Greek lyric poetry: the poems and fragments of the Greek iambic, elegiac, and melic poets (excluding Pindar and Bacchylides) down to 450 BC*, Oxford
  (1997) *The east face of Helicon: west Asiatic elements in Greek poetry and myth*, Oxford
Westrup, C. (1930) *Le roi de l'Odyssée et le peuple chez Homère*, Paris
Whitman, C. (1958) *Homer and the heroic tradition*, Cambridge, MA
  (1982) *The heroic paradox*, ed. C. Segal, Ithaca, NY
von Wilamowitz-Möllendorf, U. (1893) *Aristoteles und Athen*, Berlin
  ed. (1903) *Timotheus: Die Perser*, Leipzig

BIBLIOGRAPHY

Winkler, J. (1990) 'The ephebe's song: *tragoidia* and *polis*', in *Nothing to do with Dionysos?*, eds. J. Winkler and F. Zeitlin: 20–62

Winkler, J. and Zeitlin, F. eds. (1990) *Nothing to do with Dionysos? Athenian drama in its social context*, Princeton

Witte, K. (1907) *Singular und Plural: Forschungen über Form und Geschichte der griechischen Poesie*, Leipzig

Wofford, S. (1992) *The choice of Achilles*, Stanford

Wyatt, W. (1994–5) 'Homeric and Mycenean λαός', *Minos* n.s. 29–30: 159–70

Yamagata, N. (1994) *Homeric morality*, Leiden

Zanker, G. (1990) 'Loyalty in the *Iliad*', in *Papers of the Leeds international Latin seminar* 6: 211–27

Zeitlin, F. (1990) 'Thebes: theatre of self and society in Athenian drama', in *Nothing to do with Dionysos?*, eds. J. Winkler and F. Zeitlin: 130–67. First published in *Greek tragedy and political theory*, ed. J. Euben, Berkeley, CA, 1986: 101–41

GENERAL INDEX

Achaeans: as Helen's suitors, 140f.; generic status, 44–7, 102, 104–6, 119–21; *laos* of, ix, 2, 36, 43–7, 50, 61, 64–6, 68, 70, 74–80, 96, 102, 104, 194, 195 n. 181, 201
Achilles, 68–83 *passim*; relationship with *laoi*, 2, 10, 50, 52, 59, 64–6, 68f., 72f., 76–81, 83, 96, 98f., 145, 192, 195; relationship with Patroclus, 77–81, 130; shepherd of the people, 65f., 77; wrath, 65f., 68
achos, ἄχος, *see* grief
Acropolis, 186
Aegisthus, 104 n. 278, 119 n. 341
Aeneas, 24 n. 44, 88
Aeschylus, 22–4, 155, 171f., 179, 187; *Eumenides*, 171f., 179, 181 n. 128, 187; *Supplices*, 157 n. 43
aetiological, aetiology, 12, 55, 100, 117, 144, 163, 169, 172, 177f., 179 n. 117, 180f., 183, 185f., 188, 191, 193, 196
Agamemnon, 52–68 *passim*; attitude towards Troy, 48, 57f., 62, 68, 83, 91, 98, 145, 195; relationship with *laoi*, 10, 21, 25–7, 30, 38, 48f., 53–64, 66–8, 73, 76f., 83f., 98f., 107, 121, 133, 192; relationship with Nestor, 54, 59f., 62–4, 67, 75; shepherd of the people, 21, 49, 67, 69, 80, 104 n. 278
ageiro, ἀγείρω, *see laos*
Agelaos, 123–6, 144
agon, ἀγών, 35, 37, 154, 159, 176 n. 110
agore, ἀγορή, *see* assembly
Ajax, 74, 78
akouete leoi, ἀκούετε λεῴ, 174–83 *passim*, 202; *see also* formulae, *leos* ritual
Alcaeus, 155, 160f.
Alcinous, 115–17, 121f., 134

algos, ἄλγος, *see* grief
anax, ἄναξ, 18 n. 20, 23, 63 n. 79, 122, 197
Anchises, 127
Andromache, 88f.
aner, ἀνήρ: relationship with *laoi*, 59; relationship with suitors, 140, 142
Anthesteria, 151
Antinous, 117, 119–21, 123
apobates, ἀποβάτης, *see* sideman
apoikie, ἀποικίη, *see* colonisation
Apollo: relationship with Achilles, 50, 65, 76; relationship with *laoi*, 41, 76, 82, 154f., 157, 159f.; wrath, 50, 65; *see also* Paean
Apologoi, 133–5
apophthino, ἀποφθίνω, *see laos*
archaic and classical texts: relationship with epic, 147, 153–60, esp. 155f.; as sources for study of Homeric performances, 147
Areopagus, 171, 179, 183
Ares, 41 n. 121f., 70, 82, 86
Arete, 116
Aristarchus, 8, 72, 77 n. 150, 88 n. 219
army, *see stratos*
Aristophanes, 172, 178, 180, 182, 187 n. 158
Aristotle, 8f., 12f., 22, 24, 26–8, 51 n. 18, 170f., 180
Artemis, 158 n. 45
assembly, 28, 32–5, 37, 53 n. 27, 54f., 60, 78f., 82, 95, 97, 103f., 110f., 113, 115, 118, 148, 154, 159, 167, 170, 177, 183
Astyanax, 84, 87
atasthaliai, ἀτασθαλίαι, 92f., 103, 132
Athena: as herald, 58, 60, 70, 179; relationship with the founding people, 157, 159, 165, 171f., 179, 188 n. 160;

218

GENERAL INDEX

at the Panathenaea, 188, 191, 194; relationship with *laoi*, 41 nn. 121 and 123, 58, 60, 70f., 82, 114, 124, 126
Athens, Athenian, *see* Attic, Panathenaea
Attica, Attic, Ἀττικός, 171, 180 n. 125, 182 n. 134, 184f., 194 n. 180, 196
audience (Homeric), xi, 145f., 148, 151, 174, 189, 192, 194f., *see also laos*
Auffarth, C., 141 n. 435, 151f.
autochthony, *see laos*

Bacchylides, 7, 161–3, 176, 178
bias (narrative), 7, 26, 30, 46, 99, 131, 133f., 137; *see also Apologoi*, companions, early Greek hexameter poetry, *Iliad*, *laos*, *Odyssey*
bie, βίη, 73, 93
Björck, G., 155
blame, 26f., 30, 37f., 55f., 75, 102, 113, 127, 132f.
boule, βουλή, 63, 67, *see also* council, counsel
boulephoros, βουληφόρος, 53
Brauronia, 175 n. 105

Catalogue of ships, 36, 60f., 85, 166f. nn. 72f., 195 n. 182
Catalogue of the Trojans, 85f.
Catalogue of women, *see* Hesiod
Cecrops, 165f.
Choes, 175 n. 105, 178
Chryses, 31, 50f., 76f.
Chytroi, 175 n. 105
city, *see polis*
Clytoneus, 116
colonisation, colony, 169–71, 186
companions, 104–9 and 126–37 *passim*; and *nostos*, 105f., 120; relationship with *laoi*, 80, 95–7, 99, 104–9, 117, 120f., 125–31, 133; relationship with leader, 77–9, 129–35; relationship with suitors, 110, 128, 137; role in the *Odyssey*, 47, 100–2, 126ff., 132, 134f., 143; *see also* Achilles, Odysseus
Cook, E., 108 n. 292, 110 n. 299, 132 n. 393, 151f., 189 n. 164, 193 n. 178
co-operation: leader with companions, 130; leader with *laoi* 25, 32, 35–7, 39, 70, 83, 90; suitors with *laoi*, 114
council, counsel, 53f., 62–4, 67f., *see also boule*
crowd, *see ochlos*
Cyclops, 18 nn. 25f., 106, 108, 110, 121, 136

Demeter, 157
demos, δῆμος, 44, 58 n. 60, 114 n. 316, 164, 183, 184 n. 140, 195 n. 182
deur' ite, pantes leoi, δεῦρ' ἴτε, πάντες λεῴ, 174–83 *passim*, 202; *see also* formulae, *leos* ritual
Deubner, L., 186
Dionysius of Halicarnassus, 190
Dorieus, 169f.
drama, 178, 180, 194 n. 180, *see also* tragedy

early Greek hexameter poetry: relationship with other texts, 33, 37, 153–60, 162–4, 166f., 172; definition, 14 n. 1; use of the term *laos*, ix, 14–46 *passim*, 145, 162, 166f., 172; *see also* epic, formulae, Hesiod, Homer, *laos*, traditional theme
van Effenterre, H., 2
Epeians, 69
ephebeia, ἐφηβεία, 187
epic: relationship with other texts, 153; relationship with ritual, *see* resonance; treatment of *laoi*, 30, 46, 99, 125; treatment of shepherd 18; *see also* early Greek hexameter poetry, formulae, Hesiod, Homer, *laos*, traditional theme
Erichthonius, 190f.
erieros, ἐρίηρος, 128, 130, *see also* companions
esthlos, ἐσθλός, 128, 130, *see also* companions
ethnos, ἔθνος, 44
euandria, εὐανδρία, 186f.
Eupeithes, 107–9, 120, 122–4, 126, 132f., 144
Euripides, 155–7, 164f., 168f., 171, 181
Eurymachus, 119–24, 126, 144
Eurymedon, 115, 117, 133

219

GENERAL INDEX

fame, *see kleos*
family: relationship with *laoi*, 112, *see also laos*; of Hector, *see* Hector; of Odysseus, *see* Odysseus; *see also oikos*
Finley, M., 11
flock, 17–19
formulae, formulaic language: definition, 15f., 173f.; in epic, 15f., 47, 49, 55, 72f., 93, 102f., 107, 115, 117, 127–9, 148, 155f., 160, 173f.; in ritual, 174–83 *passim*, 184; relationship with ritual action, 173f.; *see also* traditional theme
funeral, 35, 37, 95–7, 154, 191; *see also* agon, ἀγών

gamos, γάμος, 138–41; *see also* suitors
gather (the people), *see laos*
genre, 7, 13, 72f., 146, 153–63 *passim*
giants, *see* Eurymedon
Glaucus, 4, 130
gloss: on *apobates*, 190; on *hetairos*, 134; on *laos* 24, 103, 117, 133, *see also ochlos*, *stratos*; on shepherd (of the people), 23
Goldhill, S., 4 n. 16, 5 n. 22, 6 n. 27, 108 n. 292, 147, 186 n. 151
Great Panathenaea, xi, 184 n. 141, 188–96; *see also* Panathenaea, performance
grief, 36, 83

Hector, 83–95 *passim*; relationship with family and city, 48, 57, 83–5, 87, 89–92, 97, 98f; relationship with *laoi*, 10, 26, 36f., 40, 48, 57, 73, 83–97, 99, 133; relationship with Paris, 26, 38f., 86; shepherd of the people, 86, 90
hegemon, ἡγεμών, *see* leader
Helen, 61, 88, 140f.
Helenus, 87f.
Helios, 135f.
Hera, 158 n. 45
herald: in epic, 34, 54, 58, 60, 81, 175, 179, 183, 200; in Athenian ritual, 174–83 *passim*, esp. 175, 178, 180
hero, ἥρως, 3–11 *passim*, 18, 116; and king, 6–9; existentialist view, 4; structuralist view, 5f.
Herodotus, 156, 169–71
heroic, heroism, *see* hero
Hesiod, 7f., 9 n. 42, 18–20, 28, 30 n. 67, 31f., 41–3, 45, 73, 139–41 *passim*, 162, 177; *Catalogue of women*, 9 n. 42, 42, 139–41 *passim*, 177 n. 112; *Theogony*, 28; *Works and days* 7, 31, 42, 45, 156, 177 n. 112
hetairos, ἑταῖρος, *see* companions
Heubeck, A., 1
hexameter poetry, *see* early Greek hexameter poetry
Homer: and early Greek *polis*, 11–13, 150f.; Homeric audience as *laoi* 146, 189; treatment of *laoi* 30, 43–6, 47–144 *passim*, esp. 98–100, 143f., 145; *see also* early Greek hexameter poetry, epic, Homeric hymns, *Iliad*, *laos*, *Odyssey*
Homeric hymns, 15, 18, 32; no. 5 *to Aphrodite*, 127; no. 11 *to Athena*, 70
Homeric society, 11–13, 149f.
honour, *see time*
household, *see* family, *oikos*

Iamblichus, 22f.
Iliad, 47–100 *passim*; and the fall of Troy, 58f., 87, 89, 91, 95, 98; and negative reciprocity 81, 99; ring structure 95; treatment of shepherds 18–20; treatment of *laoi*, xi, 25–7, 28 n. 60, 30–2, 36, 38–40, 43–5, 47–100 *passim*; *see also* Achilles, Agamemnon, Hector
Iliadic scholia, 8, 23f.
Ilios: not sacked in the *Iliad*, *see Iliad*; taken by ambush, 90 n. 226; *see also* Agamemnon, Hector
imbalance of interest: between leader and *laoi*, 35–7, 40, 46, 52, 79; between shepherd and master, 18f.
institutions, *see laos*
Istros, 8, 186 n. 144
Ithaca: and Achaeans, 121; and Troy 124, 192; as model for Athens, 193 n. 178; assembly of, 33, 110–13; *laos* of 103f., 114, 117

GENERAL INDEX

Jeanmaire, H., 1

king, *see* hero
kleos, κλέος, 10, 25, 38, 55f., 60–2, 64, 66, 68, 77, 99, 126–37 *passim*
kraino, κραίνω, 57, 61 n. 71, 63
kudos, κῦδος, 30, 50, 65

laas, λᾶας: relationship with *laoi*, 42f., 159f., 164–6, *see also laos*
laos, *laoi*, λαός, λαοί in early Greek hexameter poetry, 14–46 and *passim*; and negative reciprocity, 37–40, 77, 81, 92, 103, 115, 127; and stones, see *laas*; as audience, 41, 145f., 189; as a measure of well-being, 27, 40–3, 46, 102; at funerals, 35, 37, 95–7; at the *agon*, 35, 37; destruction, x, 28–32, 37–40, 46, 48, 55f., 62, 72f., 76f., 80, 83, 92–5, 98–100, 103, 107–9, 115, 122, 127, 133, 145, 198; in the assembly, 35, 37, 54–8, 95, 103f., 110–13, 118, 167; in Hesiod, *see* Hesiod; in Homer, *see* Homer, *Iliad*, *Odyssey*; in similes, 38, 84, 86, 94f., 103; in the *Iliad*, *see Iliad*; in the *Odyssey*, *see Odyssey*; inclusiveness, 40–3, 46, 95–7, 99; lack of effective institutions, 32–6, 40, 46, 99, 172; on the battlefield, 35 and *passim*; on the shield of Achilles, 81f.; relationship with companions, *see* companions; relationship with gods, 41, 74f., 58, 61, 69–71, 82, 90f., 113, 124, 126, 158, *see also* Apollo, Ares, Athena, Zeus; relationship with leaders, *passim*, e.g. x, 28–40, 46, 48, 55f., 62, 72f., 76f., 79f., 83, 92–5, 98–100, 103, 107–9, 115, 122, 127, 133, 145, 198f.; relationship with suitors, *see* suitors
laos, *laoi*, λαός, λαοί outside early Greek hexameter poetry, 145–95 *passim*; and negative reciprocity, 156; and stones, see *laas*; as audience, 176; as basis for institutions, 168f.; as measure of well-being, 156f., 159; as founding people, xi, 144, 163–73 *passim*, 177; at funerals, 154; at the *agon*, 154, 159; autochthony, 163–6; association with early social life, 162, 166, 172; association with institutional progress, xi, 37, 144, 161–3, 163–83 *passim*, 184, 195f.; destruction, 155f.; democratic attitudes, 22 n. 35, 195 n. 182; glosses 181 n. 127; in colonisation, 169f.; in poetry and prose, 146 n. 4, 153 n. 25; in prayer, 153f., 158, 167; in ritual, *see leos* ritual; in the assembly, 154, 159; in the Paean, *see* Paean; inclusiveness, 158–60, 166, 182–4; lack of social differentiation, 164, 172; on the battlefield, 154; relationship with gods, 157f., 159, *see also* Apollo, Athena; relationship with *laoi* in Homer, x, 189, 192–5; relationship with leaders, 154, 159–61; relationship with herald, *see* herald; relationship with *laoi* of epic, 153–63 *passim*
laossoos, λαοσσόος, 41 n. 123, 124
laotrophos, λαοτρόφος, 167
Latacz, J., 1f.
leader: as shepherd, *see* shepherd of the people; of companions, *see* companions; of *laoi*, *see laos*
Leiodes, 124
Lenaea, 175 n. 105
leokoreion, λεωκόρειον, 185 n. 142
leos, *leoi*, λεώς, λεῴ: as founding people of Attica, 183, 195; in Attic ritual, *see leos* ritual; inclusive nature, *see laos* outside epic; relationship with *laoi* of epic, 194 n. 180
leos ritual, 173–83 *passim*; announcements to *leoi*, 174–83 *passim*; collective restraint, 181
Longo, O., 148
Loraux, N., 6 n. 27, 128 n. 134, 185f., 190 n. 170
Lord, A., 148

Machaon, 68f., 74
man, *see aner*, suitors
mantis, μάντις, 41, 154 n. 29
master, *see anax*
menis, μῆνις, *see* Achilles, Apollo
Mentor, 111–14, 122

GENERAL INDEX

metaphor (of the shepherd), *see* shepherd of the people
mnesteres, μνηστῆρες, *see* suitors
Morris, I., 11
Murnaghan, S., 122
Mycenean, 1

Nagy, G., 1 n. 3, 2f., 4 n. 16, 6 n. 29, 10 n. 44, 16, 42 n. 127, 44 n. 131, 45, 48 n. 4, 50f. nn. 11 and 16, 60 n. 64, 76 n. 149, 78 nn. 158 and 162, 147 n. 5, 149 n. 15, 151 n. 23, 153 n. 26
neikein, νεικεῖν, *see* blame
nemesis, νέμεσις, *see* blame
neolaia, νεολαία, 187
neoleos, νεολέως, 187 n. 158
Nestor: relationship with Agamemnon, 53f., 57, 59f., 62–4, 67, 94; relationship with *laoi*, 23–5, 39, 53f., 57, 59f., 62–4, 67, 69–75, 77f., 85, 104–6, 113; shepherd of the people, 53f., 67, 104 n. 278
nostos, νόστος: and companions, 104–7, 136f.; generic status, 105f., 192f.; in the *Odyssey* proem, 132 n. 393

ochlos, ὄχλος: as a gloss on *laos*, 172, 179, 181
Odysseus: relationship with Agamemnon, 67f., 82, 107f.; relationship with companions, 105–7, 126–37 *passim*; relationship with *laoi*, 58f., 100–2, 104–9, 125–8; relationship with suitors, 120, 137–43 *passim*
Odyssey, 100–44 *passim*; narrative bias, 26, 122, 126–43 *passim*; treatment of companions and suitors, xi, 47, 100, 126–43 *passim*; treatment of shepherds, 18–20, 32; generic status, 100, 105–7, 120; treatment of *laoi*, 26, 38f., 47, 84, 86, 94f., 100, 102–4, 104–27 *passim*, 132f., 142–4
oikos, οἶκος: in the context of *laoi*, 169 n. 83; *see also* family
olese laon, ὤλεσε λαόν, x, 28–32 *passim*, 37–40, 46, 47 n. 2, 50, 55, 62, 73, 92–4, 98f., 102 n. 264, 103, 105, 107–9, 115, 127, 155f., 195, 198; *see also* formulae, *laos*

Paean, 157f., 174f.
Panathenaea, Great Panathenaea: and performances of Homeric poetry, 151f., 188–96 *passim*, *see also* performance; founding festival of Athens, 183–8 *passim*, 196; structure, 186–8
parabates, παραβάτης, *see* sideman
Paris: relationship with *laoi*, 26, 38f., 86, 89; *see also* Hector
Parry, M., 15, 148
Parthenon frieze, 187, 190f.
payment: for the shepherd, *see* shepherd; for the shepherd of the people, 35–7
Penelope, 114f., 118f., 121
people, *see demos, ethnos, laos*
peplos, πέπλος, 191
performance: of Athenian tragedy, 147f.; of Homeric poetry, x–xi, 148–52, *see also* Panathenaea, Great Panathenaea
Persephone, 158 n. 45
Phaeacians: and giants, 115, 117; and Ithacans, *see* Ithaca; *laos* of 115–17
Philochorus, 165f., 187 n. 152
phylon, phyle, φῦλον, φυλή, *see* tribe
phratry, 60
Pindar, 7, 100, 154f., 159, 163f., 166–8, 174, 176, 178
Pindaric scholia, 165
Pisthetairos, 172
pistos, πιστός, 128, 130; *see also* companions
Plato, 8, 12f., 23–5, 168
poimen laon, *ποιμὴν λαῶν, *see* shepherd of the people
polis, πόλις: and Homer, *see* Homer; and the founding people, 161–70, 192–4; in early Greek hexameter poetry, 166f.
Polydamas, 90
Poseidon: and Odysseus' companions, 135f.; relationship with *laoi*, 74–6, 82, 91 n. 236
pothos, pothe, πόθος, ποθή: for companions, 130f.; for the leader of *laoi*, 36f., 130f.
praise, *see kleos, kudos*

222

GENERAL INDEX

prayer, *see laos*
Priam: sons of, 86, 92; relationship with Hector, 92; relationship with *laoi*, 84, 89, 97
Protesilaos, 36, 60 n. 67
Pseudo-Eratosthenes, 190
Pylos, Pylians, 69–72

Quiller, Q., 12

Raaflaub, K., 4 n. 17, 10 n. 45, 11 nn. 49 and 51, 12, 14 n. 2, 30 n. 66, 50 n. 10, 66 n. 88, 69 n. 104
reciprocity: between leader and companions, 131f.; (negative) between leader and *laoi*, 37–40, 77, 81, 93, 99, 103, 115, 127, 156, 162
Redfield, J., 4 n. 16, 5f., 8f., 84 n. 199, 137f. nn. 421 and 426, 149f.
resonance: between epic and ritual, 189, 193 n. 178
return, *see nostos*, νόστος
ring composition, *see Iliad*
ritual, 173–83 *passim*; as intertext 152; definition, 173f.; relationship with epic, *see* resonance
ritual formulae, *see* formulae
Russo, J., 15

Sarpedon: not called a hero, 4f.; relationship with *laoi*, 85, 87; relationship with Hector, 86f.
Scherie, 115–17, 121, *see also* Phaeacians, Ithaca
Scully, S., 11
Seaford, R., 4 n. 16, 12 n. 54, 109 n. 295, 150
Semonides, 177
settlement, *see apoikie, synoikismos*
shepherd: in early Greek hexameter poetry, 17–20; in the bible, 20; lack of success, 19f., 28, 31f.; payment, 18
shepherd of the people: as metaphor, 17; lack of success, x, 28–32; payment, 36; task, x, 20–4, 27f.; traditional nature, 9f., 16
shield of Achilles, *see laos*
sideman, 186, 189–91
simile, *see laos*

Simon, E., 74 n. 130, 190
Simonides, 146, 189
Socrates, 21f., 26–8
soothsayer, *see mantis*
Sophocles, 168f.
Sparta, 158, 169f., 187
stone, *see laas*
Strabo, 193
stratos, στρατός, 171f., 179, 181
suitors, 110–25 and 137–43 *passim*; and guests, 142; relationship with the *aner*, 140–3; relationship with companions 110, 128, 137; relationship with *laoi*, 110–25 *passim*; lack of cohesion, 138; lack of success, 140f.
Susarion, 177f.
synoikismos, συνοικισμός, 170, 186, 196

Taplin, O., 1 n. 3, 14 n. 2, 22 n. 36, 30 n. 66, 38 n. 108, 41, 50 n. 10, 74 n. 134, 82 n. 184, 84 n. 197, 114 n. 316, 151 n. 20
Tauropolia, 175 n. 105
Telemachus: and Nestor, 113f.; relationship with *laoi*, 111, 113f., 118
Teiresias, 100–2, 104, 106, 109, 119, 123, 127, 134, 136f., 143f.
teleology (narrative): of companions, suitors and *laoi*, 138
telos, τέλος, 139–41
Theognis, 160f.
Theseus: and Panathenaea, 186, 191 n. 171; relationship with *leoi*, 170f., 180f.
Thersites, 58 n. 60
Thompson, A., 190
Thrasymachus, 23f., 25
Thrinacie, 135f.
time, τιμή, 36, 131, 138
Timotheus, 154f., 158f., 187f., 195 n. 181
Tlepolemus, 25
traditional theme, 15f., 28, 93, 148f., *see also* formulae
tragedy, 147f.
tribe, 60 n. 64
Troy, *see* Ilios

Vernant, J.-P., 137 n. 421, 147

Watkins, C., 15f.
wedding, *see gamos*
Welskopf, E., 1
Whitman, C., 3 n. 15, 4–6, 81 n. 181, 137 n. 421
wrath, *see* Achilles, Apollo

Xenophon, 21f., 26–8

Zeus, 61, 41 nn. 121f., 63–5, 75–8, 80, 90f., 157, 159

INDEX OF PASSAGES CITED

ADESPOTON TRAGICUM

Adespota fr. 428 (Kannicht/Snell)   159 n. 50

AESCHYLUS

Agamemnon
188f.	154 n. 28
516	7 n. 30
657	20 n. 32

Choephori
363–6	154 n. 28

Eumenides
15f.	157 n. 44
290	159 n. 50
566	179 n. 119
569	179 n. 119
638f.	157 n. 43, 171 n. 93
681	202
681–4	171, 179 n. 117, 181 n. 127
775	168 n. 80, 179 n. 117
996f.	179 n. 117
996–9	157 n. 44, 188 n. 160
997	168 n. 80

Persae
116–27	187 n. 152
126–30	181 n. 127
241f.	22f.
297	123 n. 353
592	182 n. 129
669	187 n. 155
728f.	154 n. 30, 155, 181 n. 127
729f.	187 n. 152
787–9	154 n. 28

Supplices
92–5	154 n. 29
366f.	157 n. 43, 168 n. 80
399–401	157 n. 43
484f.	157 n. 43
517	159 n. 50
517f.	154 nn. 28 and 29, 157 n. 43
686–8	187 n. 155
975–7	157 n. 43
976	159 n. 50

Fragments
55 (Radt)	7 n. 30
132c8 (Radt)	20 n. 32
406 (Radt)	123 n. 353

ALCAEUS

fr. 356 (*PLF*)	154 n. 28, 160 n. 55
fr. 364 (*PLF*)	155 n. 32, 160 n. 54

ANDROTION

FGrHist 324 fr. 2	186 n. 144

ANECDOTA GRAECA

AB 426	190 n. 166

APOLLONIUS SOPHISTA

s.v. ποιμήν	17 n. 13

ARISTOPHANES

Acharnians
162f.	168 n. 80
1000	202
1000f.	175 n. 105, 178 n. 114
1000–4	182 n. 135

INDEX OF PASSAGES CITED

Birds
448   202
448–50   154 n. 29, 181 n. 127
1271–7   154 n. 28, 172 n. 97

Frogs
211–19   181 n. 127
219   175 n. 105
676   146 n. 3, 175 n. 105

Knights
163f.   123 n. 353, 154 n. 28

Peace
62   157 n. 44
296   202
296–8   154 n. 29, 180, 182 nn. 133 and 135
296–300   181 n. 127
551   181 n. 127, 202
551f.   154 n. 29
551–5   175 n. 103
632   154 n. 29
1316f.   181 n. 127, 202

Thesmophoriazusae
39   146 n. 3, 182 n. 129, 202

Wasps
1015   202
1015f.   146 n. 3, 175 n. 105

Fragments
73 (*PCG*)   187 n. 155

ARISTOTLE

Athenaion Politeia
18.3   185 n. 142
42   187 n. 153

Ethica Nicomachea
1161a 12–15   17 n. 13, 22 n. 34

Poetics
1461a 9–12   51 n. 18

Politics
1285b3ff.   9 n. 39
1332b12–32   9 n. 39

Problemata
922b   9, 182 n. 135

Rhetoric
1365a13   28 n. 61

Fragments
384 (Rose)   12 n. 57, 170 n. 86, 180 n. 122, 187 n. 152

ASIUS OF SAMOS

fr. 1.3 (Davies)   197

ATHENAEUS

8.41   183 n. 138, 202

BACCHYLIDES

1.112–19   154 n. 28
1.119   168 n. 78
3.5–9   182 n. 129
9.30–5   154 n. 28, 182 n. 129
9.35   154 n. 30
11.64–8   161
11.64–76   154 n. 28, 170 n. 85
11.69–76   162
11.115–17   154 n. 45
13.228–31   146 n. 3, 154 n. 30, 176
18.8–10   20 n. 32

CALLIMACHUS

Lavacrum Palladis
130   123 n. 353

CALLINUS

fr. 1.18 (West)   28 n. 59, 36 n. 96
fr. 1.18f. (West)   35 n. 92, 154 n. 28

CERTAMEN HOMERI ET HESIODI

281–3 (Allen)   35 n. 90

DIODORUS SICULUS

12.70   190 n. 167

DIONYSIUS OF HALICARNASSUS

Antiquitates Romanae
7.73   190 n. 166

INDEX OF PASSAGES CITED

[ERATOSTHENES]
Catasterismi
13   190 n. 170

ETYMOLOGICUM GENUINUM

s.v. Ἀγησίλαος καὶ
    Ἀγεσίλαος   123 n. 353
s.v. λαοσσόος   41 n. 120

EURIPIDES

Alcestis
103   187 n. 155
Andromache
19f.   157 n. 43
1089   157 n. 44
Erechtheus
fr. 360.5–8 (Nauck)   159 n. 50
fr. 360.48f. (Nauck) 157 n. 44, 188 n. 160
Hecuba
8f.   154 n. 28
508ff.   154 n. 30
508–10   157 n. 43
510   154 n. 28
530–2   181 n. 127
529–33   179, 181 n. 127
532   202
532f.   182 n. 129
553   182 n. 129
Helen
1319–31   156 n. 40
1327–31   156f.
Heraclidae
80f.   168 n. 82
86   157 n. 43
316   159 n. 50
922f.   157 n. 44, 168 n. 80
922–5   157 n. 43
923   188 n. 160
Hercules Furens
1389   154 n. 28, 159 n. 50
1389f.   202
1389–93   154 n. 30
Ion
29   159 n. 50
29f.   165 n. 64

1140   154 n. 29, 157 n. 44
1572–8   165 n. 64
1575–9   60 n. 64
1577f.   154 n. 28, 159 n. 50
1592–4   154 n. 28
Iphigenia at Aulis
281   157 n. 43
Iphigenia in Tauris
958–60   171 n. 89, 175 n. 105
960   157 n. 44, 188 n. 160
1450–61   171 n. 89, 175 n. 105
1452   157 nn. 43 and 44, 171 n. 90, 188 n. 160
1458   171 n. 91
Orestes
846   181 n. 128
871–3   172, 181 nn. 126f.
873   154 n. 29, 202
901   182 n. 129
Phaethon
102–18 (Diggle)   182 n. 135
109–18 (Diggle)   180 n. 124
112 (Diggle)   202
Phoenissae
290   157 n. 43
1227   154 n. 28, 159 n. 50, 202
1235   156 n. 40
1238f.   157 n. 43
1239   154 n. 28, 159 n. 50
1460   157 n. 43
1467   154 n. 28, 159 n. 50
Rhesus
410   156 n. 40
426   159 n. 50
Supplices
329   154 n. 28, 159 n. 50
387   154 n. 28
467   159 n. 50, 181 n. 127, 202

227

INDEX OF PASSAGES CITED

Supplices (cont.)
467f.	157 n. 43
481	157 n. 43
664	154 n. 28, 159 n. 50
669	181 n. 127, 202
669f.	182 n. 129
677–9	190 n. 168
728–30	156 n. 40
743f.	155, 159 n. 50
744	154 n. 28

Troades
522	182 n. 129

Fragments
446 (Nauck)	7 n. 30

EUSTATHIUS

vol. I pp. 38.27–39.19 (van der Valk)	43 n. 130
vol. I p. 38.30–3 (van der Valk)	166 n. 69
vol. I p. 39.11–13 (van der Valk)	159 n. 50
vol. I p. 402.37 (Stallbaum)	109 n. 298
vol. II p. 308.24–34 (Stallbaum)	108 n. 295

EZEKIEL

Exag. 203	186 n. 151

HARPOCRATION

s.v. ἀποβάτης	190 n. 167

HECATAEUS

FGrHist 1 fr. 345	166 n. 70

HELLANICUS

FGrHist 323a fr. 2	186 n. 144

HERODOTUS

1.22.3	156
2.129.1	154 n. 28, 156 n. 37
4.148.1	60 n. 64, 169 n. 84
5.42.2	169
8.136.2	187 n. 152

HESIOD AND HESIODEA

Aegimius
fr. 301 (M–W)	197

Catalogue of women
fr. 1.16 (M–W)	9 n. 42
fr. 23(a).34 (M–W)	197
fr. 25.34 (M–W)	197
fr. 25.34–6 (M–W)	41 n. 120
fr. 30.15–19 (M–W)	41 n. 122
fr. 30.16 (M–W)	51 n. 19
fr. 30.16–19 (M–W)	28 n. 61
fr. 30.19 (M–W)	51 n. 19
fr. 33(a).2 (M–W)	63 n. 79, 200 n. 15
fr. 33(a).24 (M–W)	28 n. 61, 29, 198
fr. 43(a).58 (M–W)	197
fr. 75.11 (M–W)	199
fr. 76.4–8 (M–W)	139
fr. 76.20–3 (M–W)	139
fr. 136.18 (M–W)	197
fr. 141.19 (M–W)	197
fr. 193.1 (M–W)	197
fr. 204.8 (M–W)	140 n. 431
fr. 204.46–9 (M–W)	140 n. 432
fr. 204.58–62 (M–W)	141 n. 433
fr. 211.4 (M–W)	37 n. 101
fr. 234 (M–W)	42

Pirithoi catabasis
280.8 (M–W)	197

Scutum
27	25 n. 46, 37 n. 101
39	19 n. 27
472	199 n. 5, 200 n. 12
472–5	35 n. 92
475	199

Theogony
26	19 nn. 27 and 28
84f.	35 n. 90, 37 n. 101, 200 n. 12
84–7	28 n. 59
88f.	28, 35 n. 90
430	35 n. 90, 37 n. 101

Works and days
156–65	40 n. 116

INDEX OF PASSAGES CITED

158f.	8 n. 35	1.50	51 n. 18
158–60	7	1.53f.	79 n. 167
161–73	141 n. 433	1.54	33 n. 80, 35 n. 90
184–6	18 n. 18	1.75	50 n. 12
225–7	42, 51 n. 19	1.116f.	30 n. 66, 50 n. 10
238–43	51 n. 19	1.117	28 nn. 59–61, 61
240–3	31		n. 72, 65 n. 86,
243	28 n. 61, 29, 198		198
650–2	45	1.126	52, 53 n. 29, 79
652	33, 199		n. 169
763f.	37 n. 99, 200 n.	1.153f.	18 n. 17
	15	1.154–7	71 n. 119
768	145 n. 2, 157 n.	1.225–8	52 n. 26
	43	1.226	70 n. 115
		1.263	197
HESYCHIUS		1.312–17	41 n. 122
s.v. Ἀγεσίλαος	123 n. 353	1.313	33 n. 80, 41 n.
			124, 52 n. 23,
HOMER AND HOMERICA			65 n. 86, 199
Cypria		1.313f.	51
fr. 1 (Davies)	5 n. 21	1.345–7	78 nn. 159f.
Homeric hymns		1.375	197
h. Ap. 77f.	166 n. 72, 167 n.	1.380–3	41 n. 122
	73	1.382	30 n. 69
h. Cer. 296f.	33 n. 80, 35 n. 90	1.382f.	28 n. 61, 49 n. 8,
h. Merc. 286	19 n. 27		65 n. 86, 79 n.
h. Merc. 286f.	18 n. 23		170
h. Merc. 491f.	18 n. 23	1.412	76 n. 149
h. Ven. 54f.	18 n. 23	1.454	10 n. 44, 28 n.
h. Ven. 69	18 n. 24		61, 41 n. 122,
h. Ven. 103–6	51 n. 19, 109 n.		50, 65 n. 86,
	297, 127 n. 367		198, 201
h. Ven. 106	41 n. 124	1.505–10	76 n. 149
h. 11	70	2	34 n. 83
h. 11.1	41 n. 123	2.24f.	26, 53
h. 11.4	41 n. 121, 70 n.	2.25	33 n. 80
	107	2.54	53 n. 30
h. 29.3	41 n. 123	2.55	53 n. 31
Iliad		2.56–71	53 n. 32
1.2	44 n. 136	2.61f.	26 n. 54, 53 n. 28
1.4	5 n. 21	2.62	33 n. 80
1.8–10	49	2.79–83	53 n. 33
1.10	28 n. 61, 29, 30	2.84–6	54 n. 37
	n. 69, 41 n.	2.85	54 n. 34, 197
	122, 65 n. 86,	2.86	58 n. 58
	130 n. 384, 198	2.94	54 n. 38
1.10–12	52 n. 23	2.95f.	35 n. 90, 54 n. 39
1.11f.	31 n. 71	2.95–7	34 n. 84
1.16	31 n. 72, 197	2.96–8	54 n. 40

INDEX OF PASSAGES CITED

Iliad (cont.)
2.99   34 n. 84, 200
2.99–101   54 n. 41
2.105   55 n. 45, 197
2.110   55 n. 46
2.110ff.   75 n. 136
2.111–15   55 n. 48
2.114f.   10 n. 43
2.115   28 n. 61, 29, 37 n. 99, 73 n. 127, 198, 200
2.119–22   56 n. 50
2.120   200
2.132f.   56 n. 51
2.137f.   57
2.149f.   58 n. 58
2.163   41 n. 120, 70 n. 109, 201
2.163f.   34 n. 84, 58 n. 59
2.179   41 n. 120, 70 n. 109, 201
2.179f.   58 n. 59
2.191   33 n. 80, 35 n. 90, 58 n. 60, 200
2.198f.   58 n. 60
2.211–69   58 n. 60
2.226   79 n. 169
2.243   49 n. 9, 197
2.254   49 n. 9, 197
2.279f.   41 n. 120, 70 n. 109
2.280   33 n. 80, 34 n. 84, 199
2.362   54 n. 35
2.362–6   59 n. 63
2.365   75 n. 136
2.437f.   60 n. 65
2.438   34 n. 84, 199 n. 7
2.450   41 n. 120, 201
2.450f.   60 n. 65, 70 n. 109
2.576–80   25, 60
2.577f.   200
2.578   33 n. 80, 199
2.579f.   25 n. 46
2.580   33 n. 80, 123 n. 353, 199 n. 10, 200
2.653–70   166 n. 72
2.664   33, 198, 200
2.672–5   60 n. 67
2.675   25 n. 46, 33 n. 80, 199f.
2.684   44 n. 135
2.708f.   33 n. 80, 36 n. 96, 129 n. 373, 130 n. 382
2.708–10   60 n. 67, 79 n. 163
2.768f.   74 n. 133
2.771–9   80 n. 171
2.772   49 n. 9, 197
2.778–80   58 n. 59
2.791   85 n. 204
2.799   60 n. 65, 85 n. 205, 200
2.806   85 n. 204
2.809   85 nn. 206f.
2.816–18   60 n. 67, 85 n. 207
2.817f.   33 n. 80, 200
3.49   140 n. 431
3.186   24 n. 44
3.201   193 n. 178
3.236   197
3.318   39 n. 111
3.318–22   35 n. 91, 86 n. 209
3.318–24   61 n. 69
3.322   39 n. 111
4.27   61 n. 69
4.27f.   41 n. 120, 70 n. 112, 71 n. 117
4.28   199
4.47   24 n. 44, 84 n. 196, 89 n. 223
4.76f.   41 n. 120
4.90f.   33 n. 80
4.164f.   28 n. 61, 84 n. 196, 198
4.165   24 n. 44, 89 n. 223
4.184   28 n. 59, 61 nn. 69f., 201
4.199   201
4.201f.   33 n. 80
4.257–64   131 n. 388

INDEX OF PASSAGES CITED

4.266f.	130 n. 378, 130 n. 388	6.214	197
4.275	18 n. 23	6.223	28 n. 61, 40 n. 116, 44 nn. 132 and 137, 45 n. 143, 56 n. 49, 61 n. 69, 154 n. 27, 198, 201
4.275–9	20 n. 30		
4.279	18 n. 24		
4.287	33 n. 80		
4.296	197		
4.377	33, 45 n. 143, 61 n. 69, 198	6.269	41 n. 123
4.384	44 n. 137, 45 n. 143	6.271–311	191 n. 176
		6.279	41 n. 123
4.407	33 n. 80, 45 n. 143, 61 n. 69, 200 n. 16	6.289–95	191 n. 175
		6.305	41 n. 123
		6.305–11	191 n. 173
4.413	49 n. 9, 197	6.325–7	37 n. 100
4.430	33 n. 80, 76 n. 148, 200	6.325–9	26 n. 51, 38, 86 n. 210, 88 n. 220
4.430f.	197		
4.452–6	20 n. 30	6.327	28 n. 61, 61 n. 69, 198
5.136–40	19f.		
5.144	197	6.350	140 n. 431
5.311–13	18 n. 21	6.402f.	84 n. 198
5.464–6	86 n. 213	6.403	85 n. 201
5.471–4	87	6.431–4	88f.
5.472–4	85 n. 200	6.433	33 n. 80
5.474	85 n. 201	6.433–9	89 n. 221
5.485f.	33 n. 80	6.448f.	28 n. 61, 84, 89 n. 223, 198
5.485–9	87 n. 215		
5.513	197	6.449	24 n. 44
5.566	197	6.449f.	167 n. 73
5.570	197	6.449–53	166 n. 72
5.573	201	7.177f.	35 n. 91
5.600f.	55 n. 47	7.177–80	61 n. 69
5.643	25, 28 nn. 59 and 61, 29, 30 n. 69, 61 n. 69, 198	7.230	49 n. 9, 197
		7.234	197
		7.306	201
		7.307	55 n. 43
5.757f.	37 n. 100	7.342	33 n. 80, 199
5.758	28 n. 61, 41 n. 122, 61 n. 69, 198, 201	7.434	35 n. 92, 61 n. 69, 201
		7.469	197
5.803	44 n. 137, 45 n. 143	8.66–72	61 n. 71
		8.67	28 n. 61, 32, 76 n. 146, 198
6.76	88 n. 219		
6.77f.	88	8.75–7	41 n. 120
6.80	33 n. 80, 89 n. 221, 199	8.76	201
		8.242–6	61 n. 71
6.80–2	88	8.246	28 nn. 59–61, 61, 198
6.86	88 n. 218		

INDEX OF PASSAGES CITED

Iliad (cont.)

8.281	197		95, 74 n. 132, 197, 201
8.522	89	9.708	33 n. 80
9.13–22	133 n. 396	10.3	49 n. 9, 67 n. 94, 197
9.14f.	67 n. 93		
9.18–22	62 n. 73	10.14	198, 201
9.21f.	10 n. 43, 38 n. 108	10.14f.	74 n. 132
		10.14–16	28 n. 59, 67 n. 95
9.22	28 n. 61, 29, 37 n. 99, 67 n. 93, 68 n. 99, 73 n. 127, 198, 200	10.73	197
		10.73–9	54 n. 35, 67 n. 96
		10.79	33 n. 80, 199 n. 9
		10.170	200 n. 15
9.81	197	10.170f.	67 n. 96
9.94	63 n. 80	10.406	86 n. 208, 197
9.96	63 n. 78	10.485f.	20 n. 31
9.96–9	62	11.85	28 n. 61, 32, 76 n. 146, 198
9.96–102	54 n. 35		
9.97–9	63f.	11.92	197
9.98	63 n. 79, 197	11.186–90	90 n. 227
9.98f.	28 n. 59	11.187	49 n. 9, 197
9.109–11	94 n. 244	11.189	33 n. 80, 199f.
9.116f.	64, 77 n. 152	11.201–5	90 n. 227
9.118	28 n. 61, 50 n. 15, 64f., 68 n. 100, 198, 201	11.202	49 n. 9, 197
		11.204	33 n. 80, 199f.
		11.309	28 n. 61
9.190f.	78 n. 160	11.370	197
9.201–8	78 n. 160	11.465	197
9.211–20	78 n. 160	11.504–6	78 n. 161
9.337–9	65 n. 87	11.506	68 n. 101, 197
9.338	33 n. 80, 199	11.548–55	20 n. 31
9.417–26	75 n. 138	11.578	197
9.418–24	66	11.597–9	68 n. 101
9.424	28 n. 59, 66 n. 90, 67 n. 95, 74 n. 132, 197, 201	11.597–604	78 n. 161
		11.598	197
		11.602–4	68 n. 101
		11.649–51	69 n. 103
9.483	200	11.651	197
9.521	201	11.655ff.	54 n. 35
9.573	55 n. 43	11.701–4	71 n. 120
9.584–6	130 n. 379	11.714–17	54 n. 35, 69 n. 105
9.593	28 n. 61, 198		
9.620–2	78 n. 160	11.716	33, 70 n. 113, 198
9.630	78 n. 156		
9.644	197	11.717	70 n. 112
9.644f.	78 n. 157	11.720f.	70 n. 110
9.658–61	78 n. 160	11.754–8	54 n. 35
9.676–87	66 n. 91	11.756–61	69 n. 105
9.680–7	75 n. 138	11.758	33 n. 80, 41 n. 120, 79 n. 168,
9.681	28 n. 59, 67 n.		

INDEX OF PASSAGES CITED

11.758f.	126 n. 366	14.22	232
11.761	70 n. 111	14.34	49 n. 9, 197
11.762–4	72 n. 122	14.90–4	167 n. 73
11.763f.	54 n. 35, 72	14.93	67 n. 97
11.764	39 n. 109	14.102	33 n. 80
	28 n. 61, 77 n. 151, 198 n. 3		49 n. 9, 67 n. 98, 197
11.769f.	54 n. 35, 71 n. 116	14.423	86 n. 208, 197
11.770	199	14.444f.	18 n. 21
11.783f.	71 n. 121	14.516	197
11.796	33 n. 80, 80 n. 172, 200	15.15	91 n. 233
		15.56	201
11.796f.	44 n. 134, 54 n. 35	15.218	76 n. 142, 91 n. 236, 201
11.842	197	15.262	86 n. 208, 197
12.1–35	167 n. 73	15.311	33 n. 80, 41 n. 121, 76 n. 143
12.201	199 n. 5		
12.219	199 n. 5	15.318f.	41 n. 122
12.200–29	41 n. 120	15.319	28 n. 61, 32, 76, 198
12.218f.	90 n. 228		
12.228f.	90 n. 229	15.323–5	20 n. 31
12.243	90 n. 230	15.323–6	76 n. 148
12.299–306	20 n. 31	15.475	33 n. 80, 199f.
12.322–9	4 n. 18	15.506	33 n. 80, 199 n. 11, 200
12.471	55 n. 43		
13.47	28 n. 59, 74, 198, 201	15.546–51	18 n. 21
		15.586–8	20 n. 30
13.107f.	74	15.630–8	19 n. 29
13.108	58 n. 57	15.674ff.	74 n. 133
13.196	201	15.689	55 n. 43
13.345–50	75 n. 140, 76 n. 141	15.694f.	41 n. 121, 91 n. 234
13.348f.	41 n. 122	15.695	33 n. 80, 76 n. 144, 199f.
13.349	28 n. 61, 198 nn. 2 and 4, 201	15.723	33 n. 80
13.411	197	16.2	65 n. 83, 80 n. 174, 197
13.489–95	24 n. 44	16.38	80 n. 173, 199f.
13.492	33 n. 80, 199	16.39	44 n. 134
13.495	33 n. 80	16.129	33, 80 n. 175, 199
13.571f.	18 n. 23		
13.600	197	16.170	80 n. 176
13.674–6	90 n. 231	16.237	10 n. 44, 28 n. 61, 50 n. 15, 76, 80 n. 177, 81 n. 179, 198, 201
13.674–8	75 n. 137		
13.675f.	28 n. 61		
13.710	33 n. 80, 199		
13.822	201		
13.822f.	41 n. 120	16.237–41	77 n. 154
13.833f.	33 n. 80, 90 n.	16.240	80 n. 178

INDEX OF PASSAGES CITED

Iliad (cont.)
16.246–50	77 n. 154	18.523f.	82 n. 186
16.248	80 nn. 176 and 178	18.525–9	19 n. 29
		18.573–86	20 n. 30
16.290	130 n. 380	18.575–7	18 n. 23
16.295f.	55 n. 43	19.34	82 n. 187
16.352–6	19	19.35	49 n. 9, 197
16.367–9	91 n. 235	19.40f.	82 n. 187
16.368f.	33 n. 80	19.139	33 n. 80, 82 n. 188, 199
16.501	33 n. 80, 85 n. 203, 199f.	19.171	199
		19.171f.	82 n. 190
16.549–51	85 n. 203	19.233f.	82 nn. 190f.
16.550f.	200	19.234	33 n. 80
16.551	33 n. 80, 199	19.251	49 n. 9, 197
16.581	130 n. 381	19.289	197
16.584f.	130 n. 381	19.321f.	130 n. 384
16.714	33 n. 80	19.315f.	130 n. 383
16.777–80	81 n. 179	19.315–21	79 n. 163
16.778	28 n. 61, 32, 76 n. 147, 198	19.386	65 n. 83, 83 n. 192, 197
16.822	36 n. 97, 79, 81 n. 179, 201	20.110	86 n. 208, 197
		20.219–22	18 n. 20
17.12	197	20.221	18 n. 23
17.61–9	20 n. 30	20.283	197
17.109–12	20 n. 31	21.221	65 n. 83, 197
17.150–2	129	21.387	55 n. 43
17.220–6	91 n. 237	21.448f.	18 nn. 22f.
17.225f.	156 n. 39	21.458	41 n. 121
17.250f.	33 n. 80	22.52–5	79 n. 165, 92
17.251	37 n. 101	22.53	92 n. 240
17.348	197	22.54	92 n. 240, 97 n. 255, 200 n. 13
17.380	55 n. 43		
17.559	199f.	22.54f.	36
18.22	79	22.104	28 n. 61, 73 n. 127, 103 n. 270, 198
18.81	131 n. 386		
18.161–4	20 n. 30		
18.300–2	91 n. 238	22.104–10	10 n. 45, 37 n. 99, 39 n. 115, 92f., 115 n. 323
18.452	80 n. 173, 199f.		
18.497	35 n. 90, 81 n. 182		
18.502	182 n. 129	22.107	28 n. 61, 29, 73 nn. 127 and 129, 198
18.502f.	35 n. 90, 81 n. 183		
18.503	200	22.205–7	83 n. 193, 96 n. 248
18.503–5	34 n. 84		
18.509	35 n. 90	22.277	86 n. 208, 197
18.516	41 n. 121	22.408f.	36 n. 98
18.516–19	70 n. 108, 82 n. 185	23.6	130 n. 379
		23.132	190

INDEX OF PASSAGES CITED

23.156	201	2.26f.	33 n. 79
23.156f.	33 n. 80, 35 n. 92	2.40f.	111 n. 303
23.156–63	96 n. 249	2.41	35 n. 90, 103 nn. 275f., 104 n. 277, 110 n. 300
23.158	199 n. 8		
23.162	35 n. 92, 96 n. 250, 199	2.47	112 n. 309
23.218–25	96 n. 251	2.80f.	111 n. 305
23.257f.	96 n. 252	2.81	36 n. 98, 103 n. 276, 110 n. 300, 200
23.258	33 n. 80, 35 n. 91		
23.389	197		
23.411	197	2.87	121 n. 347
23.728	35 n. 91, 37 n. 101, 96 n. 252	2.174–6	134 n. 404
		2.230–2	113 n. 310
23.881	35 n. 91, 37 n. 101, 96 n. 252	2.230–6	111f.
		2.233f.	36 n. 98, 112 n. 308, 113 n. 312
24.1f.	35 n. 91, 96 n. 252		
24.27f.	86 n. 209, 89 n. 223	2.234	63 n. 79, 103 n. 276, 112 n. 309, 197
24.37f.	35 n. 92	2.239	113 n. 311
24.60	140 n. 431	2.252	35 n. 90, 55 n. 47, 103 n. 276, 104 n. 277, 110 n. 300, 111 n. 304, 199
24.610f.	35 n. 92		
24.611	43 n. 130, 96 n. 253, 164 n. 61		
24.654	49 n. 9, 197		
24.658	33 n. 80, 96 n. 253, 199	3.140	33, 104 n. 279, 199
24.665	35 n. 92	3.144	104 n. 279
24.713–17	97 n. 254	3.155	33 n. 80, 34 n. 84, 200
24.740	35 n. 92, 36 n. 98, 97 n. 256	3.156	49 n. 9, 104 n. 278, 197
24.777	97	3.157–9	104 n. 279
24.777ff.	35 n. 92	3.167	105 n. 280
24.788f.	33 n. 80, 97 n. 258	3.180–2	129 n. 375
		3.181	105 n. 280
24.789	199 n. 6	3.191	105 n. 280
24.789–92	35 n. 92	3.213	113 n. 315
24.793f.	97 n. 259	3.214f.	113
Odyssey		3.305	28 n. 61, 119 n. 341, 198, 200 n. 12, 201
1.1–8	132 n. 391		
1.247	193 n. 178		
1.346	128 n. 371		
2	34 n. 83	3.469	104 n. 278, 197
2.7	44 n. 138	4.24	104 n. 278, 197
2.13	35 n. 90, 37 n. 101, 102 n. 266, 103 nn. 275f., 110, 200	4.87f.	18 n. 20
		4.156	104 n. 278, 197
		4.174–6	166 n. 72
		4.174–7	116 n. 327
2.25–7	111 n. 302	4.176	200 n. 12

235

INDEX OF PASSAGES CITED

Odyssey (cont.)

4.277	90 n. 226	9.12f.	134 n. 399
4.291	104 n. 278, 197	9.15	134 n. 399
4.316	104 n. 278, 197	9.37f.	134 n. 399
4.367	105 n. 280	9.112–15	18 n. 25
4.374	105 n. 280	9.182–92	18 nn. 20 and 23f.
4.408	105 n. 280		
4.433	105 n. 280	9.224–30	136 n. 417
4.528	104 n. 278, 197	9.259	44 n. 140
4.532	49 n. 9, 104 n. 278, 197	9.259–66	105 n. 282
		9.263	24 n. 44
		9.265	28 n. 61, 29, 198
4.669–72	114 n. 318	9.265f.	61 n. 68
4.700f.	114 n. 318	9.278	107 n. 286
4.739–41	114 n. 317	9.336f.	18 nn. 20 and 24
5.7–12	114 n. 319	9.494–500	136 n. 418
5.12	197	9.502–5	136 n. 419
6.164	33 n. 80, 199	9.526–36	106 n. 285
6.194	117 n. 330	9.530–6	136 n. 420
7.58–60	103 n. 269, 115 n. 321, 156 n. 37	9.534	134 n. 404
		10.84f.	18 n. 22
		10.538	104 n. 278, 197
7.60	28 n. 61, 39, 198	11.113f.	100f., 134 n. 404
7.69–72	25 n. 46, 115 n. 324	11.113–18	137 n. 422
		11.114	134 n. 405
7.71f.	37 n. 101	11.115–17	100f.
7.322f.	117 n. 333	11.119–21	100f.
8.62	128 n. 371	11.134–7	41 n. 123, 51 n. 19, 101, 109 n. 296
8.100	35 n. 91		
8.124f.	116 n. 328		
8.125	35 n. 91	11.136f.	28 n. 59
8.382	25 n. 46, 37 n. 101, 115 n. 324, 200	11.293	19 n. 27
		11.355	25 n. 46, 37 n. 101, 115 n. 324, 200
8.401	25 n. 46, 37 n. 101, 115 n. 324, 200		
		11.376	134 n. 399
		11.378	25 n. 46, 37 n. 101, 115 n. 324, 200
8.471f.	34 n. 85, 116 n. 328, 145 n. 2		
8.472	37 n. 101	11.412	105 n. 280
8.515	90 n. 226	11.500	28 n. 61, 198
8.523–5	38 n. 104, 84 n. 195, 94, 103 n. 271	11.518	28 n. 61, 198, 200
		11.525	90 n. 226
8.577f.	134 n. 403	12.28	37 n. 101
8.581	134 n. 403	12.260ff.	136 n. 412
8.584–6	134 n. 403	12.297ff.	136 n. 413
9.2	25 n. 46, 37 n. 101, 115 n. 324, 200	12.320ff.	136 n. 413
		12.333ff.	136 n. 414
		12.377f.	135

INDEX OF PASSAGES CITED

12.426–46	134 n. 401	21.83	18 n. 20
13.27f.	116 n. 328, 145 n. 2	21.188f.	18 n. 20
		21.346	193 n. 178
13.38	25 n. 46, 37 n. 101, 115 n. 324, 200	22.45f.	121 n. 346
		22.45–9	119
		22.46	44 n. 139
13.61f.	25 n. 46, 116 n. 326	22.52	121 n. 348
		22.54	28 n. 59, 120 n. 344
13.154–8	41 n. 120, 117 n. 329		
		22.54f.	119
13.155f.	200 n. 12	22.61–4	120 n. 345
14.102	18 n. 20	22.101ff.	123 n. 254
14.245–50	105 n. 281, 117 n. 324	22.132–4	123 n. 355
		22.136–8	123 n. 356
14.248	199	22.210	124 n. 358
14.497	49 n. 9, 104 n. 278, 197	22.241	124 n. 357
		22.294	124 n. 361
15.64	104 n. 278, 197	22.299	123 n. 353
15.87	104 n. 278, 197	22.322f.	124 n. 362
15.151	104 n. 278, 197	22.326–9	124 n. 359
15.167	197	22.329	125 n. 363
15.244	41 n. 120	23.281–4	41 n. 124, 51 n. 19, 109 n. 296
15.503–5	18 n. 20		
15.510	193 n. 178		
16.25–8	18 n. 20	23.283f.	28 n. 59
16.27	19 n. 27	23.296	108 n. 295
16.77	140 n. 431	23.324	105 n. 280
16.91–6	117 n. 335	24.124	139 n. 430
16.124	193 n. 178	24.368	104 n. 278, 197
16.375	117 n. 336	24.426–8	105 n. 283, 108
17.64	37 n. 101, 118 n. 337, 200	24.428	28 n. 61, 29, 198
		24.438	108 n. 293
17.65	118 n. 338	24.456	104 n. 278, 197
17.109	104 n. 278, 197	24.464f.	108 n. 293
17.246	19	24.523–5	108 n. 294
17.476	139 n. 430	24.528–30	28 n. 61, 126
18.70	104 n. 278, 197	24.530	33 n. 80, 199 n. 11, 200
18.152	104 n. 278, 197		
18.275–7	138 n. 426	*Sack of Troy*	
19.107–14	27, 37 n. 99, 41 n. 124, 51 n. 19, 102 n. 267, 118 n. 339	fr. 4.2 (Davies)	197
		HORACE	
		Epistles	
19.108	102 n. 268	1.2.21	132 n. 393
19.114	119 n. 341		
20.74	139 n. 430	**HYGINUS**	
20.106	104 n. 278, 197	*Astronomia*	
20.335	140 n. 431		
21–2	142 n. 437	2.13	190 n. 170

INDEX OF PASSAGES CITED

IAMBLICHUS
Life of Pythagoras
35.260   17 n. 14, 22 n. 37

INSCRIPTIONS
CEG II 824.2	159 n. 50
CEG II 852	154 n. 27
CEG II 852 (ii)	160 n. 52
CEG II 890	60 n. 64, 157 n. 43, 166 n. 70, 182 n. 134
IG 2(2) 3118	60 n. 64
IG 2(2) 3744.1–4	187 n. 158
IG 2(2) 3765	187 n. 158
IG 2(2) 5006.1–4 = 466 (P–W)	185 n. 142
Marmor Parium 10	190 n. 170
The Olbia epigram [= Lebedev (1996) 264]	22 n. 35

ISTROS
FGrHist 334 fr. 4   186 n. 144

LYCURGUS
Against Leocrates
102   184 n. 141

NICOLAUS OF DAMASCUS
FGrHist 90 fr. 28   171 n. 88

ORACLES
229 (P–W)	167 n. 74
302 (P–W)	167 n. 74
363 (P–W)	167 n. 74
466 (P–W)	185 n. 142

PANYASSIS
fr. 12.7f. (Davies)	28 n. 59
fr. 12.8 (Davies)	33 n. 80, 37 n. 99, 199, 200

PAUSANIAS
8.2.1   186 n. 145

PHERECYDES
FGrHist 3 fr. 22a–c   166 n. 70

PHILO
Legatio ad Gaium
76   17 n. 14

PHILOCHORUS
FGrHist 328 fr. 93	166 n. 69
FGrHist 328 fr. 95	165 n. 67
FGrHist 328 fr. 108	183 n. 139

PHOTIUS
s.v. νεολέως	187 n. 158
s.v. Παναθήναια	186 n. 145

PHRYNICHUS TRAGICUS
fr. 5 (Kannicht/ Snell)   159 n. 50

PINDAR
Isthmian Odes
6.53	156 n. 40
6.53f.	154 n. 28

Nemean Odes
1.13–17	158 n. 45, 168 n. 78
9.31f.	154 n. 27, 157 n. 44, 167 n. 76
10.36	186 n. 151

Olympian Odes
1.89	154 n. 28
5.4	167
6.58–61	154 n. 29
6.60	167 n. 77
8.25–30	154 n. 28
9.41–6	159 n. 50, 164
9.59–66	154 n. 28, 168 n. 78
13.24–8	154 nn. 27f., 157 n. 44

Pythian Odes
3.85	22 n. 35, 154 n. 28
4.107	154 n. 28
4.152f.	154 n. 28
5.94f.	7 n. 31, 100 n. 261, 154 nn. 28 and 30, 163
8.41–56	154 nn. 27f.
8.52–5	181 n. 127

INDEX OF PASSAGES CITED

8.54	56 n. 49	**SCHOLIA**
9.54f.	154 n. 29, 157 n. 44, 167 n. 75, 168 n. 78	*Prolegomena de comoedia* XVIIb
9.121–3	139 n. 429	1 and 2
10.31	154 n. 28	(Koster) 175 n. 105, 178 n. 113, 202
12.11f.	156 n. 40, 159 n. 50, 164 n. 61	schol. Ar. *Nu.* 28 191 n. 171
12.22–4	146 n. 3	schol. Ar. *Nu.* 386 186 n. 149
12.24	154 n. 30	schol. Ar. *Th.* 39 182 n. 129
Paeans		schol. D.T. in *Grammatici Graeci* 1.3 p.
1.8f.	157 n. 44	
1.8–10	175 n. 103	
1.9f.	154 n. 27, 158 n. 47	458.26–34 17 n. 13, 23 n. 42
		schol. Hom. *Il.*
2.1–5	157 n. 44, 175 n. 103	1.10.b 1 n. 3
		schol. Hom. *Il.* 1.117 50 n. 10
2.48	168 n. 80, 175 n. 103	schol. Hom. *Il.* 1.126 43 n. 130
		schol. Hom. *Il.*
6.177–81	175 n. 103	2.85b 17 n. 13, 50 n. 10
Fragments		schol. Hom. *Il.*
42.3–5	176 nn. 107f.	2.110a 8 n. 38
133	7 n. 31	schol. Hom. *Il.* 2.579 23 n. 42
140a.55f.	156 n. 40	schol. Hom. *Il.*
PLATO		2.579–80a, b 23 n. 42
		schol. Hom. *Il.* 3.186 24 n. 44
Laws		schol. Hom. *Il.* 6.76 88 n. 219
707e1f.	12 n. 56, 168 n. 78	schol. Hom. *Il.* 6.433 89 n. 221
		schol. Hom. *Il.*
Republic		6.433–9 89 n. 221
343b–c	23 n. 39	schol. Hom. *Il.*
404b10–c2	8 n. 36	10.79a 23
Statesman		schol. Hom. *Il.*
271ff.	23 n. 39	12.153a–d 43 n. 130
Theaetetus		schol. Hom. *Il.*
174d	23 n. 39	13.629 a.1 8
PLUTARCH		schol. Hom. *Il.*
		18.219a 8 n. 37
Theseus		schol. Hom. *Il.*
13.4	183 n. 139, 202	18.301 24 n. 44
25.1 = Aristotle fr. 384 (Rose)	12 n. 57, 170 n. 86, 180 n. 122, 187 n. 152, 202	schol. Hom. *Il.* 22.54f. 79 n. 165
		schol. Hom. *Il.* 23.132b, c 191 n. 172
25.3	195 n. 182	schol. Hom. *Od.* 4.740 114 n. 318
PROCLUS		schol. Hom. *Od.*
Chrestomathia		11.235 28 n. 61, 41 n. 122, 51 n. 19
p. 103 (Allen)	71 n. 118	

INDEX OF PASSAGES CITED

schol. Hom. *Od.* 23.296	108 n. 295
schol. Pi. *O.* 9.68a	159 n. 50
schol. Pi. *O.* 9.70a–d	159 n. 50
schol. Pi. *O.* 9.70b	165 n. 65
schol. Pi. *O.* 9.70b–c	187 n. 152
schol. Pi. *O.* 9.70c	165 n. 66
schol. Pl. *Prm.* 127a	186 n. 145

SEMONIDES

fr. 7 (West)	177 n. 112

SERVIUS

ad A. 11.811	17 n. 13

SIMONIDES

Epigrams

16.10 (Page)	154 n. 30
36.4 (Page)	22 n. 35, 154 n. 28

Fragments

564.4 (*PMG*)	146

SOLON

fr. 4.1–4 (West)	191 n. 174

SOPHOCLES

Ajax

565	202
1100f.	154 n. 28

Antigone

731–4	168 n. 80

Oedipus at Colonus

741	159 n. 50
741f.	154 n. 28
884	202
884–6	157 n. 43
884–900	154 nn. 28f.

Oedipus Tyrannus

144	154 nn. 28f., 159 n. 50, 202

Philoctetes

1242f.	156 n. 43

Trachiniae

194f.	154 n. 28
783	182 n. 129

Fragments

844.1 (Radt)	202
844.1–3 (Radt)	175 n. 105

STRABO

13.1.53	193 n. 177
14.1.20	193 n. 177
14.4.3	193 n. 177

SUDA

s.v. Παναθήναια	186 n. 145

SUSARION

fr. 1 (West)	146 n. 3, 202
fr. 1.1–5 (West)	177

THEOGNIS AND THEOGNIDEA

vv. 53–6	168 n. 80
vv. 773–9	175 n. 103
vv. 773–81	160 n. 53
v. 776	157 n. 44

THUCYDIDES

1.27	171 n. 88
6.75.3	185 n. 142

TIMOTHEUS

fr. 791.206–9 (*PMG*)	158, 187 n. 156
fr. 791.206–12 (*PMG*)	157 n. 43
fr. 791.236 (*PMG*)	195 n. 181
fr. 791.237–40 (*PMG*)	154f., 157 n. 44, 175 n. 103

TYRTAEUS

fr. 11.13 (West)	28 n. 59, 198, 200 n. 12

XENOPHANES

fr. 2.15 (West)	154 n. 30

XENOPHON

Cyropaedia

1.1	23 n. 39
8.1.14	23 n. 39

Memorabilia

3.2.1	17 n. 13, 21, 26 n. 52